I Could a Tale Unfold

I Could
A Tale Unfold

Violence, Horror & Sensationalism
in Stories for Children

P. M. Pickard

LONDON: TAVISTOCK PUBLICATIONS
NEW YORK: THE HUMANITIES PRESS

First published in 1961
in Great Britain
by Tavistock Publications (1959) Limited
First published in 1961
in the United States of America
by The Humanities Press, Inc.

Printed in Great Britain

To the
World Organization for Early Childhood Education
Organisation Mondiale pour l'Education Préscolaire
O.M.E.P.

Contents

Preface

Parents and educators have long been exercised over the problem of what kind of stories of violence or horror, if any, should be accessible to young children, whether read to them or by them. Some have gone so far as to eliminate toy soldiers from their playthings in the hope of checking the dawn of militaristic interests. The problem is of first-class importance and is a part of the portentous issue with which mankind is now faced. It is becoming increasingly realized that man's control over the tremendous forces of nature has plainly outstripped his control over the impulses within himself of violence and destruction which lie deeply embedded in his nature, so that nothing is more urgent than the study of these impulses and of the agencies that may stimulate or moderate them.

We observe that children commonly listen to fairy tales with an air of fascinated horror, or even with gusto, and demand the reading to be repeated. Yet the gruesome figures of these tales, e.g. cannibalistic giants, enter into the frightful nightmares which so many children have to endure. It would therefore seem plain sense to avoid such horror-raising stimulation. But the matter turns out to be not so simple. We find that young children *spontaneously* create in their imagination, both consciously and still more unconsciously, the same images of horror and terror, and that they suffer from nightmares without ever having listened to a fairy story. Indeed it often happens that when their own phantasies are brought into the open by a smiling mother relating a tale of horror they thereby achieve a measure of reassurance by gradually learning that the imagery they conjure up does not correspond to any outer reality. There is certainly no easy or

ix

general rule that can apply to such a variable creature as the human child, but Miss Pickard's book contains much valuable information and wisdom concerning the numerous considerations that have to be taken into account.

With older children the problem is in many respects different. The wave of 'horror comics', with a strong commercial background, have created in the United States an extensive social problem. Dr Wertham's investigations there have shown that they play a significant part in inspiring the behaviour known as juvenile delinquency. The mode of operation is evidently through youngsters coming to idealize daring criminals and thus to distort their moral values. Here again is a fruitful field for research to which Miss Pickard in her studies affords valuable guidance.

ERNEST JONES

Acknowledgements

It is my pleasure to express appreciation of the five London primary schools which entrusted their top classes to me for the investigations on children's out-of-school interests; and also of the hundreds of children who transformed a formidable plan into a delightful collaboration.

Of the many publications referred to in the text, two warrant special mention because they both confirmed my own lines of thought and gave stimulating re-direction of ideas just when I was assembling data. From Praz's *The Romantic Agony* I saw the value of cross-lateral classification of types of literary character and also gained much information about sources of plots which we found were being plagiarized for horror comics. From a paper given in 1955 by Andrew Peto to the Australian Society for Psychoanalysis, entitled 'Contributions to the Theory of Play', I saw fresh links between the creative activity of artists and children. In this paper he fused the thoughts of his wife, Elizabeth Kardos (who was killed during the war), and himself in a remarkably constructive way.

I wish to thank the author and Peter Davies Limited for permission to reproduce passages from *Dew on the Grass* by Eiluned Lewis.

'The fairy-tale is a merry judgement-day on appearance and reality.'

GRIMUR THOMSEN on Hans Andersen

CHAPTER 1

Art for adults and children

The problem that necessitates a serious study of the nature of stories for children is a pressing one for all educators, particularly parents. It is the problem of horror. Do children need horror in stories? If so, how much and how soon? It is said that they will meet horror later in life and so had better be schooled to it. That the majority of them enjoy some horror is obvious to anyone familiar with children. But this does not prove that it is an essential factor in their stories; they might merely have become conditioned to expect it because we have never told them good stories without horror; or we might be giving them horror because we ourselves need it. Moreover, there are many things, such as smoking, that they enjoy but we do not think to be good for them. It is not possible to say whether they need horror or not without going into the question of why they might need it. Attempting to answer this question is a formidable task, because it necessitates going into both the sources of horror and the function of stories.

Story-telling is an art akin to the performance of music; the artist may or may not be the original creator of the story, but he is an artist in his own right during the course of its 'performance'. Indeed, for many centuries the best stories were recited to the accompaniment of music. One of the biggest stumbling-blocks to constructive argument about this art of story-telling is that people so rarely agree about what they mean by the term art. A first step would therefore seem to be that of bringing this word *art* out of the realms of intuition into the daylight of definition.

I

The following definition is suggested as a starting-point to the discussion:

ART. *A means of communication of experience, between human beings, not necessarily involving language, in which traditional and novel elements are blended so as to stimulate simultaneously 'high' (intellectual) and 'low' (not-conscious) levels of the mind, typically by a rhythmic or equivalent pattern-like construction.*

By 'not-conscious' is meant both the pre-conscious mind from which things can easily be recalled, and the unconscious mind from which things cannot be recalled without the aid of some form of depth psychology. This definition is intended to apply to all forms of art.

A work of art has two important relationships: with its creator and with its appreciator. If the work of art is successful, if it communicates through the 'high' and 'low' levels of the mind of the appreciator, then the struggle of the artist to achieve this communication does not obtrude itself upon the appreciator. But if the work of art fails in any way, then even the most receptive and cooperative appreciator begins to puzzle about what the artist was trying to communicate: attention is diverted to the artist's effort.

An artist who is free to create in whatever he considers to be the best means of communication does not have to consider the level of maturity of the appreciator; he hopes for appreciation of his message from those sufficiently mature to comprehend the communication. But a commercial artist may be severely restricted by what one might call a common denominator of maturity in the public who may wish to purchase what he is advertising. The creator of stories for children, whether writer or teller, undergoes a restriction similar to that of the commercial artist.

The difference in maturity between child and adult is a normal phenomenon which must be taken into account. Strictly speaking, maturity can be reached through balanced development at any age; in this sense we can hear wisdom from peasants or from babes and sucklings. But there are qualitative differences between the maturity of a child and the maturity of an adult that must be recognized if the child is to receive the communication *in the form of art*. For instance, every tradition is novel the first time it is encountered. The difference between hearing a nursery rhyme once and twice is not double the difference between never having heard it and hearing it for the first time. Rhymes like *Pat-a-cake, pat-a-cake, baker's man* may fail dismally if introduced by a stranger who cannot compensate the excess of novelty by making familiar or 'traditional-to-this-child' gestures.

There are many ways of surmounting the unfamiliarity of tradition for tiny children, such as much repetition within one story, much re-telling of the same story (with never a single word out of place), and much answering of questions about the story; until all is so familiar that it has become traditional. Thus, even at the very beginning with *This little piggy went to market*, the baby's subjective appreciation is controlled by the artist's objective manipulation of the balance between the traditional and the novel. Without this there is failure to achieve simultaneous stimulation of the 'high' and the 'low' levels of the mind of the infant appreciator. At the commencement there is an artist, usually a parent, communicating with a child; each knows the other personally.

Tradition and novelty are not the only aspects requiring specialized balance for children. There are qualitative differences in thinking, in feeling, and in capacity to repress unacceptable thoughts and feelings. On the intellectual side children have less ability and less experience than adults. They cannot grasp all forms of reasoning until they have reached a mental age of about seven years; and, even then, they need years of practice in fairly concrete forms of reasoning before they can reason consistently for any length of time. Nor can they grasp abstract concepts until about this age. Here they have sadly misled us. We were under the impression that the mechanical ability to multiply ninety-three by seven meant that they had grasped the principle of multiplication; we thought that their use of words such as *liberal* or *civic* in their right context meant that they understood the terms. Quite recently, in a London junior school, a class was asked to write down who was the chief civic dignitary in a borough; and one child wrote: 'Rabbit.'

The findings of such research workers as Piaget have shown that we are still very much in the dark about how children think. In the first half-dozen years or so, much of what they say is so far removed from what we think they are saying, that they are in the position of a colour-blind child who speaks of a red pillar-box because everyone else does. Such a colour-blind child may think *redpillarbox* is the name of the place where you post a letter, or may associate it with *redball* and, abstracting the movement in the absence of colour, wonder whether the redpillarbox bounces letters into other people's houses by night. Thinking along such lines, the child may ask some quite incomprehensible question, to which no reply is given. Children, like adults, dislike uncertainty, and will make up an answer if none is provided. Just as we think children mean the same as we when *we* talk, so they think we mean the same as they when *they* talk. Having laughed among ourselves over the child who said 'rabbit' instead of 'mayor', we may pause in humility over our failure to make ourselves understood.

On the feeling side, children experience far more vividly than adults. The psycho-analysts tell us that adults, even when they fall in love, do not feel and experience with such vivid intensity as children of two to four years. Moreover, inhibiting powers have to mature before feeling can be controlled or repressed. When their wishes are obstructed, children become angry with an intensity of which adults are no longer capable. An angry adult may think what he would like to do with infuriating old So-and-so; but not only has he learned many reasons for restraint – he no longer has the driving anger of the small child. No considerations deter the furious thinking of the enraged child; unrestrained by adult practice in self-control, he thinks what he will do with the obstructing person in pictures far beyond his vocabulary that would horrify those who love and care for him were they able to guess them. Then, when he swings back to more tender feelings, he is in a desperate predicament; he cannot disentangle what he wanted to do from what he actually did; nor can he be sure how much the adults knew of what went on. So this is the triangle he goes through: love, hate, and guilt. His suffering is terrible; and, knowing no other world, he assumes that the adults feel the same about him. A mildly firm parent refusing him something is assumed to be as wildly, savagely furious as he at times feels and planning equally dire revenge.

How he manages to find a solution for himself over this succession of love-hate-guilt waves is dealt with in Chapter 4. It seems that, from a much earlier age than was realized in the past, children learn the expediency of restraining some impulses. While they are learning to hold down thoughts and feelings unacceptable to the community in which they live, they go through a twilight phase in which they hold down much of what is not acceptable although they are still aware of much that they are trying to inhibit. In this twilight phase they differ greatly from adults, who have formed such solid repressive barriers that they frequently no longer know what impulses they have shut away. Consequently an artist creating for adults can touch on unrecognized thoughts and feelings, without the adult appreciator properly realizing what 'low' levels of the mind have been allowed partially into consciousness. But an artist creating for children has to exercise the greatest care, lest too much vivid feeling is called up through the less secure barriers, to the detriment of the aesthetic effect.

Today it is not enough for a children's artist just to work intuitively. He has to know some children well, and he has to become acquainted with modern findings about children, if he wishes to be a top-rank children's artist. The intellectual content of his work has to be just sufficient to stimulate thought; if it is insufficient or excessive the children become bored by too little or too much thinking. The 'not-conscious' content has to be solidly there but not in excess; an insufficiency fails to grip the children and an excess grips them to the detriment of intellectual effort. Moreover, the balance of the various aspects works on a sliding scale according to age; the creating develops from a familiar artist communicating with a familiar child to the artist creating for children. At every stage, if the communication is to be made in art form, there must be adjustment both of the novel and traditional and of the 'high' and 'low' elements. Adults who have a great aversion to a particular children's story have usually received it in childhood with some imbalance that has destroyed the aesthetic effect – and, what is more, they can usually tell you exactly who it was told them this story. The painful incident has remained with what Rousseau called 'the ineffaceable traces'.

Children are innately capable of anger; this anger can appear in the earliest months; during anger, thought is phantastically horrible and far more fierce than during anger in adults. If we accept these findings of modern research, then some of our difficulties are cleared away. The argument that we have to condition children to horrors is now seen as fallacious; there is no question of introducing them to horrors, because the horrors already known to them are far in excess of anything we experience as adults.

Now where do we turn? It is no good asking the children to tell us about these thoughts. By the time they are old enough to explain, or to realize that we do not know all about them, they already know that such thoughts are 'forbidden'. Even the most loving and understanding parent can rarely get out of a terrified child what the nightmare was about. In sleep there is a general relaxation, and some of the most pressing forbidden wishes sometimes manage to emerge a little. But by the time the child is awake enough to talk, control has usually been taken once more; and anyhow, all that matters to the child at the moment is finding that he is still loved. Yet we cannot abandon him to go through this private hell without our help. The 'aloneness' of a nightmare is one of its worst aspects.

If we cannot ask the children, we can at least recognize that each one of us underwent childhood horrors. Have we completely got over them? Or is there some way in which we need to tell each other now we are adult? Or, stranger still, are we each still in some private hell about it, so that communion has to be held with ourselves, without the fresh air of friendly discussion?

People often say that there is plenty of horror in adult art, but they rarely specify to what they are referring, other than by saying rather vaguely: 'Well . . . take Lear . . . or the Cenci.' Before we try to decide whether there is any value in horrific art, it would be well to be more specific than this. Let us begin with a visual art, since nightmares are predominantly visual.

Any art gallery has a minority of great paintings of a horrific nature. But let us be more precise still and take the famous Washington D.C. Art Gallery. Here we find a minority of horrific pictures, among them:

GOZZOLI: 'Dance of Salome' and 'Beheading of St John the Baptist'.

MANTEGNA: 'Judith and Holofernes'.

EL GRECO: 'Laocoön'.

BOSCH: 'Death and the Miser'.

MANET: 'The Dead Toreador'.

BLAKE: 'The Great Red Dragon' and the 'Woman Clothed with the Sun'.

RAPHAEL and SODOMA: St George and the Dragon. (Two very different renderings of the same theme.)

What do we see in these pictures? Their content includes a cruelly indifferent executioner about to carve through the halo of a saint, a complacent mother receiving the head of a saint, Judith dropping the head of Holofernes into a bag while gazing inattentively elsewhere, writhing dragons spouting blood, snakes overpowering naked and straining men, death and monsters battling round a dying man, a pregnant woman attacked and cursed by a sevenheaded monster, and the brave toreador an inert corpse. Each picture is a masterpiece by a great painter; every event is gruesome, and yet as impersonal as a caryatid upholding the Erechtheum – as these same caryatides reproduced at St Pancras Church, London. Do we or do we not know what we are looking at? Few of us would be unwilling to admit that we have gazed at some time with incredulous fascination at some such masterpiece. What echoes awoke in us, that we did not turn away in

7

disgust? What interest had we in receiving this communication from the artist?

A rapid survey of the local art gallery will show that this horrific minority of pictures really *is* a minority. But it is there. It cannot be dismissed as a mere minority for two reasons: because the pictures are studied with interest and because great artists have something to communicate. If both the artist and the appreciator have an interest in horrific pictures, then such pictures, though statistically in a minority, must be recognized as having importance. It would be impossible, for instance, to dismiss Blake's 'Woman and Dragon' without also dismissing Revelations, upon which it is based. Blake was moved by the twelfth chapter, which actually contains far more horrors than he put into his picture: the woman is pregnant, the child is killed at birth, the mother is driven into the wilderness and plagued, and the dragon puts a curse upon all her descendants. Such content cannot be dismissed as irrational lapses, since this kind of terror has taken hold of such artists as Raphael, El Greco, and Manet. They have clothed horror in beauty.

Are they merely sugar-coating the pill we must learn to take when we grow up? No! We ate that pill of horror first in infancy, with very little coating. Are they showing that horror can be dominated by beauty? Or is there some relationship between the two, requiring us to grasp both at once if we are to understand either? In 'To a Candle'[1] Walter de la Mare puts the relationship from the other side, from the sight of beauty awakening the thought of horror: 'A head of such strange loveliness . . . That dread springs up to see it there . . .'

Our next step, it seems, is a more detailed examination of the nature of horror in adult art. If we can throw any illumination upon the subjects of horror that still concern adults, we shall be in a better position to understand the children's problem. Since this book is about horror in children's stories, the most suitable adult medium to examine is literature. Some actual examples can give us opportunity to study the nature of this horror for adults.

The Chatto Book of Modern Poetry, 1915–55.

CHAPTER 2

Horror and beauty in literature

Human beings, whether living people or literary creations, may show marked discrepancy between outer behaviour and inner thoughts. Dover Wilson says that the words used most frequently of the man Shakespeare by his contemporaries were always epithets flowing one way: 'gentle', 'friendly', 'civil', 'brave' (that is gallant), 'dear-loved', and always affectionately 'our Shakespeare' or 'my Shakespeare'. Yet this gentle, civil man created a king who could say of his daughters:

> *No, you unnatural hags!*
> *I will have such revenges on you both,*
> *That all the world shall – I will do such things –*
> *What they are, yet I know not; but they shall be*
> *The terrors of the earth.*

> King Lear

Lear broke down and spluttered and could not even find the words for what he meant to do, like a child in a temper-tantrum. But Shakespeare also created a character outwardly as gentle and civil as himself, who bore within him passions so lurid that Macbeth by comparison seemed the more compassionate ruler. Malcolm has such grace that he is even held in high respect at pious Edward's court; yet this same Malcolm, while actually a guest at Edward's court, tells the horrified Macduff:

> *I grant him [Macbeth] bloody,*
> *Luxurious, avaricious, false, deceitful,*

9

Sudden, malicious, smacking of every sin
That has a name; but there's no bottom, none,
In my voluptuousness: your wives, your daughters,
Your matrons, and your maids, could not fill up
The cistern of my lust; and my desire
All continent impediments would o'erbear
That did oppose my will; better Macbeth
Than such an one to reign.

Macbeth

When George Sand gave the original manuscript of *Lélia* to Sainte-Beuve, who knew her well, he was startled at the revelation of her inner life. She made Lélia say of herself such things as: 'When I was with him I was seized with a strange, delirious hunger which no embrace could satisfy. I felt as if burned up by an unextinguishable flame, but his kisses brought me no relief.' Sainte-Beuve told her that *Lélia* made him afraid of George Sand; but she implored him not to think of her as Lélia, which she assured him was nothing of herself. Byron, on the other hand, did not deny the link between the villainous characters he created and himself. He modelled his own behaviour on that of his villians, whose high foreheads hid, or almost hid, their dark passions.

When arch-villains emerge in literature, powerful inner realities have taken command of outward behaviour. Moved by a furious lust to domineer, they rove the world in search of weaker beings unable to withstand their craving, upon whom they can slake their thirst for command. The myths and literature of the world are full of tales about such terrifying characters and their terrified victims. Here one sees unrestrained inner horrific phantasy become overt behaviour, and it is well worth our while to take a closer look at some of them.

DOMINEERING WOMEN

In the *Choephorae* Aeschylus says:

When perverse rebellious love

Masters the feminine heart, then destroyed is the union
Of mated lives for beast or Man.

(Tr. Prior)

The names of such women are legion: Lilith, Scylla, Cressida, Helen, Salome, the Sirens and Gorgons and Harpies, are only a few of them. These archetypal seductresses seem to have an irresistible fascination for writers. The cruel heroine in an early play by Swinburne says:

Yea, I am found the woman in all tales,
The face caught always in the story's face;
I, Helen, holding Paris by the lips,
Smote Hector through the head; I, Cressida,
So kissed men's mouths that they went sick or mad,
Stung right at brain with me . . .

Rosamund

Of Faustine, Swinburne says:

She loved the games men play with death,
When death must win;
As though the slain man's blood and breath
Revived Faustine.

Faustine

Faustine had a host of men to trample in 'the winepress of the dead'.

Oscar Wilde asks of the Sphinx:

What snake-tressed fury fresh from Hell, with uncouth gesture
and unclean,
Stole from the poppy-drowsy queen and led you to a student's
cell?

The Sphinx

D'Annunzio's La Comnena, last descendant of the decadent Byzantine Emperors, is described thus by her victims:

'Thou wast trailed like bait through sloughs of vice; thou wast steeped in the foam of all corruption; there was nothing vile or

11

desperate that thou didst not know . . . wherever thou didst touch, wherever thy fiendish flesh clung, there was destined to be a wound without hope of healing . . .'

It is quite overpowering to meet these horrors in concentrated form; yet anyone versed in literature knows that there is a seemingly unending list of great works from which quotations could be selected. These phantastically horrific women, these witches seducing men, cast spells that reduce men to sterility or impotence, change them into beasts, or annihilate them in some fearful way. They inflame men's passions without satisfying them, like Kleist's Penthesilea, Mérimée's sorceress gipsy Carmen, and Sue's Cécily. Praz, in *The Romantic Agony*, speaks of their 'murderous chastity'.

Rudwin, in *The Devil in Legend and Literature*, makes a most illuminating reference to Lilith, a character apparently dating back to Babylonian days. He says that she consumed new-born infants as well as young men. This suggests that she consumed them in some inner way as infants which prevented their maturing as young men. From the victim's standpoint, a child who never satisfactorily surmounted horrific infantile phantasies about the first woman he ever loved, namely his own mother, might suffer a recrudescence of the early horrific ideas when he fell in love as a man. Then as infant and man he would be liable to undergo a double destruction by Lilith. This may sound very improbable; but so does Lilith. Yet artists still refer to Lilith. She must have some meaning to them.

If we can accustom ourselves to the idea that these cannibalistic elements are survivals of infantile wishes, then much which appears incomprehensible in literature begins to take shape. Artists call up these figures from the cradle of civilization because artists and appreciators still have these unresolved residues from their individual cradles. In the melodic verse of Swinburne we catch the double-echo of Lilith, the mother and mistress snaring the child and man in a single mesh, as he cries:

I would my love could kill thee; I am satiated

With seeing thee alive, and fain would have thee dead.

.   .   .   .   .

That I could drink thy veins as wine, and eat
Thy breasts like honey; that from face to feet
Thy body were abolished and consumed,
And in my flesh thy very flesh entombed !

Anactoria

Even that intolerably heartless old harridan, the mother of Lord Rendal, fits into the design. She failed to know her own complete fruition in his infantile love for her (for quite good reasons, we may be sure, if we knew her clinical history). Still hungry for love, she probes and probes into his maturing adult love, ignoring his beseeching cry for respite. Inevitably the predatory old mother survives and it is the mortally wounded young lord who dies before his time. The traditional theme of the lament is enhanced by the traditional cadence of a dirge.

In *Twelfth Night* Shakespeare displays the situation through Orsino, in love with love. The play opens with him seeking death by satiation through music. 'That strain again !' he cries, 'It hath a dying fall.' In an imperishable scene, almost cinematographic in form, he unconsciously tells a woman that women cannot feel as men do. 'There is no woman's sides', he tells the attentive but disguised Viola, 'can bear the beating of so strong a passion as my heart knows.' The unsatisfactory conclusion, when he switches his undying devotion from Olivia to Viola, is a quite logical consequence of his unrealistic state, still enmeshed in infantile phantasies.

DOMINEERING MEN

Milton's Fallen Angel might be classed as the greatest villain of all, for he is lord of a host of archetypal villains. He is gigantic in physique and ambition, and he rules an infernal host among whom, 'prime in order and might', come Moloch, besmeared with blood of human sacrifices and parents' tears, Chemnos the obscene dread of Moab's sons with 'lust hard by hate', Thammuz of wanton passion for both men and women, and so on. Each one of the prime in order behaves outwardly in accordance with the most horrific inner thoughts man can experience – of hatred, lust, homosexuality, and parental inability to spare his children. The Fallen Angel dominates them all.

Many other writers have portrayed archetypal villains. Mrs Radcliffe's villains are gigantic becowled monsters, the most outstanding of whom is Schedoni in *The Italian, or the Confessional of the Black Penitents*. His figure was 'tall, and, though extremely thin, his limbs were large and uncouth, and as he stalked along, wrapt in the black garments of his order, there was something terrible in its air; something almost super-human'.

Byron often concentrated upon the eyes, through which the dark passions beneath might be glimpsed. He devotes as much as forty lines to describing the eye of one villain who had done 'some dark deed, he will not name'. The villain in Mérimée's *La Guzla* also has strange eyes; they have double pupils. Maturin's *Melmoth the Wanderer* uses his eyes as weapons. He terrifies everyone at the wedding feast with the horrible fascination of his preternatural glare; the bride dies and the groom goes mad.

The special characteristics of the domineering men seem to be gigantic physique and ambition, horrific eyes with death in their glance, sins of lust and hate, and dark deeds that cannot be named. There is a refreshing touch of sanity when one of them over-reaches himself and causes his own destruction. Mrs Shelley's modern Prometheus, Frankenstein, constructs a ghastly super-sized semblance of humanity from old charnelhouse bones; this he animates, and it destroys Frankenstein himself. As a Prometheus story it is, of course, incorrect; for in that myth Man (Hercules) finally liberates his progenitor.

What gives the nightmare-feeling to these tales is the fact that all ends in total destruction; these horrific monsters pursue their course through to collapse from which there is no hope of redemption. Byron makes a link between the 'dark deeds' and the past when he writes:

The flash of that dilating eye
Reveals too much of times gone by.

These horrible death-dealing phantasies, which Lear could not name and which Byron links with emotionally charged dilating pupils and the long-ago past, are still highly active as a theme for artists. The villainous men must be ranked for potency in adult years with the villainous women.

THE VICTIMIZED

The nightmare of the victimized is that they undergo an appalling paralysis, which makes them incapable of taking rational steps to overpower the monsters. The villains prowl round till they find people weak enough to succumb to victimization. But the victimized also speak. What can we learn from what they have to say? Swinburne is one of their witnesses. All his heroines are unrestrained, imperious, cruel beauties. Darnley says of Mary Stuart:

> . . . *nay, your eyes*
> *Threaten us unto blood . . .*
> *You are pitiful as he that's hired for death*
> *And loves the slaying better than the hire.*
>
> Mary Stuart

In the *Whippingham Papers* Swinburne shows remarkable insight into the experience of the victim. He writes, 'One of the great charms of birching lies in the sentiment that the floggee is the powerless victim of the furious rage of a beautiful woman'. So there is a charm about being victimized. When Keats healthily rebelled against his treatment by Fanny Brawne, Swinburne condemned him for his unmanly attitude, for not knowing how to love and die like a gentleman.

Keats is an example of one who was quite aware of the charms of victimization but deliberately resisted them. In his search for creative poise he became almost what he called 'an addict to passivity', and it did cross his mind that Fanny was something of

an archetypal seductress. With the feather-light gesture characteristic of his work, he only touched upon this; but he wrote to her,
'My greatest torment since I have known you has been the fear of
your being a little inclined to the Cressid'. And his immortal
requiem for those who succumbed was:

> O what can ail thee Knight at arms
> Alone and palely loitering . . .

> I saw pale Kings, and Princes too
> Pale warriors death pale were they all;
> They cried La belle dame sans merci
> Thee hath in thrall

> I saw their starv'd lips in the gloam
> With horrid warning gaped wide
> And I awoke, and found me here
> On the cold hill's side.

La Belle Dame Sans Merci

Here is the nightmare victimization, actually seen in sleep.

It is not a new idea that there is emotional gratification in being
victimized. After the plagues of the thirteenth and fourteenth
centuries, monks sought to appease divine wrath by being
flogged; but the Church, recognizing the sexual gratification
enjoyed by these flagellants, first forbade this penance and then,
when these addicts to masochism persisted, declared them heretics.
Another writer who healthily rebelled against victimization was
Southey, author of *The Three Bears* as well as *Lives of the British
Admirals*. While a pupil at Westminster School, he wrote an
essay against flogging for which he was expelled. But it is only
just beginning to be realized that it is a sign of immaturity to
have to find weaker personalities to victimize; and that addicts to
victimization will search for monsters to gratify their masochism.

This shows the persecuted maidens of literature in a rather
different light. Gretchen may have had a share of guilt that Faust
would have been very reluctant to yield to her. At Udolpho

Castle Mrs Radcliffe subjects her young heroine of untarnished virtue to 'a human figure [of a man] of ghastly paleness stretched at its length' with face 'partly decayed and disfigured by worms'. Not for many chapters is the reader allowed to learn, with the maiden, that this is only an effigy, regularly contemplated by one who wishes to expiate his sins. (The word 'only' seems a little out of place, when one realizes what satisfaction the contemplater would be getting from this effigy.) Mrs Radcliffe created a succession of such persecuted and virtuous maidens, and countless virtuous maidens relished her novels.

In *Northanger Abbey* Jane Austen mirrors the manner in which these mystery tales gripped the young ladies of her day; and she shows their confusion with the phantasies of the reader. Here Catherine is somewhat unbalanced by assiduous reading of Mrs Radcliffe's novels, and suffers severe humiliation when she herself, confusing inner with outer reality, invents a criminal mystery which is disclosed as the machination of her own mind. This book must have had very special significance for Jane Austen, because she could not bring herself to publish it. When a writer takes a very long time to produce a work it is usually assumed that this has very special significance; for instance, Grillparzer took nearly twenty years to finish his Oedipus drama *Der Traum, Ein Leben*, a popular play certainly well known to Freud; Swinburne spent twenty years upon an unpublished epic, *The Flogging-Block*; and Goethe took virtually a life-time on *Faust*. Jane Austen began *Northanger Abbey* in 1798 but did not publish it for twenty years. Being a great artist, she may well have undergone something of Catherine's obsession with mystery tales and have been uncomfortably aware of the sources of this fascination. If this is so, then her reluctance is redolent of Keats's

> *O blush not so! O blush not so!*
> *Or I shall think you knowing;*
> *And if you smile the blushing while,*
> *Then maidenheads are going.*

At any rate, the deeper awareness of motivation in human

behaviour did not become a characteristic of Jane Austen's work, even thought it might have done so.

But Mrs Radcliffe is not the only author to revel in persecuted maidens. One's thoughts turn naturally to Richardson's Clarissa Harlowe, who is drugged and violated in a house of ill-fame, and to Lewis's Agnes, in *The Monk*. Of her imprisonment, Agnes says, 'Sometimes I felt the bloated toad, hideous and pampered with the poisonous vapours of the dungeon, dragging his loathsome length along my bosom. Sometimes the quick cold lizard roused me, leaving his slimy track upon my face, and entangling itself in the tresses of my wild and matted hair. Often have I at waking found my fingers ringed with the long worms which bred in the corrupted flesh of my infant . . .'

This ecstasy of victimization, enjoyed first by the artist and then by the many appreciators, puts the persecuted maidens in quite a different category, once the camouflage of 'righteous indignation' is ripped away. We are not seeking where to lay blame, but questing for explanation. So far we have found that the domineering and the victimized are not realistic; they are horrific machinations of the imagination. Writers have linked them with the past and with sleep; moreover, they have shown that it is possible to be aware of the ecstasy of both domineering and being victimized and yet to resist the temptation to convert this inner experience to outer behaviour. While appreciating works of art with horrific content, it is possible to put up a healthy and realistic rebellion against behaving thus.

THE SOLUTION OF ANDROGYNE

In *The Monk* Lewis forewarns the reader in a preface of 'extremes in hating and in loving'. Here the lascivious phantasies are set in a matrix of the occult which is all the more horrifying because it is those who consider themselves to be beyond superstition who are most duped by ghastly apparitions. If these apparitions are compared with, for instance, the accredited criteria for apparitions drawn up by the Society for Psychical Research, they are found to be figments of the imagination. It is as figments of the imagination that one should read Lewis's vivid descriptions of wantonness and sadism among monks and nuns; burial alive, the Inquisition, blood drunk from skulls, murder, death by haunting, incest, and other inventions of Lewis's own mind are there for the reader's mind to enjoy. The climax is a visitation by the Devil. He comes to the abbot first as a young novice, whom the abbot learns to love for his wisdom; the novice then changes to a woman; and finally he is transformed into the apparition of a beautiful naked youth decked only in jewellery. Step by step the reader, securely wrapped in righteous indignation, reaches the final stage, when it is possible to have a look at that special sin of the Fallen Angel's minion, Thammuz.

The extremes in loving and in hating, characteristic of domination and victimization, produce states of tension so terrible that one solution is an almost inevitable result: to withdraw altogether from the opposite sex. There are many examples of this in mythology, such as Sappho on the Island of Lesbos, and the Delphic Priests. At various times this solution has been accepted by society. But a close examination usually shows signs of domination and victimization between the sexes; for instance, it was impossible for the respected homosexual order of Delphic Priests to make any prophecy without the sanction of one of the terrifying old Sybils.

Writers troubled by the nightmare swings of love and hate between the sexes have been fascinated by the charms of sex-reversal as a possible solution to the tension. Byron translated Catullus's *Ad Lesbiam* and addressed poems to Lesbia. Swinburne's *Lesbia Brandon* was widely read. Grillparzer's epic poetic drama *Sappho* was highly successful. Hermaphroditism, Lesbianism, and androgyny, main preoccupations at the end of the century, are themes in the poetry of Samain and Renée Vivien.

But androgyny did not bring the hoped-for mature peace because it did not come to terms with the causes of the tension. Renée Vivien admitted the sterile cruelty involved, and depicted the green-eyed jealousy of the Amazons. Furthermore, in a homosexual relationship one of the partners may be playing an almost normal role; and as the other, who is playing the opposite sex, loses youthful charm, the first may begin to see the situation in the light of cold reality. Oscar Wilde symbolically depicted the still existing terrible tension when he came out of prison after serving a term for homosexuality. He called himself Melmoth, presumably after Maturin's Wanderer, who dealt death at the wedding with his double-pupilled eyes and who cried, 'I am commissioned to trample on and bruise every flower in the natural and moral world – hyacinths, hearts, and bagatelles of that kind, just as they occur.' Certainly imprisonment had done nothing to ease the situation; this merely deals with the symptom and ignores – or even exacerbates – the cause.

Grillparzer tried an interesting experiment; he introduced a young man into the legend of Sappho. She went to the Olympic Games on the mainland and returned with the young champion. He rebelled and refused to be victimized by the domineering old woman; moreover he dealt her a mortal wound by seducing one of her obedient maidens. This exquisite tragedy has two levels of poetry, grand epic for Sappho and humble simplicity for the young lovers. It ends with the great artist throwing herself into the sea because she has failed to make her communication with the young man. It would have been even more interesting if the young man had grasped her meaning but still resisted her. However, it is a contribution; because a refusal to become victimized through nightmare-paralysis destroys one of the domineering characters; and the real situation, tension between two generations, is evident.

FAMILY RELATIONSHIPS

Mythology has many examples of domineering extending from one generation to the next. Women not only murdered their husbands, like Clytemnestra; they murdered their sons, like Althaea, and murdered their fathers, like Scylla, and murdered their mothers, like Electra working through Orestes. Or quite openly, like the Sphinx, they demanded feasts of both sexes in the younger generation. If the child-victims endeavoured to be strong by emulating their parents, they were accused of that insolent pride named *hubris* and threatened with an Icarus-fall to total destruction.

The two ends of the father-and-son relationship are to be seen in the myths of many lands. In the Greek version it is Oedipus who unwittingly kills Theseus, his father. In the Persian version it is Rustum who unwittingly kills Sohrab, his son. So great is the fascination of unwitting destruction in this particular human relationship that when Julius Caesar wrote his *Oedipus* there were forty-three extant dramas of that name. To these could also be added those which had been lost, those which had different titles but the same theme, and those on the Persian pattern. Many later dramas have been given the title *Oedipus*, for example, those of Voltaire and Corneille; and still more have borrowed the theme without the title. Grillparzer's *The Dream, A Life* uses the Persian form with Rustan as hero; and the hero does not, like Macbeth, translate all the monstrosities into action – he dreams that he has done so and when he awakens alters his plans. Horace Walpole, in *The Castle of Otranto*, which was among the first of the mystery tales, has the son killed during the marriage ceremony; and it is only a matter of seconds before the father begins his attempt to seduce the bride.

The furious passion between fathers and daughters is equally lethal. When Lear's favourite daughter refuses to put commercial value on her love for him and he has seen through the deception of the daughters who would do so, having lost his wits, he uses such terms as:

> *You nimble lightnings, dart your blinding flames*
> *Into her scornful eyes! Infect her beauty,*
> *You fen-suck'd fogs, drawn by the powerful sun,*
> *To fall and blast her pride!*
>
> King Lear

He had commenced the talk with Regan by a threatened attack

on her dead mother, showing insane awareness of the complexity of such family conflict:

> *If thou shouldst not be glad,*
> *I would divorce me from thy mother's tomb,*
> *Sepulchring an adultress.*

King Lear

Shelley was also preoccupied with this theme; in the *Cenci* the father threatens his daughter with poison and corruption:

> *I will drag her, step by step,*
> *Through infamies unheard of among men;*
> *She shall stand shelterless in the broad noon*
> *Of public scorn, for acts blazoned abroad . . .*
> > *and when dead,*
> *As she shall die unshrived and unforgiven*
> *A rebel to her father and her God . . .*
> *Her spirit shall approach the throne of God*
> *Plague-spotted with my curses.*

The Cenci

Here again are infamies unheard of, deeds without a name, because by the time one could name them one has learned to conceal the phantasies; and let it be noted that the rebellion against the father has priority over rebellion against God. Moreover, the daughter reveals that she already knows that such tension can exist between fathers and daughters, for she says:

> *I thought I was that wretched Beatrice*
> *Men speak of, whom her father sometimes hales*
> *From hall to hall by the entangled hair;*
> *At others, pens up naked in damp cells*
> *Where scaly reptiles crawl, and starves her there,*
> *Till she will eat strange flesh.*

The Cenci

Where the fury of the domineering adults is let loose not upon weakly adults but upon children then the children become, as Swinburne says, 'stung right at brain'. Children thus disturbed in their balanced development will inevitably turn to each other in confusion. Mythology is full of such tales, and they are a source of endless fascination to dramatists. Of the brother and sister Orestes and Electra, Guerber discreetly remarks, 'In fact, their devotion to each other was so great that it has become proverbial in every tongue'. Events that become proverbial in every tongue have deep human significance. Electra's devotion was of such intensity that she victimized Orestes into becoming their mother's murderer; and there was nothing unwitting about the deed as in the Oedipus and Rustum myths.

In Celtic mythology, according to *The Book of Leinster*, one of the Three Sorrowful Tales of Erin tells how the son and daughter of Lir, the old sea-god, fall passionately in love and with what single-minded devotion their two brothers serve them. This is the theme of Synge's *Deirdre of the Sorrows*, although the original relationship is disguised in order to make the play acceptable for public performance: Lir is called Deirdre's uncle, as he wants to marry her, and the three brothers are called cousins, as one of them does marry her. Writing of his dramas, Synge says that the nourishment on which our imagination lives is not easy to define; and in this particular play the tragedy is almost averted because the hero finds that speaking of his doubts has almost cleared them away. The 'uncle' is so besotted with his daughter that he does not even hear her say that she will not mate with him; an old nurse says that he brings her 'the love he has for a young child, and the love he has for a full woman'. Very tragically, he tells that he has 'a store of knowledge that is a weight and terror', that she will not find elsewhere what he, who never lies, is bringing her 'in wildness and confusion' in his own mind. She flees and lives through seven years of bliss with her 'cousin', served by the two other brothers. When the lovers finally quarrel, the age-old taunts spring up, 'It's women that have loved are cruel only . . .' he cries, '. . . that mockery is in your eyes this night will spot the face of Emain.'

Through several of his lesser characters Synge expresses the idea that the knowledgeable have lost something which is known to the humble and to the mad. There is reference to the wicked Queen Maeve of the Woods and how the father drove Deirdre to her. Elsewhere, in *The Passing of the Shee*, Synge speaks of Maeve:

> *That poets played with hand in hand*
> *To learn their ecstasy.*

In the sixteenth century Tasso described the brother and sister, Olindo and Sofronia, dying as they exchanged 'looks of insensate love'. Goethe took this theme for one of his dramas, and Tasso is constantly referred to in literary criticism. Shelley, in the original version of *The Revolt of Islam*, portrays the brother and sister, Laon and Cythna, as lovers dying bound to one stake.

Shelley divined the source within him of such works as the *Cenci* and *Oedipus Tyrannus or Swellfoot the Tyrant*. In his *Prose Works* appears his oft-quoted remark, 'Incest is, like many other incorrect things, a very poetical circumstance'. Not only was he aware of this source of inspiration, but he deemed it worthy of discussion in his analysis of aesthetic experience. There is, therefore, authoritative artistic direction for turning attention to the nature of the incorrect things underlying art, for Shelley never ceased to examine the nature of artistic creation.

It is not really surprising that the loves and hates of the first and most sensitive years should centre upon the parents and the brothers and sisters, for these are the people closest to the child during this period of violently swinging emotions. Insecurity of personal development in those closest to the child is bound to make his striving towards stability much more difficult. Such a play as *Deirdre of the Sorrows* shows very clearly how the troubled emotional state of the father-figure influences the development of the children. In such circumstances the nightmares of the children must be even more terrifying than those normally undergone. The subject of nightmares has engaged the attention of very many artists. This, too, is not so surprising, for artists are not a race apart; they differ from other people only in having more than average intensity of feeling and intelligence. Thus, as tiny children, they would have experienced with even greater intensity the emotional storms of infancy, and would have puzzled about them with a mental ability above that which children usually have for these problems. Since the difference is one of quantity rather than of quality, what they have been able to observe concerns us all.

THE NIGHTMARE

Towards the end of the sixteenth century Thomas Nashe wrote, 'The rest we take in our beds is such another kinde of rest as the weerie traveller taketh in the coole soft grasse in summer, who thinking there to lye at ease, and refresh his tyred limmes, layeth his fainting head unawares on a loathsome neast of snakes . . . Therefore are the terrors of the night more than of the day, because the sinnes of the night surmount the sinnes of the day.'

Of the relatively few writings on nightmares, the majority are so graphic that they would seem to be based on personal experience. Ernest Jones, in *On the Nightmare*, summarizes the characteristics of nightmares under three headings:

1. Agonizing dread.
2. Sense of oppression or weight at the chest which alarmingly interferes with respiration.
3. Conviction of helpless paralysis.

Among the list of traditional cures he includes scarifying the throat and shaving the head, bleeding at the ankle or administration of wild carrot, Macedonian parsley, and black seeds of the male peony. He says, 'No malady that causes mortal distress to the sufferer, not even seasickness, is viewed by medical science with such complacent indifference . . .'

There is a particularly horrifying kind of nightmare literature that arises from the ghastly vampire legends. These vampire legends have existed in Europe from earliest times and some can be traced to much earlier civilizations. The Babylonian vampire, Lilith, consumer of infants and men, has been called the princess of the succubi. A vampire is the ghost of a criminal witch or wizard who leaves the grave at night and sucks the blood of sleeping persons. Thus a vampire presents a double nightmare, a nightmare behaviour from the sleep of death and a nightmare for the sleep of the living. Krafft-Ebing, in *Psychopathia Sexualis*, connects them with sadism, which is sexual gratification to the dominating through maltreatment of the victimized. Ernest Jones points out that the very paucity of psychological explanations of vampirism in itself indicates that essential factors have hitherto been overlooked; and that the latent content yields plain indication of most kinds of sexual perversion, the form of the story depending upon which perversion is predominant.

Two very ancient legends of this type may illustrate the nightmare element. Redheaded men were believed to return from their graves as objects of loathsome hate, such as frogs or beetles, and suck the blood of beautiful girls. Presumably the auburn hair suggested blood pouring from the brain; this is a most horrific infantile phantasy. The Roman Strigas were believed to return from the grave at night to suck the blood and marrow of children. Since the second legend is not only an infantile phantasy but one told by adults to children, it is worth pausing to consider this further. The *strigidae* were owls, a *strigel* is a skin scraper, and it is widely believed that what devitalizes the spine is masturbation. A child only masturbates when in a state of tension; to be told that these owl people will come and suck the marrow of your spine for this would very greatly increase the tension. The owl-vampire story is one of the worst examples of adults using infantile phantasies to frighten children. It might almost be cited as the epitome of the wrong use of stories for children, since a reasonable degree of masturbation is of no consequence to a child at all.

The vampire legends arise not just about people who have actually died, but about people against whom one has harboured murderously aggressive phantasies in infancy. In this connection Ernest Jones writes, 'Dreams of people who are dead occur most frequently, and are most heavily charged with emotion, when the dead person represents the father or mother. They are concerned

with the deepest conflicts of love and hate, and originate ultimately in incest motives repressed from consciousness in childhood. This astonishing statement has been extensively confirmed
in actual psycho-analytic investigations of the unconscious
mind . . .'

Vampire legends should be seen as tales of hatred arising from
the primordial love, hate, and guilt triangle, through which we
have all passed in infancy. There was an epidemic of them that
reached a peak in south-east Europe during the eighteenth and
nineteenth centuries, associated with outbreaks of plague and
stink. Even today the belief in vampires is very far from extinct
in Europe. Furthermore, even with those sufficiently sophisticated
to recognize them as legendary, their 'very poetical circumstance'
of incest gives them their wide appeal to artists. Vampires are
the main themes of innumerable works, such as Kipling's vampire
poem, and they are endlessly touched on in literary reference, as
in Walter Pater's comparison of the Mona Lisa with a vampire.
In fact, this passage about Leonardo's smiling Madonna not only
states that she has been dead many times and learned the secrets of
the grave, but claims that she is the mother of such people as
Helen and St Anne. Seen from the standpoint of conflicts in love
and hate, the vampire works and references become much more
comprehensible.

In the nineteenth century many writers portrayed vampires at
their erotic deeds. Polidori's vampire is a young libertine killed in
Greece, who returns from his grave to seduce the sister of his
friend and to suffocate her during her wedding night. Mérimée's
vampire in *La Guzla* drags to destruction the woman to whom he
is attached; because she had betrayed him while he was alive, he
attacks her on the threshold of her nuptial chamber and bites her
in the throat. Both the invented name La Guzla and the attack
upon the throat suggest aggressive infantile food phantasies.

In the vampire tales we obtain a glimmer of the unspeakable
thoughts of very small children, which they would learn to shut
away by day but which might come after them, so to speak, by
night. Later we shall discuss the spontaneous way in which

children discover for themselves a way to bring these frightful phantasies under control during their play. It is now quite evident that they originate from within the children, and that adult works of art are much concerned with what one might have expected to be dismissed as childish bogies.

THE ROMANTICS

In the eighteenth century, when the Romantic Movement was born, the relaxation of taboo on 'unthinkable thoughts' brought to light a puzzling plethora of information on human desires. As the movement developed the idea was conceived that the way to resolve the tensions now emerging was to carry the inner thoughts into outer behaviour, to act out and enjoy the desires. Many of the hitherto concealed wishes were clearly recognized as ethically wrong; but it was thought possible that moralists might have been mistaken. More and more writers endeavoured to identify themselves with what the moralists condemned, in order to form their own opinions; at least, they created characters in their writings who did this. All the seductive but forbidden people of the seventeenth century, the prostitutes and beggar-maids, the negresses and witches, began to be regarded as rightly desirable.

Flaubert wrote of the ancient poetry of corruption and venality'. Baudelaire wrote of the Paris he loved as if it contained nothing but hospitals, brothels, purgatory, hell, and anguish. According to Keats, Burns also 'talked with bitches' and drank with their evil companions. Hugo saw debauchery and death as sisters who were equally terrible and fecund and who retained their enigma. Chateaubriand wrote that to love and suffer was man's double fatality. The subject of incest was so much in the air, so present to them, that it was given the special name, 'la criminelle passion'. It was said that Byron actually achieved incestuous relations; though, rather disappointingly, only with a half-sister.

This valiant attempt to face the horrific unspeakable and translate it into overt behaviour was a nobler attitude than merely to succumb to the sado-masochistic state of domination and victimization. It was an effort towards understanding which paved the way for later research into the motivation of human behaviour. Phases of apparent disintegration are frequently seen to precede true integration. But unfortunately this disintegration was suddenly precipitated into the most lamentable confusion by the publications of a man imprisoned for vicious and degrading practices, who was later to die in a lunatic asylum.

This was the Marquis de Sade. While in the Bastille, he wrote novels, plays, and an attempt at a philosophy of obscenity, the thesis of which was that virtue was negative and vice positive. Praz captures the impression of his works upon modern readers when he calls them 'a monotonous butchery'. This man cared nothing for the truth about forbidden wishes and was entirely preoccupied with sexual gratification through domineering. However, at this stage he was extensively read by the Romantics; and some tried to go even further by claiming that the purpose of virtue was the pleasure it accorded to vice in the aggressive satisfaction it gave to those who tried to overcome virtue.

The finest of the Romantics sincerely sought truth through studying the fluctuations of sadism and masochism, of domineering and being victimized. What they did not realize, of course, was that sexual gratification was to be had through being victimized as well as through domineering. Those of lesser calibre could do no more than imitate the outward behaviour of the finest without comprehension of the true purpose. Having no conception of the need to grasp both the horror and the beauty at once, they could only alternate between horror and beauty. Some of them succumbed entirely to the feasts of horror.

The literature moved from the relatively naïve stage of Richardson's moral indignation to the sophisticated relish of horrors with such writers as Schwob. Decadent scholars turned for inspiration to the *faisandé*, the putrid or decayed periods of the past, such as the Latin of the Decline, medieval criminal records, accounts of eunuchs, prostitutes, and beggars. Schwob published

Coeur Double and other volumes of tales about such vagrants and about ghastly unsolved mysteries, many of them legendary. Other writers struggled to think out new vices – a severe tax upon imagination, with civilization so old and every perversion already told in mythology, albeit in unrecognized form.

However, they succeeded in frightening themselves. They believed, as it has been believed in other decadent epochs, that the whole of civilization was about to collapse. When the great majority of ordinary people continued unperturbed to live normally healthy lives and enjoy what was beautiful, this flouting of their warnings distressed them. They were driven to write of distant lands, about which reasonable people could quote no contradictory evidence. Flaubert, writing of enchanting scenes set in jungles full of most bloody horrors, expressed the wish that he might die of cholera in Calcutta or plague in Constantinople. One must admire on the one hand the reasonable people who said that life is not like that, and on the other the artists who laboured at such pain to communicate a message that they felt to be of such vital importance.

Matters became so fantastic that those who had the integrity to persevere in the search for truth became seriously alarmed at the excesses of disintegration. They tried to stem the decadent tide by ridicule. In feeble parody, Le Gallienne wrote:

> *He dreamed of a new sin,*
> *An incest 'twixt the body and the soul.*
> 'The Decadent to his Soul' (*English Poems*, 1892)

Outstanding writers such as Janin, De Quincey, and Mérimée attempted to laugh the horrors out of countenance. But they underestimated the magnitude of their task. The fascination with horror was not just a surface symptom that could be disciplined by logic; barriers had been seriously breached and a flood was upon them. Virtue, against this exciting tide of evil, had no selling value. In fact, Janin put the writer's position in the tale of a young man, presumably himself, who had to abandon his fight for wan and puny virtue. This young man's fanatical propaganda for virtue brought such desolation and apathy into the world that life and happiness could be restored to man only by the rehabilitation of vice.

The cascade of human disturbance, an ecstasy of suffering, just had to work itself out, until finally Paul Adam wrote of it, 'There are more tongues cut out, more eyes put out, but nothing else is changed'.

ARTISTIC INTEGRATION

The reason why the whole of civilization did not collapse must have been that the forces of integration were strong enough to withstand this excess of disintegration. Many writers were striving after some means by which to avoid becoming too involved; they were trying to look at the horror without becoming carried away in horror. They used terms such as *disinterested*, *speculative*, and *detached* and felt that this was the only way in which it was possible to become aware of the horror without losing the sense of beauty. They knew that attention was gained only by rousing the senses, but that the senses must not be too much roused, lest they overwhelm thought.

Keats spoke of the need for momentous depth of speculation, and by speculation he meant something akin to the formulation of a fresh hypothesis by a scientist. He touched upon the Greek concept of the seer, blind to outer reality the better to see inner reality, and wrote of 'the viewless wings of Poesy'. Flaubert spoke of 'the great synthesis'. Shelley was so moved by the picture of the terrible Medusa in the Uffizi Gallery in Florence, where horror is with beauty, that he wrote:

> 'Tis the melodious hue of beauty thrown
> Athwart the darkness and the glare of pain,
> Which humanize and harmonize the strain.

Both Schiller and Shelley wrote of their experiences as appreciators of the spanning of horror and beauty in great art. They both wrote of their reactions to *Paradise Lost*. 'Automatically', wrote Schiller, 'we take the side of the loser; an artifice by which Milton, the panegyrist of Hell, transforms for a moment even the mildest of readers into a fallen angel.'[1] 'Milton's Devil', wrote Shelley, 'as a moral being is as far superior to his God as one who perseveres in some purpose, which he has conceived to be excellent, in spite of adversity and torture, is to one who in the cold security of undoubted triumph inflicts the most terrible revenge upon his enemy . . .'[2] Both experienced identification with the villain; Milton presented Hell and the Devil in such a way that it was possible to face them instead of fleeing in terror. This is a sublime example of how the artist may fuse the beauty and horror sufficiently for the appreciators to contemplate the strain. The nightmare sins, which we have seen are contained in *Paradise Lost*, can come up again for further review.

Sometimes even the greatest artists fail to maintain the detachment necessary for this review. Keats felt that Shakespeare had failed with *King Lear*; for him, and for many lesser appreciators, the momentous depth of speculation had, in this drama, failed to lift the play truly into the realms of artistic success. The curtain falls upon horror so terrible that contemplation is paralysed. As Shelley was moved to express the success of the Medusa picture in verse, so Keats was moved to express the majestic failure of *Lear* in verse:

> *When I am through the old oak forest gone,*
> *Let me not wander in a barren dream.*

Success in art enables the appreciator to increase the harmony between inner and outer reality; failure leaves the appreciator still in nightmare paralysed disharmony.

When artists become appreciators they make an authoritative contribution to criticism. From their personal knowledge of the creative process they are able to interpret novel elements in art that may at first confuse the general public. When the novel elements in *Lélia* appeared to the publisher Sainte-Beuve too

[1] *Selbstrecension der Raüber.*
[2] *Defense of Poesy.*

frightening, he startled the uncertain George Sand into denying her 'Satanic posturings'; he was not able to realize the revelation of deep conflicts, which was a novel element in Romantic literature. But when the artist Maurois wrote his exquisite biography of her, he called Lélia a witness not for the prosecution but for the defence. For him the presentation of Lélia's problems awakened sympathy, as Milton had awakened the sympathy of Schiller and Shelley for the Fallen Angel.

This brief review of the content of horrors presented by great artists in forms that make contemplation a possibility has revealed an impressive array of deeds without a name. They are the terrors of the earth, smacking of every sin, lust hard by hate, and every perversion; nothing vile or desperate is omitted and wounds without healing are left. Parents' tears cannot save their children from this trampling upon the moral world; the human sacrifice seems to go on without hope of cease. There is a strange delirious hunger that no embrace can satisfy, and people are driven to eat strange flesh. Over and over again there comes death at weddings, dealt by strange eyes; 'eyes threaten us into blood'; powerless victims are paralysed by furious rage. The extremes of hating and loving amount to the most appalling statement of suffering.

Before artists have been able to present this content to appreciators in endurable form, they have themselves had to undergo a rigorous self-discipline, playing with fire that might easily consume them. They tell us that it is not easy to define the nourishment upon which their imagination feeds, or with whom they learned their ecstasy. But they also tell us that speaking of these things helps to clear away their doubts. When they can find the necessary detachment, they are able to create in forms that allow the appreciator to receive their communication about these terrors of the earth; thus both artist and appreciator can come to terms with them.

These horrific literary characters are in a nightmare setting of agonizing dread and conviction of powerlessness for the victims. The domination and the victimization belong to no sane behaviour, to the outward bearing neither of children nor of adults.

On the rare occasions when these terrible thoughts are put into action, adults are deemed insane or psychotic. But with still plastic children, cure is proving so closely linked to understanding that breakdowns of behaviour no longer result in children being regarded as insane; under such stress they would at most be diagnosed as pre-psychotic.

The techniques of modern depth psychology have revealed the terrible pictures of horrific art to be closely allied to the terrible phantasies of rage which children undergo and which they learn to repress before they have sufficient command of language to talk about them. It seems that all children undergo these ghastly phantasies of cannibalism, murder, vampirism, and all the confusion of incestuous thought, in their great struggle to adjust their inner reality to outer reality. As they gain command of both realities, they split off or reject or throw away inner realities that fail to fit in with outer reality. They have no idea that some of the imaginings spring from inside themselves nor that thoughts which they have rejected could still be tucked away inside them in a form now technically known as repressed.

This error of the children is not surprising, since man has made exactly the same mistake through all civilizations, in fact until within living memory. Freud never claimed to have discovered the unconscious part of the mind; what he discovered, at the expense of intense personal discomfort, was the mechanism of repression whereby unacceptable thoughts are confined below consciousness. As we shall see later, it is precisely because children do not know that these rejected thoughts come from within themselves that they hit on a solution in their play. Moreover, until recent times very few artists have realized that the horrific themes which fascinated them were linked to their own forbidden wishes; and the countless appreciators who have been attracted to these horrific themes were equally in the dark about the sources of their fascination.

Just because adults have not realized this, art has given them a second chance to look at repressed problems, a second chance to use conscious intelligence coupled with mature experience in dealing with these problems. There was, naturally, a great outcry when it was first suggested that art sprang from forbidden wishes; it requires less effort of will to remain naïve and think the fascinating villains are nothing to do with oneself. Yet Shelley, who stated his view that forbidden things were poetical substance, died more than thirty years before Freud was born. Other very great artists have shown some awareness of this connection between artist's message and appreciator's thoughts. Hamlet stages a play to show his mother and stepfather their own thoughts and is so successful that all aesthetic distance is lost for them. It may be that Shakespeare was saved from prostituting his dramatic ability through creating a stage character who planned a drama with a lethal wound to inner reality, arising from his own uncomprehended infantile aggression.

It now begins to be a little clearer why both the creation and the appreciation of art require great effort and great integrity. Extremely personal material of a frequently painful nature is being reassessed in the light of further maturity. There is in all of us a streak of inertia, a 'don't-let's-go-through-all-that-again', which frequently makes us postpone creation or appreciation of high calibre. Theoretically artists suffer more in the struggle than appreciators; in actual fact, it is very likely that many unknown appreciators suffer more than many well-known artists. Because of the nature of the processes involved, art requires sustained effort towards integration if it is to result in greater understanding. Where communication is achieved the loss of nightmare loneliness would in itself reduce tension, apart from the nature of the message communicated.

It might be profitable to spend a little time studying an artist of the pre-Freudian era who was aware of the problems of childhood, of adult domination-victimization imbalance, and of the constant struggle necessary for attainment of aesthetic distance. Keats was such a man.

CHAPTER 3

An artist as an appreciator

> *There was a naughty boy*
> *And a naughty boy was he*
> *For nothing would he do*
> *But scribble poetry . . .*

John Keats, in his early twenties, apologized to his young sister Fanny for writing such rubbish to her and said he was too tired with his walking tour to write sense. The whole poem was to remind her of their early expeditions round their grandmother's country home in search of goldfinches, tomtits, minnows, mice, salmon, and 'all the whole tribe of the Bushes and the Brooks', of which he could now say, 'but verily they are better in the Trees and the water . . .' When Fanny was nearly eighty she herself wrote: 'I well remember . . . our pleasure in keeping little fish (called minnows I think) and his love of birds, especially a favourite Tom Tit.'

Since few people had noticed John Keats when he died, little is known of his family. What authentic information there is suggests that his parents were liked and respected by, for instance, the enlightened schoolmaster who had care of their three sons. The father, Thomas Keats, was head ostler to John Jennings, proprietor of the *Swan and Hoop* at Finsbury Pavement, London, and married Frances Jennings, daughter of the proprietor. The marriage was apparently without parental consent, as it took place in a church some distance away and the Jennings do not figure as witnesses; but the parents soon accepted their son-in-law.

Many years later a friend of the poet recalled the father as a man of remarkably fine common sense and native respectability with a lively energetic countenance. The mother, Frances Keats, has to be seen in historical perspective, for she was a woman of property in days when the possession by women of property and the attendant independence were frowned upon by men. On the one hand she is reported as lively, talented, impulsive, and full of gaiety; on the other hand she was darkly hinted to be 'the Slave of other appetites'. The sinister hint seems to be based upon the fact that she actually said that she must and would have a husband.

When Thomas Keats was killed in an accident, she was left with three little sons, John, George, and Tom, and the infant Fanny. She quickly made a second and unfortunate marriage. The grandmother took the children from her and when she left the second husband to rejoin her children she lost the greater part of her property. She was undoubtedly a woman of impulse, but the impulse to send the children to old Mrs Jennings was a very sound one. There the children grew up with an unusually close bond of affection for each other and with a lively interest in the world around them. Their mother was not strong and for years after she joined them she was confined to bed with rheumatism, finally dying of consumption. There is a tale that five-year-old John, hearing that the doctor had ordered her absolute quiet, himself stood guard at her bedroom door with the aid of an iron sword. There are also tales of his violent tantrums at about this age, and George said later that their mother gave in to his every whim, 'of which there were not a few'. Dorothy Hewlett, in her biography, gives yet another quite well authenticated tale of John, when learning to talk, repeating a word and adding to it a rhyme, and then laughing.

It was well for the children that they could be so united, for within the short space of ten years they were to lose both parents, both grandparents, and their adored uncle who had been a lieutenant in the Navy. The three younger ones looked always to John for leadership, though George, the least belligerent, had often to restrain John's violent outbreaks; being stronger he could take the simple measure of sitting upon him till he was again laughing.

Before John and George were breeched, their parents selected a progressive boarding-school at Enfield for them. As Cowden Clarke, son of the headmaster, was to become a life-long friend to John, there are fuller records of him from this time. He had a brisk, winning face and was a favourite with boys and masters alike. He was a most orderly scholar and put great energy into playing, particularly into fighting. One friend speaks of his violence and vehemence, his extremes of mood, being in either passions of tears or fits of outrageous laughter; this coupled with his great physical beauty captivated the boys, and no one was more popular. The three boys – for Tom soon joined them – were so close that they had few intimate friends. Those whom John had, had to prove themselves first by their readiness to fight; once having done this, it was not fighting which he expected of them but a sort of grotesque and buffoon humour. Cowden Clarke saw John's rages and fights as superb picturesque exhibitions, comparable with the polished performances of his idol Edmund Kean. He gives an account of Tom having been rude to an usher and having his ears boxed: 'John rushed up, put himself in the receiving position of offence, and, it was said, struck the usher – who could, so to say, have put him into his pocket.'

George wrote of their mother that she was 'a most excellent and affectionate parent and as I thought a woman of uncommon talents'. John left no comment upon her. When he was fourteen he spent his last holiday with her, sitting up whole nights in a great chair, suffering nobody to give her medicine but himself; he cooked and did everything for her. During her intervals of ease he read her novels. He must have thought that he could compel her to live, for when, during the next term, he heard she had died, he was completely shattered; his impassioned and prolonged grief moved all to pity.

It was about this time that he gave up violent physical activity and turned to books. He had always read a great deal but now he began to study. He quickly exhausted the school library. He translated long sections of the classics quite voluntarily; he devoured the half-yearly prizes for amount of work done, which always came to him, such as Kauffman's *Dictionary of Merchandise* and Bonnycastle's *Introduction to Astronomy*; he poured over any reading matter he could find, such as Leigh Hunt's *Examiner*, a periodical of wide and often controversial interest. The headmaster subscribed to this paper and spoke up for the Hunts when they were imprisoned for persistent attacks upon the character of the Prince Regent. John Keats must have had some interesting discussions with the head over this paper; when later John met Leigh Hunt it was through him that he was introduced to Shelley. After he left school to study surgery the boys remembered him as a formidable bruiser, the masters remembered him as a brilliant scholar, and his fellow apprentices saw him as an idle, loafing fellow, always quoting poetry.

Here, then, is the picture of a healthy, lovable boy, utterly unaware that he will become one of the greatest poets of all time. The difference between him and other healthy, lovable children is not qualitative; all children love excitement, discovery, opportunity for physical activity, and gangs of friends; in the course of normal development all children feel closer bonds to the family than to those outside. It is only in adolescence that Keats's striking quantity of ability begins to show: his high intelligence, voracious reading, boundless imagination, and awakening sense of purpose. At first glance it might seem that anyone could become a successful poet with all those gifts; but the more there is to integrate, the greater the task of integration. One friend thought he would become a distinguished admiral, others thought he would become a surgeon – he might have been either, or have distinguished himself in many other spheres. He chose to become an original thinker in the world of art, and, when he had made the final decision for poetry, he dedicated everything to this with high purpose.

There is just a handful of letters covering those few short years of poetic production, written from 1816 to 1820, which tell the inside story: a mere two to three hundred letters that he wrote to

his family and to a few friends. More than forty are to his sister
Fanny and nearly forty to Fanny Brawne. These letters are
bubbling with vitality; they abound with such vivid comments
that it is difficult to believe that he was a sick man who had to
contend with the most overwhelming depressions. Indeed, it was
not his intention that the recipients should be burdened with his
problems. If he could tell them in ways sufficiently entertaining to
ward off too much suffering in sympathy, he would do so; if not,
then he refrained from writing. Moreover, he hoped that his
friends would exercise the same restraint in maintaining distance
when communicating with him. This artistic distance, para-
mount in his works, was integral – and consciously so – to the
man. He wrote *There was a Naughty Boy* to Fanny a couple of
days after he had sent to George the sonnet on the tomb of
Burns; he had been so completely overwhelmed by what he
learned of Burns that he felt robbed of creative power for a time.

Some of his gayest comments have become proverbial far
beyond the world of literary criticism: 'I am about to become
settled, for I have unpacked my books'; 'The wind is in a sulky
fit'; and, of a performance of *John Bull* at Drury Lane, 'Musicians
began pegging and fagging away at an overture'. All that he
would say of his exhaustion and depression would be such
comments as: 'Truth is I have a horrid Morbidity of Temperament' or 'I am in that temper that if I were under water I would
scarcely kick to come to the top' or '– and now I am never alone
without rejoicing that there is such a thing as death – without
placing my ultimate in the glory of dying for a great human
purpose'. If he found himself getting too worked up he would
write: 'I will speak of something else or my spleen will get higher
and higher.' On one occasion he made the exquisite comment:
'I carry all matters to an extreme – so that when I have any little
vexation it grows in five minutes into a theme for Sophocles.'

He was sufficiently confident of his ability to appreciate his
own work to rise above the criticism of others. 'Praise or blame',
he wrote of *Endymion*, 'has but a momentary effect on the man
whose love of beauty in the abstract makes him a severe critic of

his own Works.' However, to those who were near him, he made the most engaging comments about that momentary effect. When Leigh Hunt and Shelley were being excessively critical because – he suspected – they were offended at his not consulting them, he touched on a childhood game with his brothers, '... they appeared much disposed to dissect and anatomize any trip or slip I may have made – But who's afraid? Ay! Tom! Demme if I am.' On another occasion he quoted *Henry VI* of the critics, 'I see swarms of Porcupines with their Quills erect like lime-twigs set to catch my Winged Book'. He could trust the appreciation of his friends, who were known to him; it was the unknown Public which he distrusted: 'When I am writing for myself,' he told his congenial friend Reynolds, 'for the mere sake of the Moment's enjoyment, perhaps nature has its course with me – but a Preface is written to the Public; a thing I cannot help looking upon as an Enemy, and which I cannot address without feelings of Hostility.' In the Preface to *Endymion* he stated his own evaluation of the work as a feverish attempt rather than a deed accomplished.

What he could not accept was barrenness in art. Of Leigh Hunt, whose ambition to achieve fame as a poet was not supported by lyrical ability, Keats wrote, 'Hunt does one harm by making fine things petty and beautiful things hateful ... This distorts one's mind – makes one's thoughts bizarre – perplexes one in the standard of Beauty.' But for the fruitful suffering of coming into contact with reality he had the greatest compassion. He was so deeply moved by the poetry of Burns that he was consumed by a fire of pity for all he went through, and wrote, 'His misery is a dead weight upon the nimbleness of one's quill – I tried to forget it – to drink Toddy without Care – to write a merry sonnet – it won't do – he talked with Bitches – he drank with blackguards, he was miserable – We can see horribly clear in the works of such a Man his whole life, as if we were God's spies.' As if we were God's spies! This depth vision which he experienced in appreciating Burns, though it caused him anxiety, did not prevent him persevering in depth appreciation of poetry. He was so upset about Burns that he wrote, 'it is impossible to make out that sorrow is joy, or joy is sorrow'. In a strange mood, half-asleep, he wrote the sonnet on Burns, saying, 'All is cold Beauty; pain is never done'.

This sonnet to Burns is not ranked as one of his great works. He was suffering too much sympathy at the time. He felt that Shakespeare also had become too involved when writing *King Lear* and so had failed to achieve a final momentous conclusion. Keats found that he could come to his own momentous conception of the truth only through application, study, and thought. His speculative power waned if he became too involved in human relationships; he could attain universal depth of feeling only if he stood back from the impact of close individual contact. In his opinion one of the finest things Byron ever wrote was:

> *I am free from Men of Pleasure's cares,*
> *By dint of feeling far more deep than theirs.*

But there was no question of his regarding poets as a race apart in this; he tried to achieve detachment with his friends but he also tried to get them to achieve it themselves. He complained of Reynolds that he had no sufferance. He was deeply touched when Bailey wrote him a gloomy letter and then tore it up to write again more cheerfully. This, he said, he would never forget. 'You were at the moment', he replied to Bailey, 'estranged from speculation.' He was also very much aware of the danger of this detachment, should it become excessive; at one time he feared that he might lose all interest in human affairs. This was when he called himself an addict to passivity.

His letters give remarkably precise information on how he attained this state for 'the innumerable compositions and decompositions which take place between the intellect and its thousand materials before it arrives at that trembling delicate and snail-horn perception of Beauty'. He said that the quality needed for a Man of Achievement in literature, such as Shakespeare, was a *Negative Capability*, to be capable of being in uncertainties, mysteries, doubts, without any irritating reaching after fact and reason. He believed Shakespeare to be *enormously possessed of this negative capability.* Of Reynolds's quarrel with a friend he said both were in the right and both were in the wrong. Of the unfriendly criticism which had made Bailey gloomy, he said the sure way was first to know a man's faults and then to be passive. He maintained that what occasioned the greater part of the world's quarrels was simply this: 'two Minds meet and do not understand each other time enough to prevent any shock or surprise at the conduct of either party.'

His concept of the poetical character itself contains these apparent contradictions, the attention and passivity and waiting and application essential for the innumerable compositions and decompositions to evolve. He said of the poetical character:

'. . . it is not itself – it has no self – it is everything and nothing – It has no character – it enjoys light and shade; it lives in gusto, be it foul or fair, high or low, rich or poor, mean or elevated – It has as much delight in conceiving an Iago as an Imogen. What shocks the virtuous philosopher delights the cameleon Poet. It does no harm from its relish of the dark side of things any more than from its taste for the bright one; because they both end in speculation . . . When I am in a room with People if I ever am free from speculating on creations of my own brain, then not myself goes home to myself: but the identity of every-one in the room begins to press upon me that I am in a little time annihilated – not only among Men; it would be the same in a Nursery of children.'

The reference to the nursery of children suggests that he was aware of this poise between self and not-self at a very early age. In a letter to his sister when she was just fifteen he makes a most interesting reference to their childhood equivalent of the 'virtuous philosopher' who does not understand this self-and-not-self game. He had taken her out to visit Well Walk and she had rather injudiciously let her severe guardian know that they had not only been to Well Walk.

'I do not mean', he wrote when he heard she had been in trouble for this, 'that you did wrongly in speaking of it, for there should rightly be no objection to such things: but you know with what People we are obliged in the course of Childhood to associate; whose conduct forces us into duplicity and falsehood with them. To the worst of people we should be open-hearted: but it is as well as things are to be prudent in making any communication to any one, that may throw an impediment in the way of the little pleasures you may have. I do not recommend duplicity but prudence.'

So the need to side-step praise and blame from uncomprehending virtuous philosophers was something known to him from the nursery years. This self-and-not-self game was a task of immense importance which could bring fruition, to the child as to the man, only if he were left to work things out for himself. Of his conscious determination to find his own solution with *Endymion*, he wrote, 'Had I been nervous about its being a perfect piece, and with that view asked advice, and trembled over every page, it would not have been written.'

In order that he might preserve himself to himself, being everything and nothing for creation, his rapier-sharp humour, originating in the outrageous laughter of childhood, was raised to the highest poetical level. Thus he learned to sustain the negative capability through which he could span extremes with impartiality. In the unsuccessful Burns sonnet he captures his own failure to speculate when he says that all is cold beauty and pain is never done. During the process of developing his humour as an aid to negative capability, he became deeply interested in the problem of humour.

He came to see that there might be an inner truth in the distorted that might be lacking in the outwardly well-proportioned. 'I can never', he wrote, 'feel certain of any truth but from a clear conception of its Beauty – and I find myself very young minded even in that perceptive power – which I hope will increase – A year ago I could not understand in the slightest degree Raphael's Cartoons – now I begin to read them a little.' He said that he learned to read them through 'seeing something done in quite an opposite spirit'. He suddenly realized that a picture of saints by Guido, missing all the heroic simplicity and unaffected grandeur of Raphael, appeared canting solemn melodramatic mawkishness. Then he chanced to see a book of Milan frescoes, and felt that he had never known greater pleasure outside Shakespeare. He found them 'grotesque to a curious pitch' but full of romance and most tender feeling, with magnificent draperies and making a finer whole than more accomplished works, because more room for the imagination was left. Those inclined to raise an eyebrow at the implication that the Milan frescoes were not accomplished would do well to consider the influence upon the history of aesthetics which this speculation of Keats has had. Today we accept as axiomatic something that Keats arrived at through his highly developed power to see things in 'quite an opposite spirit'.

Keats undoubtedly felt that his mature attitude to art had roots deep in childhood play, in the kind of play that is likely to be misinterpreted by some of the People with whom children are obliged to associate. The way in which some of the critics were niggling over his trips and slips in *Endymion* made him feel that, had he been obliged to associate with them, *Endymion* might never have been written. It is now time to turn attention to this highly serious business of children's play, from which there can arise such mature *negative capability* in adult creation and appreciation.

CHAPTER 4

The psychology of children's play

Less than a decade after Keats died, Froebel published his view that the play of children was not trivial but highly serious. This was a novel idea. Throughout many civilizations children have been left to play, the adults merely thankful that they could occupy themselves happily. The serious activity for them was believed to be their educational learning. Only in relatively recent times have educationists begun to realize that, in the revolutionary words of Froebel, play is a very serious business; even now, the nature of the seriousness is not widely understood. As it happens, it has in some ways been greatly to the advantage of the children that they were left in peace to play, because uninformed interruption of a serious business can have most harmful effects.

There are certain familiar characteristics of children's play that have always been recognized as indication of its importance to the children. These include the ecstatic pleasure that it gives them at times, the passionate and sustained effort that they will put into solving problems, and the tireless repetitions that they will carry out. It is as if they were out-manœuvring some invisible enemy. At times they seem very happy and at times they seem lacerated with anguish. But happy or unhappy, some ecstatic delight carries them on – unless something goes seriously wrong and play stops, or has to be stopped. These characteristics are constant whatever the age, from the two-year-old discovering how to jump down the last stair to the twelve-year-old playing shipwreck round the playroom furniture.

There is a clearly marked evolution that can be only crudely classified in years. During the first two years bodily movement is the most noticeable characteristic. During the next four or five years, though movement is almost as much in evidence, phantasy begins to play an increasingly important part. Then the gang stage sets in, with rules not merely tolerated but welcomed and invented; in addition to the socially recognized games, such as hide-and-seek or tag, and club activities, such as Brownies and Cubs, secret societies are convened and booklets of dos and don'ts carefully scheduled. As the second, the phantasy, stage retains much movement, so the third, the 'rules', stage retains much of both movement and phantasy.

Throughout this evolution there are periods of progression and regression, when characteristics of the next or previous stage predominate. A child of eighteen months who repeatedly puts her father's hat on the hall stand, on her head, on the hall stand, and on her head, is almost certainly working out some phantasy as well as moving. A child of twelve, waiting to receive his plate at lunch, who beats and chants a rhythm of *Chig-a-ti-bom! Chig-a-ti-bom!* with knife and fork upon the table mat is probably regressing to both earlier stages, in an idle and placid moment. Adults, for that matter, experience a strong element of earlier stages of play when they enjoy Walter de la Mare's *Do-diddle-i-do, Poor Jim Jay* or Edward Lear's *Far and few, far and few, Are the lands where the Jumblies live* or many other such poems which spring to mind.

It is generally accepted that the first stage, the period when movement predominates, is the common link between the play of humans and the play of animals. For both it seems to serve the dual purpose of releasing surplus energy and helping to gain mastery over the play-objects. The infant in the pram struggling to grasp a suspended rattle and the kitten pouncing upon a thrown cotton reel are experimenting with as yet unfamiliar neuro-muscular mechanisms that will later be used in the business of living. They are also releasing energy not yet required for looking after themselves. During this time much mental effort goes to learning how to estimate and manipulate the environment. Most of us have no recollection of discovering, for instance, that if you hold your finger between your eye and the door knob, the one you do *not* focus upon has a double image. Yet it is by such experiments that a child learns to estimate position in space about him. When the first steps are taken, and hitherto unattainable objects can be investigated, the child goes through a veritable orgy of grasping which can be very distressing to an adult not wise enough to remove unsuitable objects.

By the phantasy stage a child has learned a great deal about how to manage people, in order to get what he wants (or as much of it as possible). If he smiles at his mother he is more likely to get what he wants than if he screams. As there were errors in grasping objects, so there are errors in assessing his mother's expression. For instance, if she says 'No' even ever so mildly, he may assume that her unsmiling face means that she is as wild with rage as he is when he refuses her what *she* wants. He neither knows nor cares what his own face is like when he is angry. During the long period of learning he discovers that not everything that he experiences is part of him. If he bites his own finger, he cries out; if he bites his mother's finger, she cries out; if he bites a brick, nothing cries out.

The discovery that not all is self but some of it is not-self happens at a very early stage; and this is a childhood discovery that is rarely detected by adults other than experts. In a nursery where there were two identical wooden engines, a two-year-old straddled one and started going round the room. Another two-year-old got on to the other and started going the opposite way round the room. In due course they met head on and stopped. The reflection-like image before the first child puzzled him; the engine might have been a reflection, but not the child upon it. After a long pause he pointed slowly at the other, saying, 'That's Jimmy,' then pointed slowly to himself, saying, 'That's me'. The teacher's comment was, 'It is not often that you can catch a moment of realizing the self from the not-self'.

Another essential discovery by the child is that certain impulses must not be carried out if certain desired ends are to be gained. This may just concern the material environment or it may involve people. If a brick is almost out of reach, it is exciting to stretch out and touch it; but if the objective is to grasp it, then the great temptation to make the easier movement of pushing it farther away must be resisted. This is frequently seen when a child sits on an adult's knee at a table and plays with objects. What might be mistaken for a piece of childish stupidity is actually a major intellectual exercise, and like many later exercises it is liable to be sadly impeded by outbursts of emotion. If, however, the desired object is a sweet in the possession of an adult, and it is wanted with almost intolerable urgency, then the temptation to stamp must be resisted. With the brick physical laws are being formulated, but with the sweet psychological laws are being formulated. When adult behaviour is inconsistent, the newly forming laws of behaviour become infinitely more difficult for the child to establish.

The whole business of learning to manipulate the environment of objects and people in order to satisfy as many wants as possible is the child's adjustment to outer reality. It is a laborious and often painful process, because he is driven forward by imperious inherited inner drives and driven backward by frustrations too strong for him to surmount. If he cannot surmount them then he is forced to compromise. The compromise that he makes is to repress some of his impulses; the impulses are still forceful but no longer being expressed. He knows no more of how he does this than he knows of how he circulates his blood; moreover, nobody can explain to him how he is to do it. His own mind has to do this battening down below decks of impulses that work out as unprofitable to the child. Needless to say, there are many errors that the tiny child makes in these decisions as to what is acceptable and what is not. The greatest help that parents can give is to spare him unnecessary frustrations. This is done by letting him have plenty of what he needs for development and by being consistent when frustration is deemed wise.

The technical name for this self-learned process of compromise between inner and outer reality is ego-formation. During the development of the child's ego he compromises for long-term gains, and what he represses continues to be active in the unconscious part of his mind. Since the repressed wishes are energetic in confinement, much energy is required for holding them down. But so far as the child knows the impulses have vanished; they are disowned, de-selfed, gone. Like all humanity prior to the last few decades, the child believes the rejected impulses to be gone.

Eventually so much of his ego is split off and disowned in this way that he has insufficient energy to hold down the whole noisy crowd of living repressed impulses. His dilemma is this: expressing the impulses caused him anxiety so he 'forgot' them; but now holding down so much forgotten desire inside himself is beginning to cause him even more anxiety than expression did. The solution comes through his not knowing of the continued existence within him of all these split-off and repressed parts of himself. If these split-off bits of himself could emerge in some slightly changed form, he might not recognize them as his own wishes. He could then think they were something from outside. Not knowing that they were anything to do with him, they could appear as something socially acceptable; he could then have another chance to consider them, to make the major decision as to whether they must be rejected in entirety. 'Split-offs' emerging as their original selves would, from past experience, immediately be banished. But split-offs *changed* to something rather less disreputable and seeming to be outside himself could not be recognized as his own impulses, because he knows that he has rejected being anything like this. The technical name for this split-off process, whereby repressed mental processes not recognized as of personal origin are ascribed to the external world, is 'projection'. Such unrecognized projections are naturally of great interest to the child since they are his own transmuted desires.

From the point of view of play this is exactly what happens. The split-offs come out as real or imaginary 'outside' objects, and no anxiety is felt because no responsibility is known. In such a way the larrikins turn up in the nursery, and the children will chat for hours to them or even discuss them with adults. A child of four had a larrikin called Mr Daceman, of whom she could – as we now understand – explain little. He seemed to be always present and it was assumed that he was in touch with the adults. 'Give it to Mr Daceman,' she would say of any difficulty, 'he's sure to know what to do. He can take anything.' In due course, having served his infinite-coping capacity, he vanished. Usually the adults can find no clue to the appearance, disappearance, or even the extra-ordinary names of these inventions. But in this case the child was highly intelligent and had a dearly loved adopted aunt, a retired educationist, who managed to gain a little insight into the matter. With utmost delicacy and casualness she managed to trace his moment of origin and something of the symbolism of his strange name.

The child's family had moved house when she was only three. (Children of three should not see a home broken up; having no data for assuming the damage can be repaired, they undergo terrible emotional strain and the new home is liable to be first viewed as something liable to break up.) In the primordial upheaval of her environment, the shrewd child noted one thing that seemed to restore some measure of calm to the disturbed adults concerning the disturbed objects. Of any piece of furniture with which they did not know what to do, they called to each other, 'Put it in the basement.' 'There is plenty of room in the basement.' 'Thank God for the basement!' God bless Mr Dace-man! Only a person could be so helpful.

The split-offs can equally well be projected on to objects, on to a piece of string, a bent gas-pipe, a dog, or a teddy bear. Countless split-offs can take possession of an object in rapid succession; a feather is thrown up as a tossing kite, laid to rest with a hummed lullaby, grasped fiercely and told to create fairyland, or crushed underfoot and instructed to annihilate all the rice pudding in the world. Thus repressed wishes – in these examples, perhaps, to fly away from trouble, to be loved to sleep, to have omnipotence of domineering thought over even smaller people, and to reject for ever a hated food – can rise again to consciousness. The wishes can, as it were, have a second chance to be integrated into the child's personality instead of being totally repressed. A second chance? Sometimes they seem to have thousands of chances as the child plays the same tireless repetition over and over, day after day. Even though, time after time, the game, which is not yet played out, has to be deferred, and the original impulse repressed again, the repressed wishes have had an airing and some of the work has been done. Moreover, the child has had a temporary respite from the labour of maintaining repression.

The illogical but completely 'psycho-logical' phantasy play is often followed by apparently inconsequential but basically relevant questions:

'What would happen if there were no rice pudding in all the world?'
'The people in China would be very sorry, because they like it and eat a lot.'
'Couldn't there only be rice in *China*?'

To limit instead of totally to annihilate rice is clearly a step towards integration; but it is a step that might never have been taken without the split-off game with the feather.

The objects, real or imaginary, on to which the split-offs are projected may be transitory or permanent symbols of the inexpressible, the unutterable, the horrible because not-acceptable. The phantasies rise spontaneously, unbidden by the child, and are accompanied by the ecstatic pleasure that has had to remain bottled up ever since the original desire had to be denied expression. They can be completely hallucinatory in strength, because of the vivid intensity with which children experience and can obscure reality. Mr Daceman could hide things by standing in front of them. The whole process is so remarkable that it would be incredible if one had not met countless cases of children behaving in this way, creating unaided their own phantasies of such great intensity.

It is a laborious task for children, learning to distinguish between the always interesting phantasy and the often uninteresting outer reality. Wise adults often enter into the phantasy as a means of communication with the child, if interruption is considered advisable. A light jest such as: 'All the best Red Indians finish their dinner before going hunting,' will not be mistaken by the child for a lecture on ethnology; it will be accepted as a very understanding remark and the Red Indian will probably finish his dinner. The ecstatic power of feeling rising from the unconscious part of the mind and flooding the ego is a power to be reckoned with, if unnecessary conflict between adult and child is to be avoided.

Phantasies can rise when the child is awake or when he is asleep; but they may get seriously out of hand when he is asleep and become nightmares. The reason for this is very interesting. When he is awake the child is not merely regressing to the situation when the split-off first happened; something happens that fundamentally alters the situation. He is receiving new impressions from outer reality and has gained new skills in mastering outer reality, while entertaining the unrecognized part of himself; and his intelligence is fully occupied in bringing all three together. But in sleep he is receiving no new impressions and his intelligence is not fully operating. Consequently a pleasant split-off can be dreamed with enjoyment but he is more or less defence-less against an unpleasantly unacceptable split-off. The original rejected impulse can rise in much too recognizable a form and he wakens in terror over this forbidden thought, which comes at him from outside – or so he thinks. Once fully awake he has repressed it again, so that it is impossible for him to explain to the anxious adults. For the split-offs to rise again to consciousness in a helpful fashion, he must be fully awake and ready to work hard or – as it is called – to play hard.

It is no wonder that so many children go through a phase of suddenly refusing to go to sleep or of being afraid of the dark. It is in the dark that they experience these insufficiently transmuted desires, which they assume are attacks from without by horrible, unspeakable things doing deeds that must not be named. They are warding off the external circumstances that they know precipitate these monstrous attacks, by keeping awake or by staying in the light. Sometimes a child who is afraid of the dark wants something so badly that he is willing to endure the dangerous circumstances necessary to obtain it; such an act is of the essence of courage, which should be recognized. In *Anthony* Lord Lytton gives an account of the four-year-old boy wanting a fez to which he was very attached, that is to say a fez on to which his split-offs were projected in a relatively permanent way. It was evening, the fez was in the bedroom, and the child suffered from night fears. Between where the family were sitting and the bedroom there was a winding staircase upon which stood a full suit of armour. Nearly all the Lytton children were scared of this knight in armour who was not there. On this particular evening nobody would fetch the fez for Anthony, and he 'needed it for some game', so he went himself. All the way up the staircase he maintained contact with the others by carrying on a running commentary; in the room they could hear him still talking hard. Finally he called out, 'I sees it everywhere but I can't find it!' showing the hallucinatory strength of the phantasy. When my college was evacuated to this house I mentioned this incident to Lord Lytton, standing by the gaping vizor of the knight, and he said, 'We were surprised that he was brave enough to go'. Yes, indeed! To go to the region of untransmuted split-offs in the dark in order to fetch the symbolizing object for creative activity was a most courageous deed.

Seen from the child's point of view one of the obvious problems upon which the child must work is the great difference between child and adult. The adults appear so big, strong, well-informed, disciplined, and authoritative. By comparison the child appears so small, weak, uninformed, and undisciplined; even to the adult he appears like this. But to the child himself, as the adult seems far greater than he really is, so he seems to himself far smaller than he really is. The first erroneous judgements made by the child ascribe to these super-beings gargantuan storms of love and hate of which, even were they still willing, the ageing parents are no longer capable. It is only by means of further reviewing by split-off play that the child is able to correct these first misjudgements.

Since these first erroneous impressions of adulthood are caused by the nature of the developing child's mind, even the most benign of parents must undergo this misassessment. A child in the high chair, shaking his head at the proffered spoonful, may become so worried because the mother, thoughts elsewhere, continues to hold it there, that he will himself do what he is expecting her to do next – take the spoon and actually ram it down his own throat – and then scream with rage! With this sort of thing going on in a child's head, it is no wonder that children develop food-phobias. Spinach cannot be nourishing in such an emotional turmoil. Even the authorities concerned with physical health agree that a child who has taken a dislike to some food had better not be fussed to finish it up.

With these facts in mind, it becomes easy to see why states of misunderstanding develop between parents and children. An uninformed parent, wishing to be the all-seeing, all-wise figure remembered from childhood days, may be completely unnerved by the apparent unwillingness of the child to behave with due deference. The real situation may be that the child is so unduly impressed by the magnitude of the parent that he is fighting with all the little might he thinks he has for survival. An unnerved parent behaves irrationally, sometimes too leniently through regret and sometimes too sternly through anxiety; in varying thus he greatly adds to the child's problem, the formidable task of formulating laws of permissible behaviour. When the misunderstandings arise parents and teachers should review their own consistency and ask themselves whether they are being sufficiently consistent about what must be insisted upon; and they should see the matter from the point of view of the child struggling to make generalizations.

Games such as Mothers and Fathers or Schools, if adults eavesdrop, are very revealing, and of course can be remarkably wounding to the adults, if they do not realize what is going on within the children. In my early days, under the impression that I was running a very modern infant and junior school, I was truly horrified to see myself parodied as a dragon of a teacher during play-time. The caricature was quite unmistakable: *Stand up! Sit down! Put your things away! How thoughtless of you!* Disobedience is often as guiltless as any other *faux pas*, and we should spare the severity for the few times when it is really advisable. The wiser the adult, the fewer the occasions for severity that arise.

Parents may hear themselves bullying the children, commanding them to bed *whatever they are doing*, beating them for smoking, hounding them to eat all the food or be starved to death, and so on. This is most valuable information on how what one does strikes the child. A child may be seen alternately beating the teddy bear and being beaten by the teddy bear. It is all part of their very serious split-off work. After being a bullying policeman for a week, a child may reach a stage when he can be the anathematizing driver.

Play, as understood by the lay population, is not a really good term for what the child goes through in these first years. Words are inadequate to describe the complex mental processes at work. What one needs is a series of films superimposed upon each other, a working model of interacting fountain jets or, better still, an algebra for child development. For instance, in the case of the game switching from policeman to driver, the skill with which the child now pours contumely from driver to policeman suggests that as policeman he must have realized before the end that the driver also had a point of view. Thus, if A represents rude policeman and B represents rude driver and C represents courtesy of the road, then the process gone through is as follows: A–AB–B–ABC–C. Even as adults we are constantly being fooled in personal relationships through not realizing that C is on the way, if we would only wait; but no, we constantly wound ourselves by mistaking A or B for the end-product and losing our tempers, largely in panic.

Infant-school authorities who incorporate serious play in their day's programme correctly call it *Creative Activities*. With most children, interested in all the skills they are learning about the manipulation of outer reality, by primary-school age only a part of the time need be spent in violent, disintegrative play. The greater part of the time is spent in play that helps them to master outer reality. Thus writing and reading and calculating are found to be going on during play for quite long stretches of time. This is a most valuable contribution in helping them to advance the quality of their split-off play. As he heaves and builds and balances bricks, a child is learning the beginning of physics: weight, gravity, size, substance, density, through relating weight to size of different materials, and so on. As he achieves what he has in mind, adapted as with adults according to circumstances, he is filled with the ecstatic pleasure attendant upon all split-off work. At night, by the bed, there may be a little museum of friends who have stood up to this work: a bear, a penknife, a couple of large nails, a train and the old, bitten, but adored lamb.

By the junior-school stage, creative activity should still be catered for, but of course with outer reality playing a much larger part and self-discipline much more in evidence. An author-producer of ten learns far more of the craft of play-writing when his leading lady, who seems to lack vitality, gives him a sharp retort, 'How *can* I get dramatic when all you give me to say is "Oh, dear"? Give me something to get worked up with if you want a show-down!' But creative work of this kind can only be carried on in practice when the principles are understood. Too many crises occur for ready answers to be given for all contingencies. Once the principles are understood, the kind of answer required is obvious and the actual wording in the particular event can be improvised on the spot. With a little practice it becomes quite as automatic as the rude old-fashioned shouting. However, very young parents or teachers often have to work out what they ought to have said afterwards, in order to do better next time.

What has to be understood is this: where play is successful, fresh realities interact with old split-offs while joyous energy floods the ego. Where play is not successful, certain conditions are lacking. There must be no direct reality gratification; and no feeling, particularly fear, must become too real for pleasure. Well-meaning adults who, seeing the children wolfing at a dolls' tea-party, provide real food, arrest the game; real food cannot be wolfed in the split-off way. Split-off eating is split-off eating, something the adults do not allow. Children will sometimes laugh till the tears roll from their eyes over some greedy boy in a story who chokes over a bun; they know he has mixed reality and split-off behaviour.

Many adults have described excess of fear which has ruined play. In *Dew on the Grass* Eiluned Lewis describes Lucy's intolerable panic over hide-and-seek, with the precision of self-knowledge. The account ends:

'. . . useless to say that this was only Maurice or Delia after you, worse than useless, because at bottom you knew that it was something really dreadful, something infinitely disastrous that would catch you in the end, however fast you ran.'

One of the problems of social development which children must face is that the threshold of 'too much fear' varies with individuals, not only according to age and environment, but also according to temperament. Lucy is no happier with trains than with hide-and-seek:

'They ran round and round the walled garden; only when she was finally cornered in the potting-shed and had flung the yellow flag from her did the inexorable engine apply its brakes. "What did you think would really happen to you?" he asked, roused for once from his own imaginings by her white face and obvious distress. She could not explain . . .'

Even if the children playing together are of the same age, temperament, and environment, in order to play together successfully they must learn some measure of attuning their split-off work. They can agree to Let's Pretend but their pretending must have some common factors or they will not fit together at all. Only with some community of interest can their playing together have the curative integration of successful play. If one child needs to play something over and over again, while the other is finished for the moment after two or three repetitions, then play breaks up and each goes his own way. That is as it should be. Force them to go on playing together, and the frustrations they are causing each other will make them hate each other. The delicate task of maintaining flexible and diverse oscillations cannot be sustained under such painful stress.

Where circumstances allow the delicate oscillations, the innumerable compositions and decompositions, to be sustained, play seems interminable and pointless; it may go on for hours without any outward sign of achievement. The inward achievement is the permanent widening and closing of the boundaries of the ego. For brief periods the conflicts appear in disintegrative play with reality; and the outcome of this disintegrative activity is that some of the conflict can be dissolved, for integration of valuable impulses into the child's personality. Because the child has been able to play both cruelly domineering adult and cruelly victimized child, his realistic grasp of the child-adult relationship has been increased. In an immense variety of situations he has gone through A–AB–B–ABC to a better comprehension of C. This could never happen without split-off play. The crux of the matter is that the ego copes with these rejected parts of itself *while disowning them.*

With this extraordinary fact in mind, it is extremely impressive to watch a child or a group of children carrying out their apparently pointless games which arrive at no visible successful climax. But what is more important is that, knowing this, one is more respectful towards their activity and much less inclined to intrude unless there is some very good reason. By means of this Let's Pretend the child is able to think about what he thinks is not himself, but which is himself. With integration comes greater intellectual clarity because a problem has been successfully faced; and part of this clarity consists of recognizing that what was thought to be outside is really coming from inside.

Loss of ability to pretend may be just a temporary break in activity. But chronic anxiety may cause the loss to become permanent. In this case, the precarious balance of inner and outer reality essential to play being lost, it may become impossible for the child to fit the phantasies to the real or imaginary objects. The child then withdraws from the outer world, or seeks wild reality-gratification like Billy Bunter, or becomes mentally lame. Lameness or paralysis of activity means that the child has repressed the unchanged impulses again, because there has been no interaction of outer reality and phantasy. This means that much energy is diverted to maintaining the repressions in original form. This is a partial death redolent of W. H. Auden's 'We must love one another or die'.

In 'Aggression in Nature and Society' Turquet writes: '. . . the human organism is profoundly malleable, responding to cultural conditions . . . In the Western world, the early experience of aggression conflicts with what has been called "the primary ethical imperative of society" (Parsons 1947) – love thy father and thy mother.' If the child is unable to pretend some outside object which is angry with the family, then malleability is lost, the family conflicts remain unsolved, and the child comes to need specialist help. The task of the play-therapist, in such a case, is to reinstate the capacity to pretend, so that normal widening of the ego boundaries can progress, conflicts be coped with as they arise in play, and intellectual progress be made.

It would seem that the Golden Age of Childhood is a myth of the most unrealistic kind. In 'Contributions to the Theory of Play' Kardos and Peto go far more deeply into the mechanisms of play than is appropriate to a study of this nature. Reference is made to the conspicuous but misleading element of happiness during the disintegrative phase of play, while conflicts rise and the temporarily released feelings flood the ego with ecstasy. In fact the child is no happier than an adult struggling to resolve a complex problem, or an artist painfully achieving a creative work, or a patient and analyst during a difficult session. People occupied in this way are ecstatic but not happy until there is integration. These writers point out the basic problem of happiness, which seems to emerge as soon as it can be realized that complete satiation, reality-gratification, is unpleasant. They maintain that all the elements of play, the ecstatic pleasure, the sustained effort, and the tireless repetition, are present in elementary form at a very early stage – even as early as when the nearly satisfied infant begins to play with the nipple, losing it and finding it playfully. This game, at a time when the infant is believed to be too young to play, has greatly puzzled thoughtful parents. It would seem that the problem of happiness requires Let's Pretend almost from the beginning.

Of course, there is a sense in which one can speak of the Golden Age of Childhood. Children have the technique for dissolving the boundaries of the ego and can pursue an ego enrichment through disintegrating, followed by synthesizing activity; and ecstasy accompanies this process. Their often painful happiness consists of a transitory disintegration, followed by further integration; and the technique used is a form of denial, a pretending. As early as 1925 Freud revealed the importance of 'it is not true', of 'let's pretend'. He regarded this as a basic defence mechanism and called it *Negation*, a term startlingly reminiscent of Keats's *Negative Capability* without which a man could not achieve literary success. Negation's full creative importance, as conceived by Freud, permits creative oscillation between reality and illusion, whether in children's play or in artistic creation or in scientific detachment.

The theory of children's play put forward in this chapter is quite avowedly one dependent upon depth psychology. Francis Galton, the father of scientific psychology in Britain, said: 'When you hear a fresh statement about human beings, ask: Is it based on experimentation? If not, suspend judgement. Is it confirmed by statistics? If not, beware of trusting it.' The views on play expressed here are a much over-simplified statement of the findings in clinical and other research. But during the last decade or so there has also been an increasing amount of orthodox experimentation concerning the development of children.

Over a hundred boys and girls ranging in age from six to fourteen years were asked to make up fairy stories. Between them they made up 461 stories. Only those who were more intelligent and better adjusted could express their views in the socially accepted form of a fairy story. When the stories failed to conform to a structure suitable to the age of the children, the failures were found to be due to such causes as: actions and feelings being somehow incongruous; bizarre atmosphere of failure and frustration with avoidance of difficulties or with existence of unpleasant emotions; unnecessary disasters and difficulties with destructive actions reiterated; stress on the happiness of the characters irrespective of incidents or stress on the unhappiness of characters despite happy circumstances. When the children who had not succeeded in creating a successful story were questioned they showed an incongruous amount of fear, or failed to produce any response, or else entered into excessive descriptions of irrelevant details. D. M. Vernon (1948) who conducted this investigation, suggests that possible causes of disruption in the stories might be either failure of imaginative invention to function adequately or a tendency for imaginative invention to 'take charge' of the children.

In another study over a hundred boys and girls ranging in age from six to twelve were studied for their attitudes towards the family. Some were normal, some neurotic, and some delinquent. It was found that, on the whole, the normal boys and girls had strong self-assertive trends, lively conflicts with their parents, and ambivalent swings between love and hate for their brothers and sisters. Their attitudes and emotions appeared to have been reasonably well integrated, resulting in balance and freedom and a generally constructive attitude towards outer reality. For them self-assertion was a constructive impulse. But the neurotic and delinquent children showed signs of disturbed relationships within the families. The delinquent children showed an unusual degree of detachment from their families; and the neurotic children showed an unusual degree of attachment to their families, which was frequently of a sado-masochistic nature.

The conflicts of both the delinquent and the neurotic boys and girls remained in a state of confusion instead of being integrated, and this was reflected in their attitudes towards people and life in general. Self-assertion had become predominantly a destructive impulse and this was borne out by later social studies of these children. L. Jackson (1950), who carried out this work, points out that treatment would have to go in opposite directions for the delinquents, who were too detached from the family, and for the neurotics, who were too attached to the family. Play-therapy would have to help weaken the restrictive bond of the neurotics, who were clinging too closely to the family, and help strengthen the bond of the delinquents, who were moving away from the family too fast. Before either could be done it would be essential for good *rapport* to be established between child and play-therapist.

Since disturbed children have lost the delicate balance of self and not-self, the power to oscillate between composition and decomposition, between integration and disintegration, their play with the therapist frequently appears to the uninformed alarmingly destructive. This may be an essential phase in the process of reinstating the capacity to widen the boundaries of the ego. During the war, when I was treating a neurotic boy of six at Guy's Hospital, the Psychiatric Social Worker, who had been seeing his mother while I saw him, came to me after a couple of months and said: 'Good news! His mother complains that he is getting rowdy at home!' Incidentally, the very first spontaneous remark which I got from him, after weeks of play, was: 'My Mum got some *liver* tod'y.' The way he said liver made *my* mouth water. Next came some information about a little boy in his road who *swears* – and 'swears' was said in a hoarse stage-whisper. The discrepancy between the reticence of his outward behaviour and the lurid quality of his inner thoughts was most dramatic.

Much can be done in the ordinary routine of school to give the children opportunity to display something of their inner thoughts. Puppetry is a very obvious form of split-off play, which can be shared while being guided. Quite recently two young post-graduates, training for primary-school work, took puppetry with seven-year-olds in different schools. Both invited the children to keep diaries of their puppets 'instead of keeping diaries about themselves'. Both were inundated with more than forty lengthy, vivid diaries of rich material. Any of it might be quoted, but one example from each school must suffice. In the first school, a boy wrote on three successive days about trouble his puppet had had over eating fish: day one, he refused to eat his fish, so his mother sent him to bed hungry; day two, he refused to eat his fish, so his mother smacked him and he ate it; day three, his mother asked him why he would not eat fish and he said because it smelt like dustbins, '*so he never had to eat fish again*'. In the second school the student, from Ceylon, had never met progressive education until this course; she asked the children to give her a puppet dream, confessing afterwards that she had not expected anything interesting. At least half the dreams were bad dreams, some children stating that the puppet was good though the dream had been naughty or bad. Here is a typical one:

> My puppet is a boy. His name is Robert. He is a naughty boy. Last night he had a dream. It was about a burglar. One night the burglar robbed Robert's bed and him. The burglar opened his bag and put Robert into it and tied his bag. He took a kniffe and killed Robert and that was the end of my pupet. When his mother got up and saw Robert killed the burglar took his knife and killed his mother and that was the end of his mother and Robert.

Note the break-down of spelling when the burglar attacked him. At the beginning and end he spelt both knife and puppet correctly.

What does one do with such material as this? More than twenty of the seven-year-olds' dreams commencing their diaries were as bad as this. Education is an art, and the first step is to exercise a 'negative capability' in recognizing that the aggressive material is there, within the children. Just understanding is a far greater step than is generally realized. We know from our adult relationships the immeasurable assistance that we receive from friends who really understand, although there may be nothing they can actually do. This is an immeasurable assistance that we can give the children, once we can disabuse ourselves of the traditional role of Virtuous Philosopher, of ceaseless adviser. By now the nature of this assistance becomes clear.

Let us see what happened with the students and their puppetry classes. The students chose to help the children make puppets for two reasons: the children would learn manipulation of outer-reality material in the craft and they would spontaneously use their own puppets as split-offs, which we can now recognize as their projected inner realities. The students knew that, their schools being formal, the children would have had little opportunity for ecstatic creative work in school. This meant that much anxiety would pour out of them; they therefore invited the children to begin their diaries with dreams, because it is quite socially acceptable to have queer dreams, and anxieties could be expressed without guilt; perhaps one should say without much guilt, since some felt called upon to exonerate their good puppets from their bad dreams.

Exactly as planned, the children were ecstatic about their puppets, working like slaves to complete them; and bad dreams poured out from half the children. By just understanding that puppets can be naughty and bad, the students set an example in negative capability; furthermore, they demonstrated that this game is known to adults. In this way the students made for the troubled children a genuine outer reality of the self/not-self game; the children, with none of the tricky process put into words, would be encouraged to persevere in the delicate process of arriving at integration. Exactly as these two students hoped, the children themselves moved quickly forward to integrative work; though they could often be seen turning back the pages to read again the extraordinary dreams that their puppets had experienced at first.

Clearly, a sound educationist must have a sound ego-formation; without it one is not equipped either to set a good example or to see what environment should be prepared for the children. The time is rapidly passing when students trained for progressive education can remain unaware of the mechanisms whereby they are assisting children towards realism through creative work.

Strangely enough, there is one sphere of this educational split-off work much used by those in charge of children, where the children are so far below subsistence level that they will take material of any quality, good, bad, or indifferent. This is story-telling. When we tell children a story we project characters and events upon which they can in their turn project themselves. Here again, we perform that subtle task of initiating them into the idea that other people, even adults, have inner realities some of which cannot be permitted. They are so starved of this story-telling assistance that they will hang upon every word, even when the story-teller may be projecting quite unsuitable phantasies in quite unsuitable ways, as many an adult with faulty ego-formation will do. Why do they go on listening? Because a starving person will eat strange food that the well-fed would never touch.

In order to go farther into this curious state of affairs we should examine in detail some such teller of tales. We could scarcely do better than look at Hans Andersen, for his stories are world-famous, and this renowned story-teller was a profoundly disturbed person.

CHAPTER 5

Hans Christian Andersen: success and failure

Far out in the sea the water is as blue as the petals of the loveliest of cornflowers, and as clear as the clearest glass; but it is very deep, deeper than any anchor-cable can reach, and many church towers would have to be put one on top of another to reach from the bottom out of the water. Down there live the sea people.

The man who wrote this story in 1835 was thirty years of age and so short of money that he could not pay the rent; nor could he buy decent enough clothes to go to the houses of friends who offered him free dinners. For sixteen years he had been struggling to earn enough to live on in Copenhagen to allow him to write poetry. His artistic antennae had gone out in many directions: actor, singer, playwright, poet, novelist; and now, as pot-boilers, he had tossed off four of the many tales he told to his friends' children while minding them out of the kindness of his heart.

When a friend who was a professor of physics said that if his novel *The Improvisator* would make him famous, these four tales would make him immortal, he was frankly incredulous. When they caused such a stir that they seemed to be distracting attention from what he regarded as his major works, he wished he had not written them. 'Those trifles!' he said irritably of *The Tinderbox, Big Claus and Little Claus, The Princess and the Pea*, and *Little Ida's Flowers*. They were no more than tales he had heard as a child or had woven round some incident, which he had put down exactly as he told them to the children! Yet these very tales, and many others to follow, were to be more frequently translated and more widely read than any other literary creations in the world, excepting only the Bible and Shakespeare, and possibly also *The Pilgrim's Progress*.

What lies behind this strange story of a great poet unable to make true critical assessment of his own creation? This is the very antithesis of Keats's ability to judge his own works. The story, as it unfolds over many years, cannot be told briefly. He was a giant, and giants cannot be put into thumbnail sketches. Still cruelly short of money, he brought out a second volume, containing *Thumbelina*, *The Naughty Boy*, and *The Travelling Companion*. He had to, because he was hungry. When this, too, was acclaimed as highest art, his friends managed to convince him that his gargantuan imagination had touched fresh springs of universal appeal. Cornered into using a literary medium unknown to his generation, he poured his heart into it.

Next came *The Little Mermaid*. 'Nothing I ever wrote', he said, 'has so moved myself while I was writing it.' He had dipped into his own bosom. He was no longer writing only for children; not even primarily for children. As an old man he wrote in his diary, almost contemptuous of the children: '. . . my fairy-tales were as much for older people as for children; these children only understood the *stuffage*, and not until they were grown up could they see and grasp their full meaning. The naïve was only a part of my fairy-tales; humour was the real salt in them.'

Now, in order to find out what had happened we need a great deal of information, which can be gleaned from a number of biographies; and for the purpose of this study we need it in very concentrated form. Unlike Keats, Hans Andersen lived to be a very famous old man, so there is a wealth of information about him. But these facts will strike our modern eyes very differently from the way in which they appeared to his contemporaries. It would assist us to assemble them in a modern idiom. This liberty will not offend the Danes; all they ask is that the world should try to understand their magnificent genius. They know even better than we do that not all his tales are suitable for children.

Let us, then, take one moment in his youth when, in 1819, at the age of fourteen he set out for Copenhagen to become a famous poet. We can assemble the facts as they would be presented at a child guidance clinic conference, where experts pool their information.

Very well, then. On a golden September afternoon in 1819 Hans Christian Andersen, against the advice of almost everyone, set out, aged fourteen, from his native village of Odense; he was bound for Copenhagen, where he was sure that he could become a famous poet. Now we take him a hundred and fifty years forward to 1969 and make an appointment for him. He will be seen first by the psychologist and then by the psychiatrist; the psychiatric social worker will visit his mother. Then the three specialists will hold a clinic conference at which they will try to diagnose the situation. The setting is a game – moreover, a game that requires no irritating reaching after fact and reason. But the findings of our three experts are well-known facts from the life of Hans Andersen.

PSYCHIATRIC SOCIAL WORKER'S REPORT

His mother, Ane Marie Andersdatter, was very friendly and gave me a great deal of information, which I have tried to put into some sort of order. She is a washerwoman, both capable and cleanly. Her own family was very poor indeed and she used to be sent out as a child to beg, which she hated doing. But she was afraid to go home without money and recalls having hidden under an arch for a whole day, weeping in fear and misery. She is deeply ashamed of one sister who seems to be of easy virtue. She herself had an illegitimate daughter by a potter before she met and married a cobbler named Hans Andersen; this daughter is now in a foster-home. Her marriage was in 1804 and their son was born two months after the wedding. Her husband died when young Hans was eleven and she married another cobbler a couple of years later. Both her husbands seem to have been considerably younger than she and unable to stand up to her bossy, motherly personality. The second husband appears to be something of a disappointment; he seems negative and expects her to do more washing now in order to keep them both.

Of the first husband, father of young Hans, she repeated over and over again that he was very, very clever but so very sad. In addition to being intelligent and depressed, he was utterly indifferent to his cobbling craft. She said impatiently that she was more likely to find him reading one of the books that he kept above his bench than cobbling. As she herself is illiterate, she was unable to tell me the exact titles of any of the books, but she remembered Holberg and was sure that all the books were philosophy and the Scriptures. Then she added that there were one or two translations of German novels which he would sometimes read to her – and then she could have a good cry. She never saw him smile except over his clever books; but she could never understand why he found them funny and he could never explain.

He used to read a great deal to young Hans and spent most of Sunday either reading to him or making him toys: puppets, a theatre, and things of that kind. There were often tears in his eyes, for instance when the Latin School boys went by. He said a great many queer things which everyone knew were wrong, such as there being no hell or devil but what people carried in their own hearts. When the big comet came eight years before she and her neighbours were out discussing what disaster it meant, and just as she was warning the boy that it might knock the earth to bits his father came by and 'explained scientifically', but of course nobody believed him; so he said that the worst comets he knew were drink and lotteries – and went on home.

There was one thing upon which he insisted: The boy must travel; and he must do whatever work he liked, no matter how silly it might seem to other people. 'In the end', she said bitterly, 'he went travelling himself, but it did him no good. He went to the wars, ruined his health, and came home to die when our Hans was eleven.'

Her father-in-law had apparently been a great trial. To begin with he had been quite well to do, but he was struck by financial disaster and become unbalanced. He had managed to make a little money hawking round wooden figures that he carved himself. But he did odd things, like decking his hat with flowers, so that the boys followed him and jeered. When he came to their house he always made faces through the window; and he never addressed one single word to their son, young Hans, except once when he apparently failed to recognize him. He was never dangerous, so they did not have to have him chained up; and mercifully he died some years before her husband. But her mother-in-law is a sweet, gentle, blue-eyed woman. She is on very good terms with her grandson and often used to take him with her to tend the garden of the neighbouring lunatic asylum or to see her friends who worked at the town prison. She spent many, many hours telling him tales about the days when her family were gentry. (I have looked up records and there seems to be no evidence that her family were gentry.)

On young Hans himself she was so voluble that it was impossible to get down everything. She vacillated between two attitudes. On the one hand she was filled with pride that he reads so much, sings so sweetly, tells such marvellous tales, writes such clever plays, is listened to by the gentry and called the Nightingale. But on the other hand she was filled with anxiety that he was not a little more like other children, had no friends of his own age, and got so wildly upset if anyone said the slightest thing against any of his stories. The neighbours said he would go the way of his father and grandfather, though they liked his stories well enough. The boys called after him in the street and nearly scared him out of his wits.

He apparently had a normal birth and seemed just like other children for a year or two. He had cried a good deal at first, in spite of the fact that his father started reading Holberg to him when he was two days old. When he could talk he occupied himself endlessly in chattering to himself and playing with his toys, particularly the puppets his father made for him. At night he lay on their bed in their one room with the curtains drawn, talking to himself or listening till he fell asleep. Their bed stood on a rough bier that had been made to hold a nobleman's coffin – it still has some of the black cloth hanging from it.

When he had temper tantrums he got so much worse with scolding that they had to let him have his own way. He had terrible nightmares – still has them – about countless things: fierce men and boys, dogs and chains, horrible hairy mouths and suchlike. There seems to have been one strange recurring dream, about his having a baby that had either been born dead or had turned into a wet cloth when he held it. He was always terrified of the dark and ghosts and goblins; and he seems very frightened about dying; though, she says, she took him to church regularly, and taught him to say his prayers regularly and never to forget God.

I asked whether she could account for any of the fears, for instance the fear of dogs and chains. At first she said she had no idea, but then she remembered something. One day, when he had gone to the asylum with his grannie, he was peering through the bars at a chained woman whose back was turned; she suddenly whipped round, rattling her chains, and growling at him. She thought it could have been this; at any rate, he had gone quite rigid with terror at the time. Then she remembered something else, though this was an incident of which she was very proud. She and her neighbours had gone gleaning and an angry steward had chased them with a dog-whip. But Hans was barefoot and could not run over the stubble; so he turned on the man and said: 'How dare you hit me when God can see you!' For that he got a smile and a penny from the steward and boundless admiration from the neighbours. One thing that puzzled her was that many of the things that frightened him by night fascinated him by day, such as candles, fire, sparks. She also felt that some of his fears were so peculiar; for instance, he did not like very open places and even made trouble if the end of the pew in church was not closed properly.

I asked whether he had made any fuss about food. At first she said no, none at all; but then she said he did not like sweet soup, because it made his teeth ache. Then she said he could not eat when upset. When pressed, she recalled an example. It was a christening at the prison and though she could not remember how old Hans was, he had been small enough to be carried home after the party. She could not say what had upset him but it had been so disappointing, because there were all his favourite foods and he could not eat a thing.

Almost as an afterthought, she said they had for a time thought he must be epileptic, he got into such 'states'. His father had wanted him to be taken to the doctor but she did not hold with them. She preferred to take him to the old witch for magic cures. She used to measure him with magic wool and express surprise at the enormous length of his limbs, because he was growing so fast. The witch said they must dip him for three successive years in a certain fountain up in the hills. She went once, but a child had a fit before they could get him into the water and it upset Hans, and somehow they never went again. Anyhow, nothing seemed to do him any good.

When he reached school age, she took him to an infant school and told the old dame that she must never, never beat him. He learned his letters quickly. But one day she hit him, so he came straight home and refused to go back ever again. Then she took him to the poor school for Jewish children and he was happy there. He used to get into trouble for what she called 'being away', by which she meant day-dreaming. Once a friend was being punished and he got into one of his states, which caused such a commotion that the friend had to be pardoned. When he seemed too big for school, she tried to get him to take up a trade. But the men made coarse jokes and said he must be a girl with that voice; they tried to undress him to see, so he ran away and refused ever to go back there.

But for all his queerness, she said proudly, the gentry think highly of him and lend him books and listen to his plays and invite him to come and sing to them. Some years ago, she said, a gipsy had looked into his coffee grounds and said the day would come when all Odense would be illuminated for him. Yet, in spite of her pride, there was no doubt that she was profoundly anxious about his going off to Copenhagen alone. However, he had pleaded and pleaded so much, and reminded her of the gipsy and of his father saying that he must travel and do whatever work he liked, no matter how silly it might seem. Anyway, he did not get on with his stepfather, who thought he ought to be at work. So, one way and another, though she felt guilty about it she had said very well, then, if he was determined, he could go; and she gave him the most worldly advice she knew to counteract his innocence: *See and not hear, hear and not see, if you want to get on in the world.*

PSYCHOLOGIST'S REPORT

When he came into my room I was astounded at his great height, his mop of whitish blond hair and the tiny eyes, set so far under his brows that he almost seemed blind. He loped to a corner and very carefully put down his bundle, which I imagine contained clothes as cared-for and ill-fitting as those he was wearing. Then he came and sat down with a striking mixture of uncertainty and confidence. Although he seemed intensely anxious to please, he either answered so swiftly that he did not seem to have given himself time to think, or else seemed to miss noticing that I had spoken. This variability of attention made sustained concentration impossible. He fidgeted with things on my desk and made determined efforts to lead the conversation to some writings that he wished me to read. Finally I took them all from him. But this upset him so much that I asked him to draw me a picture, hoping to put his mind at rest. Immediately he became utterly absorbed in drawing a picture of his home in Odense. It was remarkable that his huge hands could produce anything so delicate. When he had finished, he passed it across to me with a really lovely smile; the smile so transformed his face that it changed from peculiarly plain to most beautiful.

Then he helped himself to another piece of paper, took my scissors, and made a folded paper-cut, to show how he often decorated the inside walls of the house. It was highly elaborate and again done with remarkable care – definitely too much care.

There was a great deal of practice behind these movements. He had made a double (mirror) cut-out of a tree and swans and a dancing ballerina. Suddenly he looked up intently and asked if I had been reading his plays while he was working. I had glanced at them and seen that the writing was almost illegible and the spelling outrageous; I had managed to decipher the last two lines of one play, which were: 'Death I now perceive, all my limbs to cleave!' He informed me that this was a Shakespearian tragedy that he had written three years before. I asked how he had come across Shakespeare and he said the pastor's widow had lent him the translations. In another play I had caught sight of a strange mixture of languages, so I asked about this. Apparently he had sought to make his court scenes most regal in tone and badgered everyone to tell him how royalty spoke, till in the end his mother had said she thought they spoke German. He had found a French-German-English phrase book and written in all three languages, cemented with Danish. Thus there were remarks such as, 'Guten Morgen, mon pere, har De godt sleeping?'

He informed me that he had, at the time, planned about twenty-five tragedies with titles such as: *The Evening Promenade or the Cook and the Count, The Two Murderers, Qvarto and Laura, Zemire from Bagda,* and *The Temple of Honour.* This was when he was eleven and twelve. I asked if he had ever seen royalty and his face filled with ludicrous disgust as he said yes, but they wore ordinary clothes and were nowhere near as regal as his characters.

His felicitous choice of words could be humorous or macabre or exquisitely poetic. I inquired about 'the gentry' who, he told me, liked him to sing to them; he described one woman as a 'little black coffee-pot, boiling over with excitement'. I asked if he liked the sound of words, though it was quite obvious that he did, and he replied, 'Words are an Iris arch'. Then I asked about his father, who had died at the time when this impressive literary programme had been conceived, and he said that he was dead, that the ice maiden had beckoned him through the peepholes they had made on the frosted windowpanes with hot pennies. He said he had seen his father lying dead upon the bed where they had all three slept till Hans was too long to lie across its foot; he lay dead on the nobleman's bier, which still had the bits of black stuff from the first funeral. 'I don't want to die!' he suddenly said, with a nervous tremor. Then his face brightened and he said gaily that he would like to get on to a cannon-ball and ride through the spheres.

I asked about school and he said that he never quarrelled with any boy. Again the transforming smile as he added with a twinkle, 'But then my legs are longer than theirs and they could never catch me!' This was followed by a mutter in a puzzled voice, which it was hard to catch. He said that some of the other pupils peeped at the books; it annoyed him; but – he wondered if he would not do it himself, except for the shame of being caught doing it; yet he wished 'the masters would catch the others – which was a base trait'.

He said he used to do his homework between lessons. I asked about spelling. Yes, he got into trouble about spelling; but he forgot all about it while writing. The masters got angry when he was lost in thinking out his own stories. During all this conversation he kept jumping up and gesticulating to explain what he meant.

Because of his state of excitement it would have been impossible to make any objective assessment of his level of intellectual ability. He either concentrated too much or failed completely to concentrate. However, there was sufficient material for some tentative conclusions. His verbal ability seems to be phenomenal; his vocabulary is very rich, his speech is very fluent, and he selects words with remarkable precision. His imagination is outstanding and his imagery seems to be equally auditory, visual, and kinaesthetic. He also seems to have drawing, handwork, and musical ability well above average. The paper-cutting and drawing were done with meticulous care that indicated a high degree of muscular coordination. It may be that the clumsy movements of the whole body result from the excessive speed with which he has grown in recent years, together with the evident emotional disturbance, rather than from lack of ability to coordinate his limbs. In spite of the impression he gives of being naïvely unaware of himself, he possesses considerable powers of self-analysis, for instance in the introspection on cheating.

All this suggests a level of intelligence well above average.[1] But it is impossible at present to estimate the part played by special verbal ability; this may be far above the general level of intelligence, or it may be that lack of emotional discipline is impeding an equally outstanding general intellectual ability.

PSYCHIATRIST'S REPORT

Having failed to display his histrionic talent to the psychologist he took no chances with me. This curious, quivering apparition came in talking hard, parked his bundle with scrupulous care in the corner of my room, still talking hard, and announced firmly to me that he was a passionate lover of the theatre. It seems that he often went to the theatre with his father and when there was no money to spare he begged handbills from the theatre and made up his own dramas at home, while wishing he was at the theatre. He regards his own as almost as good as real theatrical productions. 'I can play you a scene from *Cendrillon*!' he called out, jumping up and pulling off his long boots, to be freer in stockinged feet. 'I love that play. I have seen it played by the Royal Players at Odense.' And he danced round and round, his long brown frock coat whirling out behind him. His gestures were wildly, wildly uncoordinated and he just improvised both words and music as he went along. What a shocking ego-formation! Because he felt like Cinderella as he talked and danced and sang, he assumed that he must therefore look like her.

I thanked him and invited him to sit down again. At this he stood stock-still; and as he looked at me his eyes filled with slow tears. Without a word, he put on his boots again as the great tears rolled down his cheeks. I had failed him, utterly and completely. He had expended so much energy on the performance

[1] It is interesting to note that C. M. Cox in *Genetic Studies of Genius*, vol. ii, p. 7 of chart facing p. 60, gives the following estimate of Andersen's intelligence: A1 – I.Q. 130; A2 – I.Q. 145.

that there were no reserves for withstanding the terrible blow. I have never seen so much courage in displaying so much vulnerability. I wondered how much he knew. Were pride and humility already completely divorced? Or was he at least in some measure aware of the terrible transition from one to the other as he wept?

His physique is drawn up 'dwindly', as gardeners say of a sapling in the shade. I quite see why the witch felt she must measure him with her magic wool, though I did not myself stop to make anthropometric measurements today. His nervous system is hysterically sensitive, so that he must live both pleasure and pain to the most abnormal limits; rather like a child removed from the nursery to adult circumstances. His daily imaginings must take him to regions never known to the majority of adults; and these imaginary regions are undoubtedly hallucinatory in strength.

However, he soon started talking again. He leaned forward eagerly, fidgeting with the things on my desk, and pouring out his hopes and dreams. The relief of being given a hearing after all brought the euphoric phase back in full flow. He is to be a famous actor-author-poet and will shortly be returning to Odense to be fêted. Yet he kept dropping his voice to a mutter and saying such things as: life is a fairy-tale; poets have to suffer a little and then triumph; the best always happens. One would have thought that suffering was some mere trifle unknown to him personally, though the tear-stains were still damp on his face as he talked.

When I asked him about his home he seemed to undergo a wave of anxiety, a horror that he might have to go back. Only the future really interested him, and I had to keep dragging him back to the past. He said that his grandfather was mad and the boys hooted at him. I asked if the boys hooted at him too and his face changed to a mask of terror, the colour of his eyes lost in the black dilation of pupil; but he said with quivering firmness that the boys were his friends and liked his stories. He would not have it that his father was mad – only sad; he described how he used to do everything he could think of to cheer him up and win from him some little encouragement. Then he began to pour out happy

78

recollections of the home to which he was terrified of returning: his mother, the neighbours, tales round the fire, the village pump, and the spinning wheel; the dead pastor's library, the letter now in his pocket from the printer to a famous Copenhagen actress. All he had to do was to get to Copenhagen and the best would happen.

He seems completely unaware of his ambivalence towards his home; unaware that for him travelling is running away from a reality that refuses to conform to phantasy; Copenhagen spells Promised Land. Yet his talk of travel had an excitement in which delight was laced with terror. 'Your worries turn out to be nothing,' he said. 'I will write to my mother and someone will write her a letter to me. No need to look for torment. God will provide.' He talked of God as if he could see nothing to prevent this benevolent deity from giving him exactly what he required.

With some difficulty I got him to talk about the local asylum and prison. He recounted quite clearly the fascination and horror with which he used to peer at the chained and locked-up lunatics. He said that when he was taken to the prison he used to feel that he was entering a robber's castle; it gave him a 'tickling sensation of terror and delight'. No wonder his super-ego demanded retribution by taking away his appetite; and at a time when he was so little that he had to be carried home! To be aware of the meaning of prison at such an early age supports the idea of his intelligence being high.

About his dreams he was much more voluble. Some were wonderful, particularly one about a lovely smile, over which he became so excited that I was inevitably reminded of the Giaconda Smile, which Walter Pater saw as that of the archetypal seductress and Freud believed to represent the mother of Leonardo da Vinci. But there were some paralysing dreams about which he could scarcely speak: a bat growing bigger and bigger till it overpowered him like a vampire; all his teeth falling out; things that trickled icy cold through him, carrying a dead child from him; riding a hippopotamus which was trying to eat his leg; thinking he was joining the King on a naval cruise and finding too late that he was on a slave-trader.

Our problem is this: exactly how far has the psychopathic swing between elation and depression become hysterically consolidated? The unrecognized aggression in him is stupendous; he weeps and boasts and throws stones. He either attacks everyone else or attacks only himself; and when he, with everyone else, attacks himself, he is driven to self-preservation by completely rejecting the entire attack upon himself. What hereditary chances of recovery has he got? The mother is, completely unwittingly, a domineering woman who seeks husbands more like sons than lovers and who 'over-loves' her own son; there is too much of the mother in her love for men and too much of the lover in her attachment to the boy.

The father, overpowered by his own father's unrealistic escape, gave up almost all outward attack. The few shots he makes at his uneducated associates are far beyond their understanding. However, he did better than his own father. He found true consolation in his erudite books and formed a real relationship with the boy, though at times he was decidedly unwise, for instance in sharing his ice-maiden phantasies of death beautifully beckoning. Moreover, he had a salty humour for those who could appreciate it. He said to young Hans, of the half-sister who is apparently becoming a harlot, that she was 'a woman who suffered from attacks of unrequited love'; and there were the comments upon drink and lotteries. But the fact remains that he was incapable of being insistent with his wife; he just let her take the boy to the witch instead of the doctor. He must have been aware of how he was letting the boy down, otherwise he would not have given the counsel of despair that he must be allowed to do what did not seem sensible to them, to travel and to do what work he chose.

The trouble with the boy himself is that the Plimsoll line of his conscious mind is pathologically low; and added to this, the circumstances of his upbringing have done little to help him integrate outer and inner reality. One might go so far as to say that many events of his childhood have been such as to unbalance a far more normal child. At present his notion of the meaning of art is completely at the infantile level: art is tumultuous recognition. If he is ever to widen the boundaries of his ego, to form a realistic attitude to life, he must create. If he does not create, he will annihilate himself by death or insanity.

Perhaps he has suffered most of all in ordinary social development with his contemporaries. From them he has been trebly estranged: his superior gifts take him into realms of literature unknown to most village fourteen-year-olds; his feminine sensitivity makes him a laughing stock to normal boys of his age; and he is liable to lose all discrimination between the self and the not-self. Just think of a great lanky boy of fourteen having no idea that he is not looking like a dancing Cinderella when he feels like one! He gave evidence of having hallucinations sufficiently powerful to suggest actual physical distortion of perception. This was particularly so concerning pride and shame, feeling big and feeling small, which he has split off and attached to happenings outside himself. He gave most graphic accounts of sometimes seeing everything enlarged, till stones were horses and reeds were ships' masts with fluffy pennants; and sometimes seeing everything as microscopic. The intensity with which he described it all was reminiscent not only of Swift's Gulliver but also of Swift's breakdown. There was the same lack of responsibility in some of the gruesome phantasies, in which horror was not mastered or enjoyed but treated as non-existent; for instance he told a tale of a butterfly that longed to be a flower but achieved this tranformation only when dead and mounted upon a pin.

THE DECISION

The discussion of this information would be directed towards deciding what hope there was of successful treatment and how long it might take; this would have to be weighed in the balance against how many less disturbed children could during the time be put securely on the road to sound and steady development.

The alignment of evidence might well take some such form as this:

(*i*) *Against taking him on*. No appreciable results could be expected in less than half a dozen years; it could take much longer; there might never be complete success at this late stage. He was in no mood to see the need for intensive and often painful application. This plethora of get-famous-quick phantasies would be difficult to dislodge. If he were to be returned to nineteenth-century Copenhagen, with its renowned classical tradition and patronage of impoverished artists, he might find a patron in spite of the shocking state of his manuscripts and the unreality of his dramas. His screams of pain over criticism and furious overcompensations of violent attack on others would only be mistaken for vanity. It is highly improbably but just conceivable that he might succeed on his own.

(*ii*) *For taking him on*. Although his family spoilt him, they did so in despair, and were motivated by the basic Danish respect for personality. Though his father exposed him to some unfortunate phantasies arising from his own depression, he had a good relationship with him over toys, reading, expeditions to the theatre, and so on. He was too old for play-therapy but his literary aspirations would be a great asset not only as a tool for treatment but also as a worthwhile goal in undergoing the rigours of treatment. Such an original personality might well be helped towards contributing something quite novel to art – though it would be impossible at present to have any idea of the direction in which this novelty might lie. The possibility of this outcome might well outweigh the possibility of failure in treatment.

Well ... they never had a chance to decide whether they should take on this major task of attempting to help a potential genius to integrate inner and outer experience through therapeutic art. But any clinic team might well have hesitated to take on such a patient, through sheer humility for their own capabilities.

Hans Andersen completed his twenty-four-hour journey to

Copenhagen with just enough money in his pocket for a couple of nights' lodgings. How much the Danes were able to help him, in spite of his chronic disturbance, and with what personal anguish he found his new form of art, can be read in biographies by Toksvig, Reumart, and many others.

For four years he hit his head against disaster and near-disaster because, of course, he always mistook advice for complete and utter rejection, reacting with self-preservative violence. Acting, dancing, singing, and playwrighting all ended in fiasco, not only because he mistook every helping hand for a belligerent fist but because he had no technique for getting outside himself and seeing what he was doing. His patrons included professors, artists, administrators, and even royalty. They fed him, clothed him, and gave him money for education. But he could see no point at all in wasting precious time on education, when success was permanently with him in hallucinatory form – or at least, just round the corner. It finally took the King himself to bring home to him his desperate need for mental discipline. Hans was informed by Collin, a reserved and respected administrator, that the King had granted some money for him to go back to school – at the age of eighteen.

He told the terrible story of his schooldays only to his diary. The cruel headmaster, the jeering little boys, the terror of speaking before them; underfed and misunderstood; baby-sitting for the headmaster's children and resisting the attempts at his seduction by the headmaster's licentious wife; forbidden to write poetry and tortured by guilt after writing a little poetry that harked back to the joys of infancy; sent, as a toughening-up process, to watch a triple execution where the victims were made to sing hymns by their own coffins – an incident destined to start yet another lifelong haunting for him. Two letters from his schooldays stand high in dignity, worthy of his great gifts. One is to the cruel headmaster explaining that anger only makes him worse. The other is to Collin, mentioning in passing that he needs new trousers. Fortunately, after a couple of years a new master was so shocked by what was going on that he reported the real facts to Collin the following vacation. Hans was immediately taken away.

Then the impossible happened. Collin, probably moved by the self-discipline of the youth's uncomplaining, took him into his own household, informing him that he was a member of the family and instructing his son Edvard to be a brother to him. This busy, far from rich home, where poverty did not matter and culture did, was so much his home for the rest of his life that it was possible for him to battle his way through some of his worst tensions there, without breaking his bond with it. With his own father unbalanced, the cruel headmaster such a recent experience, and his own affliction of mistaking helpful criticism for total rejection, it is not surprising that Collin, Edvard, and the head-master should figure as cruel symbols of fatherhood for him at times; they figured more frequently than any other symbols in his nightmares for the rest of his life.

The only tragedy of his entering that home was this: whereas he was utterly unable to see that his 'states' made these well-disciplined Danes withdraw into themselves, they were utterly unable to see that their withdrawal increased his 'states'. Yet the integrity of the family, as individuals and as a whole, was such that they were able to retain their affection for him while consistently refusing to become embroiled in his emotional storms. This combination of unshakeable affection and detachment from excessive feeling brought him some of the security that he so desperately needed; he was saved by what he mistook for heartlessness.

Prostrate with anxiety about his approaching examinations, he carried on a ding-dong fight with Edvard, who took his father's injunction that he should be a brother to Hans very earnestly. 'I can't!' 'You can. You must.' 'I *can't!*' 'You must.' He passed the first examination about the middle of the list; but not without terrifying emotion, a nose-bleed, and a swoon. After the examination, like a burst gourd, writing poured out of him, helter-skelter, without form, like a cascade of free associations, a conversational prose. In many ways it was bad, without frame-work and with confusion of his own with other people's ideas;

but it had the unmistakable touch of genius, his special genius for personification. There was even a touch of salty humour about his critics, which was an immense step forward: a Jesuit fox was advising a novice fox and said, 'My son, you must above all cultivate the art of appearing enormously modest; the world loves nothing better than this noble crawling...' In this technique of cascading free associations he might be regarded as a fore-runner of Joyce, of, for instance, some of the private-thoughts passages of *Ulysses*, which run on and on from one thing to another as the human brain in idleness is liable to tick over.

With the first works of real promise there came the first serious criticism. For the next ten years he wrote plays and novels merit-ing both favourable and adverse comment. On the one hand, the censure caused such terrifying feelings of annihilation that he retaliated with wildly ill-aimed counter-criticism of the critics. On the other hand, he wallowed in the praise like an insatiable child, sponging it up and asking for more, without according it any more balanced assessment than he was giving to the censure. He would storm into one or other infantile state, whether the criticism was penetrating or superficial. He dodged back and forth on the surface, altering his style, his plots, or anything else called to account, and never pausing to decide whether he agreed with his critics.

As was to be expected, with literary electromagnetic storms raging between irate poet and affronted critics, the first sober assessment of his worth did not come from the Danes but from abroad, where the personal entanglements were not known. This is today a cause of shame to the Danes, but it should not be. As every clinical therapist knows, the one who does the dirty work of assisting a disturbed person towards self-discipline comes in for a good deal of mud-slinging. With superficial and penetrating critics alike bespattered, the atmosphere at home could scarcely be sufficiently tranquil for objective assessment of his true worth to be made. There would have been nothing of worth to be recognized but for the generous help of the Danes to their un-couth genius.

In all this turmoil Andersen conceived the notion that there was a conspiracy of non-recognition against him in Denmark and decided to put it to the test. He wrote a couple of anonymous plays, and both were accepted by the theatre that would accept nothing with his name as author. Moreover, both were successes. Starving in the mêlée, he tossed off the fairy-tales, literally to get a pot boiling for himself. Just when he had proved beyond shadow of doubt that he was being persecuted, people expected him to bother about 'those trifles'.

When the success of the first booklet of fairy-tales was finally brought home to him, his attitude became almost vengeful. Very well then . . . he would address the adults exactly as he talked to children, since they were prepared to read such stuff. He was in no state to consider, let alone accept, the fact that his exquisitely sensitive poetic gifts could not be sustained through the three acts of a play. In rage and fury he was cornered into developing his own medium of deep message in simple language. Only his diary shows what he was going through. 'Injustice wakes all my self-confidence . . . Madness devour my brain that I may forget . . . Completely furious, an insane night. Sensually wild. Despair . . . Diabolical weariness of life . . . How loose and light my thoughts are. I think so much – I know so little . . . I am still innocent but my blood burns. Dreams boil in my soul . . . the blood's wild Bacchantes which I am afraid of writing down.'

His true medium had been discovered in time for him to write the immortal tales but too late for him to know unalloyed pleasure in success. There are literally thousands of examples of his torturing fears, the night fears of tiny children, and his ambivalence towards living and dying. He had a tooth out – and wanted it back. He put a note by his bed, 'I am not dead, only sleeping'. He would arrive two hours early for a train or return again and again and again to see if he had put out the candle. By now he was sufficiently aware of himself to see it happening, though not to resolve the trouble. 'I try in vain', he wrote in his diary, 'to find something with which to torment myself, something forgotten for the journey.' He believed that fame had cost him the joys of youth; it was not fame, but his attitude towards fame, which nearly destroyed him.

Outwardly he fell in love with many women; inwardly he never fell in love with any woman. Dreams of the exquisite smile continued but he never detached himself from infantile fixations sufficiently to form a mature relationship with any adult, man or woman. The adult's wild Bacchantes of the blood could find no fruition because the infant's deep emotional problems were unresolved. This state of affairs caused a paralysis of behaviour over marriage. Consciously he longed for marriage but unconsciously he was not sufficiently free to take on the responsibility. Every time he approached a likely woman he would make some slip guaranteed to put her off matrimony. He would tell one that his friends informed him he was in love with her, another that he wished to make her his heiress, yet another would have the colour of her eyes mixed with somebody else's eyes, and so on. They invariably turned him down. In his plays he portrayed the heroine's characteristic of unattainability by making her an abbess or giving her a name such as Annunciata. He named himself *Robert le Diable*, which was the name given in many legends to the violent and cruel father of William the Conqueror, a father said to have been dedicated by his own mother to the devil. To a sixteen-year-old girl he thought of marrying, Andersen gave Byron's poems as a confirmation present.

He came nearest to adult relationship with the father and son, Jonas and Edvard Collin. They disappointed him endlessly by refusing to reciprocate his infantile concept of love, though they helped him towards maturity by endlessly refusing to reciprocate his infantile hatred. He came through to some measure of maturity, battered and bleeding and not fully alive. On one occasion Jonas Collin unwittingly brought him to within an ace of recognition of the impossibility of his demands for appreciation. He had discovered Goethe's *Faust*. Finding the tension between intellect and emotion offensive, he dethroned Goethe in his mind. He told Jonas violently that he had decided that Goethe was not a good poet, and Jonas quietly replied that this could well be, but he felt himself to be no authority upon the subject. 'Oh, God!' cried Andersen to a friend, 'How cheap I felt! I can never forget it; not a word had I to say.' Such an emotional response to such a restrained reply suggests that he had denigrated Goethe for aggrandizement of himself, and now realized this.

Edvard steadily did for him what he could. He acted as his amanuensis, which was no small task with that calligraphy, and he attended to all the business of publication. He ignored all Andersen's letters from abroad beseeching him for protestations of unstinted adulation. He just quietly lived his own life, fell in love, and married. When Andersen heard of his engagement he wrote home with painfully conflicting emotions, trying to wish Edvard well yet unable to conceal his antagonism to the marriage. 'My eyes fill with tears as I write this,' he said. 'Like Moses, I stand on the mountain and look into the promised land, whither I shall never go myself . . . All this happiness will be yours . . . But my feelings are as strong as yours; as you love Jetta, I too have loved; but it is only self-deception . . . I fly South, Italy is my bride.' Where he was wrong was in saying he had loved as Edvard loved Jetta; for he had never become mature enough to love in that way. Copenhagen, the promised land of the fourteen-year-old, had proved too painful in reality; for the rest of his life he made one country after another his bride and journeyed continuously from harsh reality. He refused to attend Edvard's wedding because, he wrote with an irrepressible gleam of humour, it would make him feel like a homeless cat, destined to temporary shelters and odd meals, with never a hearth of his own.

With Edvard's approaching marriage and with his first volume of pot-boilers distracting from his proof of the plot of non-recognition against him in Copenhagen, he dipped into his own bosom. Out poured the tragic tale of the little mermaid who could not marry her prince because she had a tail. Nothing ever moved him so much, for he was the little mermaid and he had to lose his prince to Jetta. Himself lacerated by doubts about eternity, he ends the story in a mist of mysticism utterly unsuitable for children.

After this story his masculine side asserted itself in a virile attack upon a colleague, a tale which he called *The Emperor's New Clothes*. Having, so to speak, the inside story of the confusion in Andersen's mind, it is not surprising to read in Ernest Jones's biography of Freud (1957) that Freud examined this very popular tale but did not find it basically honest, because at the daydream or dream level it is the naked person who discovers for himself his own nakedness and feels defenceless. Andersen, not integrated enough to face his own nakedness, let himself be the little boy who discovered a king's nakedness. Here we strike the crux of the difference between Keats and Andersen. Keats could be Imogen and Iago, playing either or neither, but Andersen, in deadly earnest, saw himself as Imogen and everyone who did not see him thus as Iago. This is not a matter of historical setting, for Keats was writing on speculation when Andersen first arrived in Copenhagen; it is a matter of Keats's maturity, through constantly widening integration, which reached a level unattainable by the gifted but mentally maimed Andersen.

It was said at the end of the last chapter that children are below subsistence level for stories. How this came about will be dealt with in Chapter 10. What is true today was even more true when Andersen wrote his tales. Though much in them was never addressed to children and much very unsuitable for them, the children fell upon them. They were translated into Chinese and Peruvian, into Japanese and Afrikaans. All over the world the adults read them to themselves and to their children; and the children read them to themselves and to the smaller children. The fact that much of the stories was addressed to adults would do the children no harm. Children have always gained immensely from listening to adult communications. What caused many of the children to suffer nightmares were the occasions when Andersen's own unresolved problems came through in inartistic form. For instance, there are some lurid accounts of death beckoning, of the gallows, of murderous treatment of grandmothers. It is all understandable when facts about Andersen are known, but it is not artistry for children. He loved his blue-eyed grandmother, but it was she who took him to the asylum and the prison through which he suffered so much. His resentment comes out, for instance, in a tale in which a robber hits the grandmother on the head, uses her corpse for climbing on to reach the money, and even finds a second grandmother to slay. He also suffered through the witch, and thus one reads, 'The witch's lower lip hung right down on her chest . . . so the soldier cut off her head. There she lay! But he tied up her money in her apron . . .'

What was it he brought to the children that his stories made such an extensive appeal? He wrote with simple exactitude, giving just the right precise information to set the imagination moving along lines preparing the stage for the next event. Much that was obviously the personal experience of this man who never grew up was just right for childhood attention. In *The Tinder Box* alone can be seen the poverty, the riches, the true friends, the threat of gallows, and the shoemaker's son to the rescue. Little Claus loses his horse through showing off. Curiosity is held in a deliciously brief pulse of suspension with such sentences as, 'Now we must hear how these two got on, for it makes a regular story,' or 'The shoemaker's boy wanted the fourpence so he darted off to get the tinder box and gave it to the soldier, and – now we shall hear what happened.' Where anxiety-assuaging repetition is used it has the subtle variation of music: 'If he struck once, the dog came that sat on the chest with the copper money, if he struck twice the one that had the silver came, and if he struck three times the one that had gold.' Experiences known to the children are dwelt upon. 'So Little Claus climbed up on the shed, and there he lay down, and rolled about in order to lie comfortably . . .' And the tiny bed of the tiny Thumbelina is 'a splendid lacquered walnut shell for a cradle, blue violet petals for a mattress, and a rose-petal for a counterpane'. What is said is so interesting to the children that there can be dramatic pause while the feelings unfold and power the imagination.

With his humour intended for adults the situation is rather different. Remarks such as 'She was so pretty anyone could see she was a real princess' or 'The soldier couldn't help it, he had to kiss her, for he was a genuine soldier' entertain the adult while reading to the children; but they do not specially appeal to the children. However, in a tale to be read to children, it is good to have the two levels of entertainment, for those who are being read to and for those who are reading.

It is curious that, reaching such perfection, he ever fell below it, or rather that he seemed to have no idea when he had fallen below it. The fact is that he enthralled the children who gathered round to hear his tales without being very aware of them, so long as they stayed quiet. There is a story of one little girl sitting on his knee, gazing up at him in absorption; and when she managed to get a word in she said, 'You talk too much!' Edvard once said that he doubted if he even cared for children at all. He was really entertaining himself. If a child did or said anything not in accordance with his present occupation he could whip out a verbal cat-o'-nine-tails. Decades later one of these children recounted how, walking happily beside him through the country, listening to his talk, she chanced to pull a flower. He turned upon her with vituperation for her heartless cruelty in causing not only the death of this lovely flower but tears to all the flowers in heaven for the sufferings of their poor little sister. The macabre, ambivalent lack of logic, in assuming that it was a matter for tears to be banished to heaven, together with the wanton cruelty of the attack upon the preoccupied child, inflicted a permanent mental wound. At Andersen's death a man, who had undergone a similar childhood experience at his hands, made the caustic comment that the world would now be a better place for children.

It is impossible to leave Andersen without a word about Grimms' *Fairy Tales*, almost as extensively read and far, far more upsetting to children as first published than anything Andersen ever wrote. Andersen once met one of the Grimm brothers and was staggered to find himself unknown to them. Whereas Andersen posed as a writer of tales for children, the Grimm brothers had no such pretensions. They were philologists. They aided the extensive and important movement by which folklore was retrieved from the common people after its partial eclipse through the invention of printing. Old songs, ballads, myths, legends, customs, and rituals were being rescued from total oblivion by experts, because they were now recognized as remnants of an earlier but highly developed stage of art and religion.

What they were doing must be explained, if it is to be understood why the stories were not suitable for children and how children ever got hold of them. A single example should suffice. The song *London Bridge is Falling Down* was retrieved; taken in conjunction with various English, Breton, and Norse legends, it was found that this song was an expression of interest and wonder experienced by the Britons at the marvel of Roman architecture spanning the Thames and their incredulity when King Olaf the Dane was able to capture it in the tenth century. A leader in this romantic revival of folklore was Herder, the German poet and critic, an ardent Hellenist who had been a pupil of Kant. He once chanced to say prophetically of a collection of such tales that they would one day be a Christmas gift for young people.

This is exactly what happened. A collection of remnants of adult culture, as passed on by cottagers through half a dozen centuries, were given in mutilated form, without any proper setting, direct to the children. Despite the grizzly horrors, the slaughter and death and cruelty, the stories were lapped up by a whole generation of children before they were toned down by some measure of editing. Even the edited editions left much to be desired. But in the absence of anything more suitable, the children read them. The value for adults of these tales, apart from their historic interest, lay in their stimulus to such literature as Goethe's lyric *Heidenröslein*, Coleridge's ballad *The Ancient Mariner*, Synge's tragedy *Deirdre of the Sorrows*, and many masterpieces of similar calibre. At the end of the seventeenth century Perrault had published his *Histoire du Temps Passé* for children, which included 'Puss-in-Boots', 'Sleeping Beauty', 'Little Red Ridinghood', etc; but he did not mention the folk source of the tales he had re-written. The Grimm tales were published over a century later, without any adaptation for children.

In this romantic revival of folk tales Andersen's position was unique. Grimms' *Tales* were first published while he was growing up in a cottage at Odense, but it was not these that he heard; what he heard were the uncollected remnants of ancient culture, round the hearth and the pump and the spinning-wheel; these so fired his imagination that he made up his own stories. When he published his first volume of trifles for children, Grimms' *Tales* had been available for twenty years. Andersen's tales, which were much nearer to what the children needed, found a market with many parents deeply troubled about the fascination their children felt for Grimms' *Tales* in spite of the subsequent nightmares. He was not himself critical of Grimms' *Tales*, because he had been suckled upon such tales; this in part explains some of his lapses into what would now be regarded as lack of distance over horrors.

Andersen's simplicity of style had far-reaching effects upon adult literature. Wherever his stories were read, in Denmark and in countless other countries, they brought back a simplicity that had been lost when the invention of printing undermined oral tradition. His style brought the directness of spoken communication, which is brief, graphic, and free in rhythm. It was not lack of gifts but problems in his personal development that prevented him from achieving his ambition to be recognized as a writer for adults. He reached his summit in the third volume of fairy tales, of which Grimur Thomsen, the Icelandic literary critic, wrote: 'The fairy-tale is a merry judgement-day on appearance and reality, on the outer shell and the inner kernel. A double current flows through it: an ironic upper current jesting and sporting with great and small, playing at shuttlecock with high and low; and then the deep, serious undercurrent, putting "everything in its right place" with truth and justice.'

CHAPTER 6

Children's comic papers

We should be much freer to express our virtuous indignation at the way in which nineteenth-century parents had allowed so many children to be scared out of their wits over Grimms' *Fairy Tales*, if mid-twentieth-century parents had not done something remarkably similar. It is quite annoying to be denied the luxury of righteous indignation in this unsuspected way. Over the business of comic papers and the horrors in them, we have behaved rather like adults admonishing children seen drinking the city river-water. While virtuous philosophers have sincerely shouted: 'Naughty children! It is poisoned! You will die!' irresponsible merchants who found it remunerative to tip the refuse this way shouted, not quite sincerely: 'Don't be mean! Children relish germs! We all drank germs! What they need is more germs!' Hardly anybody seemed to notice that the children were dying of thirst, and whereas all of them would become mentally ill without enough of the right tales only a few of them would be unable to withstand polluted sources.

Enough of the right tales: this is the operative concept. Imbalance in diet, mentally as well as physically, results in greed. Children in Great Britain are spending annually more than five million pounds sterling of their own pocket money on comic papers. Moreover, it is estimated that, on an average, each copy is read by at least eight children. If this astounding information does not shake the adults out of virtuous admonition, they – the adults – are surely doomed. Let us inquire into this matter, adopting an attitude comparable with that of John Keats, being and not being

94

concerned; or comparable with that of Grimur Thomsen, sporting and jesting with a serious undercurrent. Perhaps five million pounds is not nearly enough and the children should be advised to spend ten or twenty millions of their pocket money on comics!

During the first decade after the recent war, a time of major social readjustment to civil life, the subject of children's comics suddenly blew up to hurricane force. Discussions in the press, on radio and TV, and in organized meetings turned into distressing emotional battles. Some shouted that comics were entirely bad, citing irrefutable examples; while others shouted that comics were entirely good, citing equally irrefutable examples. The sheer quantity of emotion, let alone its quality, should have drawn attention to the seriousness of the problem. In all the confusion it was extremely difficult for thoughtful people to gain a hearing.

There was a threefold question, to which nobody seemed able to give authoritative reply. Do comics do more harm than good, more good than harm, or absolutely nothing to children? There were two reasons why nobody could give an unbiased answer. First, only the producers of children's comics had given them serious adult attention. Naturally they would be somewhat biased towards believing that children needed them for survival. (In fact, they supported this view with a veritable ju-jitsu of logic.) Then, those others who were passionately for or against comics for children were much clearer about *whether* they were for or against than *why*. *Their* arguments were so outstandingly illogical, whichever side they took, that it was quite clear something was being 'forgotten' or repressed. From study of the psychology of children's play we now know that the fact that something is repressed does not prove that it *should* be repressed; it merely proves that the subject is of considerable importance. Maybe it should be repressed; maybe it should not; but it is certainly going to disrupt sound argument if it cannot be brought somewhat into the daylight. The ignorance as to *why* comics mattered so much, either way, was what stopped these impassioned arguers from carrying on a discussion; they could neither present their own case clearly nor make sense of the way in which the other side was presenting theirs.

Amid all this 'split-off' commotion, it took reasonable people a whole decade to present a balanced view of the facts to the public. For the first half-dozen years the modest request for an official inquiry was turned down flat. They would not even risk an inquiry! It was, of course, beautifully rationalized, as happens with irrational behaviour; we were told that the freedom of the press must be respected. (This so-called freedom was not being granted to the children's milk supply; children were being allowed only tuberculin-tested milk.)

By the early fifties the battle had engaged attention in very high quarters. In 1952 Lord Chief Justice Goddard, summing up at the murder trial of sixteen-year-old Craig, said that films and comic papers had very little to do with the case. But in the same year the Member of Parliament for Coventry quoted in the House such horrific data from certain comics, which he held in his hand as he spoke, that he expressed the hope that he might not be reprimanded for unparliamentary language. His attention had been drawn to these comics by the Coventry Parent-Teacher Association.

The following year the Under-Secretary for the Home Office endeavoured to stall parliamentary action by saying that the responsibility for the moral welfare of children rested primarily with parents and teachers, and there was a limit to what law and government could do in this field. By this time pressure for an inquiry was coming from parents and teachers all over the country; they were of the opinion that an inquiry was not beyond the limits of law and government. That same year, however, Sir David Maxwell-Fyfe stated publicly that he had no doubt in his own mind that some films and comics were contributory factors in the alarming rise of juvenile delinquency.

Material that was too unrestrained for parliamentary language was too hot for the press to handle for long. However, after successive waves of publicity from a press not in the least scared of losing its freedom through an inquiry, something had to be done.

When the archbishops were persuaded to examine some of the comics the Government found itself in a position strangely analogous to that of the child who is holding down so much repressed material that it feels greater anxiety about ability to maintain the repression than about behaving incorrectly before the public. Suddenly, to the somewhat incredulous surprise of those who had battled so long, opposition collapsed and in 1955 a rather indifferent Children's and Young Person's Act was hustled through Parliament – without there ever having been an official inquiry at all.

This Act of Parliament stemmed a tide of decadent obscenity for the moment; but it did nothing to explain how or why this tide ever flowed. Unless something of its causes is understood, the children's market remains exposed to the danger both of a fresh tide of this nature and of being robbed of comics that are not obscene. The vigilance payable for freedom requires that the public be informed. The first step might well be to examine something of the history of comic papers. The remainder of this chapter is concerned with that history. This alone is insufficient; the next two chapters will be concerned with what this predominantly visual form of story means to children.

THE EARLY HISTORY OF COMICS: 1890 AND BEFORE

Amalgamated Press Ltd claim that their first issue of *Comic Cuts*, published on the 17th May, 1890, was the first children's comic paper ever to be produced. It was originally intended not for children but for ordinary working-class men and women. It ran for about three thousand issues and was always read by adults; but it was so much enjoyed by children that the publishers very soon began to adapt it to children's interests. Comparison of the original issue with a typical 1951 issue shows such adaptations as the following: it became smaller and so easier for children to handle; the amount of type was reduced and the amount of pictures increased, so that it became less dependent upon reading ability; the content of the pictures became more interesting to children. A typical 1890 picture shows a well-dressed young man with an enamoured expression, under which there is the caption, 'Latest Botanical Discovery: the Blooming Idiot'. A typical 1951 picture shows a small boy laughing helplessly at a grumpy elderly man who has sat on a newly painted park seat having ignored the boy's information that the paint was wet. *Comic Cuts* was such a success that it was followed only six weeks later by *Illustrated Chips*, which was also immediately adopted by the children and ran till 1954. Amalgamated Press can really claim to have published the first two comics for children. In view of what is now known about children's interests, one naturally wonders who had the vision to open up this potential world market, hitherto never suspected.

Alfred Harmsworth was this man. In 1887, while still in his early twenties, he founded the Pandora Publishing Company; this later developed into Amalgamated Press Ltd, now Fleetway Publications. His first two comics were published before he himself was twenty-five years of age. He was evidently a man who had not 'forgotten' the games of childhood. George Garish, his junior sub-editor for these two comics, was at the time of their first issue only seventeen years of age, and is today regarded by Amalgamated Press as the greatest living authority on children's comics. In 1894 Alfred Harmsworth and his brother Harold took over the bankrupt *Evening News*; in 1896 they founded the *Daily Mail*; in 1908 Alfred Harmsworth, by then Lord Northcliffe, became chief proprietor of *The Times*. During these major publishing ventures the firm continually brought out fresh comics designed for children. In addition to the original two, they brought out thirty-five different comics, six of which were still running at the time of the investigation described in Chapter 7.

Amalgamated Press claim that Alfred Harmsworth deliberately campaigned against the penny dreadfuls by publishing suitable entertainment for working-class adults and for children, whom he found basically healthy, jolly, and kindly. This claim is sometimes jeered at by those who think they know the unscrupulousness of big business. But in view of his initial insight into simple, healthy entertainment for children and of the high standard maintained in the comics to the present day, the claim is probably entirely justified. Harmsworth's intention was to produce funny pictures and stories with no harm in them, to make people laugh. They were designed as pantomime with strong melodramatic outlines of hero and villain. It is worth noting that George Garish, who through the years played an increasingly important role in the production of these comics, did at various times both play in and produce pantomime. The fact that these first comics held the children spellbound was not due to chance but to understanding the nature of children.

Harmsworth was by no means the first to campaign against Penny Dreadfuls. The Oxford Dictionary defines *penny dreadfuls* as an elliptical reference to story-books full of horror; and a 'penny-a-liner' was a hack writer of these cheap and superficial tales. The term *superficial* seems strange, when the roots of horror are known to be so deep; but the superficiality lies in merely stimulating feelings of horror without attempting to resolve the problems involved. Many adults were deeply troubled about this form of alleviating without resolving tension. There were many children's periodicals before 1890 designed to draw attention away from penny dreadfuls; these were primarily intended to instruct though the majority included a few items to amuse. The amount of admonition in them seems almost nauseating to modern eyes; even their titles lacked humour. *The Youth's Monthly Visitor*, which first appeared in 1822, ran for eighteen months. Its stated policy was 'to attend to the solid improvement of the youth of both sexes' by 'combining instruction with rational amusement'; the editor protested against 'the cheap and ephemeral publications of the day'. It is not surprising that it did not last, for humour and amusement spring from the irrational.

By 1877 the first edition of *The London Press Dictionary and Advertiser's Handbook* listed 373 weekly, fortnightly, and monthly periodicals published in London alone. Forty-three of them, that is about twelve per cent, were published for children, mainly by religious societies. A few of the titles will give some indication of the sponsorship of these periodicals for children:

Children's Companion and Juvenile Instructor
1*d*. illustrated. Religious Tract Society.

Children's Own Magazine
½*d*. illustrated. Sunday School Union.

Band of Hope Review
½*d*. illustrated. Temperance Stories for Children.

Band of Hope Treasury
½*d*. illustrated. More Temperance Stories.

Bible Class and Youth Magazine
1*d*.

Good News for Young and Old
1*d*. illustrated. Evangelical Truths.

Although there were no children's periodicals designed primarily to amuse or even to instruct through amusement, there were many adult satirical papers. *Punch*, which was founded in 1841, is probably the most famous of all. Thus it can be seen that the word comic was not applicable to children's publications. How it came to be used in connection with children is interesting, since it became so firmly attached to them that it was used of many periodicals that were in no sense comic. For a long time the terms humorous and comic were used interchangeably of adult satirical periodicals. Between 1871 and 1890 *The London Press Dictionary* alternated between the two terms in their classified lists; but in 1891 a final change was made to 'humorous and satirical' for adult papers of an amusing nature. The list included *Ally Sloper*, remembered today by many adults who must as children have looked at their elders' funny paper. Before 1890 the term comic was used in one children's paper only, namely *The Boy's Comic Journal*, a collection of sensational stories clearly intended to interest through horrifying rather than to amuse. The fact that comic was no longer the official term for adult satirical papers, coupled with the fact that the first satirical paper for children was actually called *Comic Cuts*, seem to have been the deciding factor in reserving the term comic for children's publications.

The difference between Harmsworth's campaign to distract the attention of children from penny dreadfuls and previous campaigns was that he understood the children's need for satire at their own level. Refer back to the grumpy old man on the newly painted seat, and realize that children often warn adults of danger only to be snubbed for their pains; a picture showing an adult in difficulties for this offence to children can strike children as so funny that they go right off into gales of uproarious amusement. Such laughter is a safety valve for their pent-up annoyance. When the first satirical paper for children appeared in 1890 there were thirty-four satirical periodicals regularly giving outlet for pent-up adult emotion. Harmsworth was far ahead of his time in seeing that children needed their own satirical periodicals.

If a search is made for the sources of modern comics before 1890, then it is clear that good juvenile literature is not the sole source, greatly though it contributed, because it was predominantly instructional. Children were also looking at adult satirical papers, which were not instructional; they were reading penny dreadfuls and other sensational literature. The source of comics seems to have been fourfold:

(*a*) Juvenile literature of good quality, such as *Aunt Judy's Magazine*, *Little Folk's Weekly Budget*, and *The Boy's Own Paper*. These contained interesting stories and information for children and some amusing sections.

(*b*) Adult satirical papers, such as *Ally Sloper* and *Scraps*. The first issue of *Comic Cuts* greeted both these papers as old friends.

(*c*) Penny dreadfuls, paper-backed books recounting sensational stories, many of them stated to be 'true' as their source was the criminal records of the *Newgate Calendar or Malefactor's Bloody Register*. (Criminals such as Dick Turpin and Black Hawk still figure as sensationally interesting characters in today's comics.)

(*d*) Mystery classics, such as *The Castle of Otranto*, *The Mysteries of Udolpho*, and *The Monk*. Far from being penny-a-line hack stories, these mystery tales are ranked as classics. Since the high quality of writing was so vividly descriptive, these could be even more upsetting than the penny dreadfuls.

Much that is to be praised in modern comics can be traced back to good juvenile literature and adult satirical papers of this period; and much that is to be condemned can be traced to the penny dreadfuls and the mystery classics. In the juvenile literature what was of value included interesting and exciting stories; serials in which right triumphed; information of interest to children from such experts as W. G. Grace, the cricketer, and C. A. Read, the historian; there were puzzles and games for children to work out on their own; the illustrations, though in the elaborate style of the day, were good; there were strip cartoons of human and animal adventure; and there were humorous sections. The aims of publications containing these elements were in accordance with the high moral traditions of this country.

Elements that would be condemned today have to be seen in historical perspective. Nineteenth-century writers sincerely believed that the way to preserve children from certain errors was to outline for them the consequences of backsliding by means of cautionary tales. It is only in our generation that the satisfaction enjoyed by the adults in the course of this admonishment is realized. The children would intuitively appreciate the *bona fide* intentions of the adults, and this would in some measure act as a protective cloak. It would be far more deleterious to indulge ourselves with this heavy admonition today. Those early comics differed from the better-quality comics of today in their attitude to animals, which appeared as scientific specimens or in strip cartoons ending in their discomfort and in many stories and illustrations of human beings which dwelt on feelings of aggression, rejection, and guilt to no constructive purpose. For instance, in *Our Folk's Weekly Budget* (which by 1876 bore the slogan, 'To

Inform. To Instruct. To Amuse.') there was a strip cartoon called 'Croc's Shocks or Jacko's Whacks. A crocodile tale cut up in six pieces in six comic cuts.' Here Jacko amuses himself by cutting up the tail of the crocodile for fun. One issue of *Our Young Folks* had a very detailed series of drawings of the scandalous treatment of Hop o' my Thumb by his parents, depicting rejection and desolation in the child. Even *The Boy's Own Paper* sometimes had unnecessarily gruesome illustrations, such as a large picture of a decapitated man, with blood spouting from the trunk. In *Boys Will be Boys* Turner cites a long passage in this paper on taxidermy which casually gives such details as, 'Some people crush the skull to make it [the brain] come out easily, but this I do not advise . . . Pull the eyes out of their cavity . . .'

Examples such as these show that wrong attitudes were being built up because dangerous material was being used to gain interest, not to progress to more constructive situations. The Hop o' my Thumb example is inexcusable, because this is a folk tale which Perrault had already re-told for children in a form widely known in this country; there was no excuse for reverting to the folk form. Even when full allowance has been made for the impact of modern research about children, which has made us so much more aware of our ignorance about them, it is hard to excuse the blind spot of the Victorians. They became so engrossed in the fascination of warning children of the dangers of life that they seem to have completely overlooked the possible adverse effects of all the grisly details upon a sensitive child. The extent of their fascination with these dangers is indicated by the fact that nobody seems to have raised a voice on behalf of children upset by the tales.

THE FIRST FIFTY YEARS OF TRADITIONAL BRITISH COMICS: 1890–1940

During the first half century of the publication of children's comics in this country a tradition was built up that the pictures and stories should be full of harmless – or at least fairly harmless –

gaiety. The comics were designed for children up to a mental age of about eleven or twelve. It was realized that older children also read them, but only such, it was thought, as were immature. Actually, many adults could be seen reading them, on the dockside or outside factories. The producers set out to put the child's point of view, so naturally most of the characters were either children or animals behaving like children. Occasionally there might be an adult character, perhaps helpful, perhaps obstructive, but little else. Many of the childish pranks and adventures were in the middle pictures misinterpreted by the adults, but by the end of the strip all problems were solved and relationship with adults was once more harmonious. Very occasionally an adult would be incomprehensively antagonistic; then would come the downfall of the adult, to the glee of the children.

A 1924 example from *Tiger Tim* will show how extremely understanding the adult role could be. Mrs Bruin will not allow the Bruin Boys to bathe after supper, so they plan a secret midnight bathe; during this escapade they become very frightened and their clothes are soaked; traces of their adventure can be seen in the dormitory next morning. But does she admonish? Oh, no. (As many adults today remember, she is a remarkably understanding bear.) She sees past the wet clothes to the very frightened animals and says nothing. It is interesting to note that the name Bruin comes from Bruin the Bear in Reynard the Fox, a folk tale which was centuries old when Caxton first printed it in 1481; and there are a dozen other animals in the story. The Bruin Boys would seem to have a long and noble ancestry.

The technical quality of British comics in this first half century remained extremely high. Original drawings by fine artists were printed by means of excellent blocks. These blocks are known in the trade as cuts, hence the title *Comic Cuts* for the first one. Such a high standard could be achieved only through using expensive printing plant. But the readers of comics were only a limited section of the public, namely children of about six to eleven years and a few adults; they were too few to warrant special establishment of elaborate printing machinery solely for them.

Thus the comics had to be undertaken by established publishers, who already had plants in operation.

Amalgamated Press experienced no serious competition for over forty years, during which period they brought out between thirty and forty different comics. A few small firms attempted to compete, but the difficulties were too great and only Odham's *Mickey Mouse* is still running. Towards the end of the thirties D. C. Thomson Ltd., a well-established Scottish firm, brought out three comics: *Dandy* in 1937, *Beano* in 1938, and *Magic* in 1939. *Magic* had to be suspended very soon because of the war, but *Dandy* and *Beano* are still very popular. Traditional British comics opened a new field of publication and the standard was both set and maintained by the first firm to publish them.

The D. C. Thomson publications adopted a number of characteristics from the many juvenile publications edited by James Henderson, such as *Our Young Folk's Weekly Budget*, which was well established more than a decade before the first comic appeared. This periodical had large, clear, and entertaining pictures of animals such as Jacko the Monkey, which were stories in themselves, whether one could read the captions or not. D. C. Thomson introduced Biffo the Bear and Korky the Cat, improving on Jacko the Monkey not in quality of printing but in simplification of both drawing and incident. James Henderson had also used an elementary form of verbal play, as in the previously mentioned 'Croc's Shocks or Jacko's Whacks'. In *Dandy* and *Beano* there are personalities such as 'Dennis the Menace' and 'Wuzzy Wiz; Magic is his biz.'; and there are rhyming captions such as 'Roger can't get on the train – all his dodging's been in vain.'

Amalgamated Press never introduced rhyming, although George Garish had come to Harmsworth from Henderson and later worked in pantomime, where this kind of rhyming is constantly used. This was a sound decision on their part. The rhyming found in folklore, pantomime, children's games, etc., is not something to be made up afresh; it is the decadent remnant of a culture before the invention of printing in which rhymes were used as mnemonics in passing on orally the great traditions of religion, ritual, art, and law. Children do not have to memorize what they read in comics; nor is their reading aided by the rhymes, since the exigencies of rhyme distort the natural order of the words as most easily comprehended.

TRADITIONAL AMERICAN COMICS

Comics in America developed along lines quite different from those of this country. This has lead to a different use in America of the word *comics*, which has greatly puzzled people over here. Because the official language of the United States and Britain is English, we tend to assume that both lands mean exactly the same by familiar terms. This is very far from true. We mean, for instance, exactly the opposite when we say *suspenders* or *braces*, and if you ask for one in New York you will be given the other. Moreover, words extremely familiar in one land may be virtually unknown in the other. In a well-known test of intelligence standardized in America, high among the difficult words comes the word *limpet*. It is a word known to many children here who have no notion of the meaning of the surrounding difficult words. No one in this country can be as much as a hundred miles from the sea, practically everyone has been to the shore, and *cling like a limpet* is a standard cliché. Curious to know just how unfamiliar the word was in America, I asked an American scientist and writer what a limpet was. At first he said he had no idea, and then he said slowly, 'Wait a minute . . . aren't they gasteropod molluscs? I think they collect food by means of a radula with a couple of thousand glassy hooks.'

In the horror-comics hurricane many people over here tiraded against *American comics*. In so doing they offended the Americans because they were applying the term to a certain section of comics as if all American comics were of this kind. It is necessary to trace the development of comics in America, not only to see how we came to make this mistake, but also to find out why the word *comic* is now liable to be used for extremely un-funny books not even intended for children.

The geography of America has presented difficulties of a kind almost unknown in this country. The isolation of settlements, particularly in the early days of expansion but also today, has made schooling for children and further education for adults extremely difficult. For instance, America was the first country to start public libraries, a farsighted scheme of which Americans are justly proud. Yet a survey made just before the war shows that the rural population was so dispersed that ninety-two per cent of the country people were out of reach of libraries.

The difficulties in attempting to weld such isolated groups in a homogeneous culture were, and still are, a formidable worry to educationists. These difficulties are increased by the variety of languages spoken. In various large communities the mother-tongue may be French, German, Spanish, or English, and there are smaller groups speaking other European languages. Much of the illiteracy and semi-literacy is believed to be due to thinking in one language and being expected in school to read and write in another. In fact, since this problem does not exist here, Americans are astonished to find that literacy is any problem for us.

It was found that many American adults could interpret stories only if they contained many pictures in self-evident sequence with a minimum of type. Cheap picture periodicals with captions in English flourished, the content of which was designed for adults. The small amount of reading involved could be managed by foreign-speaking adults of average ability; it could also be managed by English-speaking adults of below average ability. These booklets sold extremely well. They were very sensational, of course, to stimulate the intellectual effort required. They were a species of penny dreadful and it was these which were labelled 'comics'.

The early-settler stories could have made first-class exciting adventure tales for picture books of much better quality. They were a source of material for those who could read, in the works of such writers as Fenimore Cooper. But many people in the isolated settlements were either sustained by fanatical religious beliefs or intellectually and spiritually at a loose end. Very soon historical facts became infiltrated with incidents of mythological quality, basic to the early development of the human mind. Supernatural and sensational incidents crept in, such as those known to us not only through penny dreadfuls and mystery classics but also through our own myth cycles. There were spectral riders, apparitions, vampires, pointless murders, people dying more than once, sinister relationships between the sexes – in fact, all the basic plots touched upon in Chapter 2. The simplicity of the pictorial medium, together with the poor quality of the cheap production, precluded any integration of horror with beauty. For many who did not even possess a Bible this was the sole source of reading matter. The stories became known as cowboy or Western stories, and the booklets as cowboy or Western comics.

What nobody noticed was that a form of tale that could be interpreted by average foreign-speaking adults and below-average English-speaking adults could also be understood by the chronically story-starved children. Writing during the last war on 'Comics as a Social Force in America', S. M. Gruenberg says, 'About the only thing that is unique in the emergence of the comics as a social phenomenon is the fact that they came upon us silently and grew to considerable dimensions before the "guardians of our culture" were aroused by them.' Concerning the children who were reading them she says, 'For a century we have looked to the schools to develop a national unity in our heterogeneous population by inculcating children, as they grow up, with common concepts, doctrines, attitudes, sentiments. But the comics, claiming to be no more than toys, have been doing just that, reaching continuously more than the schools, more than the newspapers . . . for reasons peculiar to themselves they have become almost universally intelligible.'

It was not until the Americans began to make surveys concerning children reading adult comics that they began to realize the appalling extent of these 'considerable dimensions'.

In 1949 J. Franks, in 'Comics, Radio, Movies and Children', wrote:

'Today fifty-million comics magazines are sold on the news-stands every month. It is estimated that of the seventy-five million purchasers of such magazines annually, about 40% are children between the ages of eight and eighteen. Of course, each book has many more readers, since children circulate them by "swopping" or resale as long as the pages hold together. Surveys point to the likelihood that 98% of all children between the ages of eight and twelve read comics. These readers come from all types of homes and cultural backgrounds . . . Intelligence quotients seem to make no difference, for comics are read by bright and dull children alike, although the bright children are likely to outgrow them earlier.'

Americans had had comic or funny strip cartoons in their periodicals well before the first issue of *Comic Cuts*, and these were enjoyed by adults and children alike. When the publishers realized that children were reading the Westerns, they produced children's comics along the lines of traditional British comics. These sold well but did not stop the children also reading the Westerns. The Americans use the terms *comics* and *funnies* interchangeably; this is another source of misunderstanding. They began to produce whole supplementaries, generally known as *funnies*, with their newspapers. In the Scottish report 'Studies in Reading' it is stated that only two of the two thousand three hundred American daily papers are without these funnies.

AMERICAN AND BRITISH RECIPROCAL INFLUENCE:
BEFORE 1940

The wages for penny-a-line hack writers of sensational stories in the nineteenth century were so low that it was more profitable for American and British writers, and incidentally those of other nationalities as well, to plagiarize each other's stories and merely change place-names. In a footnote to *Boys Will be Boys* Turner gives a striking example of a lawsuit reported in *The Quarterly Review* during 1890. An English story had been plagiarized in America and this same story was plagiarized by an English hack writer who was not aware of its original source. During legal proceedings it transpired that the original English writer had plagiarized the plot from Germany. Since this settled the Anglo-American dispute, nobody pursued the matter farther back.

The Americans imported penny dreadfuls and the British imported detective, space, and Western fiction. Many British characters of fiction, such as Dick Turpin, Jack Harkaway, and Sexton Blake, were given American adventures by British writers, possibly to forestall plagiarization. By the end of the nineteenth century the Aldine Publishing Company had introduced such American characters as Buffalo Bill and Deadwood Dick, and had started a Buffalo Bill Library, with some of the worst crudities eliminated. Early in the nineteen-twenties D. C. Thomson started publishing cowboy stories with supernatural elements. Whereas the American stories that came to this country appeared as adventure stories with some illustrations, the British stories that went to the U.S.A. appeared not only as adventure stories but also as American comics. Dick Turpin and Black Hawk, originally of Newgate Prison fame, both appeared in America as strip cartoons in comics. Anything less comic than the original careers of these criminals it would be hard to find. By now the term comic had become a generic term in America for a particular form of publication requiring little or no literacy, which covered both tales for immature adults and tales produced specifically for children. Since in Great Britain the term was used only for traditional British comics, this was to lead to more misunderstanding.

In the decade before the 1939 war a number of eminent Americans had begun to realize the dangers to which American children were being exposed by access to inartistic publications not originally intended for them. During the war, comics in America became increasingly violent. As the war drew to a close more and more American societies began to take steps to draw public attention to the extent to which children were reading these violent comics. Shortly after the war the American General Federation of Women's Clubs reported meetings, conventions, and attempts to assess suitable and unsuitable comics for children in places as widely dispersed as San Diego, Virginia, Los Angeles, and Cleveland. They reported activities by librarians and by Church bodies such as the Federal Council of Churches of Christ in America, the International Council of Religious Education, the National Catholic Youth Council, and the National Jewish Youth Conference. In 1949 the Americans decided upon an official inquiry. They set up the Joint Legislative Committee to Study the Publication of Comics.

One of the most distinguished workers in this campaign was the now world-famous Director of the Lafargue Clinic, Dr Frederic Wertham. He believed that a public health law alone would save the situation, and advocated that it should forbid the sale and display of all crime comic books to children under the age of fifteen years. On 14th December, 1950, the *New York Times* headed an article 'Psychiatrist Asks Crime Comics Ban'. In it was reported Dr Wertham's pleas to the Joint Legislative Committee that they should support this health law. He defined crime comic books as those depicting crime, whether their setting be in the jungle, the West, or interplanetary space. He maintained that the issue was one of public health, since our task is to educate and protect the young, and to the publishers of these comics children are seen only as child buyers. He said that in the forty to eighty million crime comic books sold monthly, the hero is nearly always 'regular-featured and an athlete, pure American white man' and 'the villains, on the other hand, are foreign-born, Jews, Orientals, Slavs, Italians and dark-skinned races'. Referring to the comics known to the young delinquents who came under his care, he cited a comic in one boy's possession that contained nineteen murders (ten by shooting, nine by choking, stabbing, and being beaten in the face) and forty-five threats of murder with a gun, and seventeen deaths by hanging and being dropped alive into acid.

A year later, on 4th December, 1951, *The New York Herald Tribune* gave a report of Dr Wertham's address to the same Committee. He said that the comic books were encouraging drug addiction and racial hatred among children and instructing them in brutality, sexual sadism, and crime. He displayed a switchblade knife, such as had been used for 140 stabbings in New York the previous year; he explained that, though it was illegal to sell such knives to children under sixteen years of age, he had obtained it merely by answering under an assumed name an advertisement in one of the comics. On the same day the U.S. *Daily Mirror* reported him as adding that the comics teach use of these knives and saying, 'The children get a very raw deal. They are sent to reformatories and asylums, while the crime book interests have gotten away with murder.'

The following year American newspapers published the officially stated rise in the American crime wave. At the same time the New York Joint Legislative Committee on Comics reported that the comic-paper industry had failed to curb their output of sex-sadistic literature, and that the Committee would continue its agitation for legislation to protect the children and bring the erring publishers within reach of the law. Meanwhile private efforts continued to support their work. In Cincinnati, inspired by Dr Wertham, a panel of experts was formed, which consisted of psychiatrist, psychologist, teachers, parents, and others. They brought out an evaluation list of comics, as a guide for thoughtful parents in selection of less upsetting comics for their children. This was later to become a guide for private efforts in this country.

The human mind is so constructed that it cannot suddenly take in too much of this horrifying information. There is a tendency to say this is not true, it cannot be, it is exaggerated, and anyway it is not my fault; then the mind slips into that easy solution of repressing the major part of the details. How could one be funny about this? Yet those responsible – if only obliquely responsible by unawareness – had to face the fact that large sections of the rising generation were having attitudes built up against anyone not a Nordic blond of the type Hitler idealized. The confusion into which human minds can be thrown is demonstrated by the fact that Hitler himself was not of the blond type he advocated. The tragedy for children in America was that the majority, not being ethnically of this comics-hero type, were actually building social attitudes against themselves. They were tending to identify themselves with the villains. Thus they were being coerced into delinquency in ways that precluded healthy widening of ego-boundaries.

It was hard enough for the press in Britain to handle the subject of crime and horror comics for any length of time. But in the United States the situation was far worse. To their great credit, when it was realized that the problem was too frightening to be considered at length, certain individuals brought humour to their aid. The humour had a gargantuan attack in it, but it was levelled against a gargantuan problem. One of the pioneers of this approach was Tom Lehrer, at the time Lecturer in Mathematics at Harvard University. He took the various subjects of crime from the newspapers and round them wrote irresistibly comic songs for the entertainment of his students. No crime was too serious for him to make it sound irrepressibly, scandalously funny. Here was a break-through of the younger generation, a detachment of the very quality that lessens the chance of repression. According to the legend on the record of his songs, there was a widespread attempt to suppress his outspoken satire; but fortunately the attempt failed. All reasonable people have to listen and to laugh, which means that they will remember instead of repressing the material that comes under his gun-shot. (However, a club in a women's section of London University was closed after an American visitor had sung some of his songs there.)

Several years after Tom Lehrer's songs became widely known the Americans produced *West Side Story*, their finest musical so far. Here both humour and beauty are fused in directing attention not towards crime comics but upon the young criminals whose social attitudes Dr Wertham claimed were being in part moulded by the crime comics. It was the story of Romeo and Juliet among the juvenile delinquents of New York. The conflict between Montagues and Capulets was not over religion but over race – Jet Teddy-boys versus Puerto Ricans. The conflict was underlined by a Shakespearian contrast in the clothing worn by the two gangs, and by a contrast of bop and jive with Latin-American dance and song, in which there was a remarkably high level of music and movement. The dramatic sequence and emotional evolution are so masterly that the audience is carried right into the gang situation with deep sympathy.

The balcony scene was played upon the fire-escape of a slum tenement. The weapons of the fight were those very flick-knives advertised in comics. There was frequent use of the play within a play, and never more effectively than when a young murderer who had been picked up by the police returned to mime for the gang how he was passed from judge to psychiatrist, from psychiatrist to social worker, and so on. Anxious to convince a policeman that they were not really to blame for their behaviour, they went through it all. At intervals the prisoner thought he had got to the root of the problem, calling out, 'I'm distoibed!' or, 'I got a social disease!' or, 'Hey, I'm depraved on account of I'm deprived!' But the lack of real comprehension could be heard in the music, as they sang with the same cheery enthusiasm, first:

> We ain't no delinquents, we're misunderstood,
> Deep down inside us there is good!

and later:

> It ain't just a question of misunderstood,
> Deep down inside us we're no good!

The scene swept with pathological excitement to the conclusion that they had better punish the policeman.

The implication sometimes made in Britain that in America the problem of children and crime has not been taken seriously is very far from true. The energy with which they have taken action, the virility of their humour, and the deep sympathy for the disturbed children to be seen in such works as *West Side Story* are most impressive. With regard to the part played by comics in the children's alienation from society, those who have read Dr Wertham's book *The Seduction of the Innocent* will realize that responsible citizens were up against a major social problem, unscrupulous big business in the comics industry.

During the last three-quarters of a century American and British influence on the publication of comics has been reciprocal in beneficial as well as deleterious ways. When the Americans found that their comics for immature adults were being relished by children, they produced comics designed for children on the lines of comics traditional to Britain. When Americans found that their children were still increasingly reading the ones not designed for them, they held a public inquiry, and offered guidance to parents by means of evaluation lists. When, as will be seen in the next section, American comics reached Britain, we sought an inquiry and brought out evaluation lists.

BRITISH COMICS: 1940 ONWARDS

During the 1939 war production of traditional British comics was suspended, as they were considered unnecessary to the war effort. Those which were occasionally brought out were inferior in technical quality because of paper restrictions and labour shortage. The fact that they were only occasional was a more disruptive factor than the temporary lowering of the standard. Children had a ration of inferior sweets and should have had a ration of inferior comics, because the material was of great significance to their mental growth and also because regularity of supplies is of great importance to the security of children. The over-eleven-year-olds suffered the same deprivation with regard to their adventure papers.

The American soldiers stationed in Britain were issued with the comics to which they were accustomed as part of their essential supplies. These comics were of all kinds, from bound copies of funnies from daily papers to Western and crime comics of every variety. When they had finished with them, the soldiers passed them on to British children as a gesture of friendliness, often with a packet of candy. The glossy paper, the brilliant colours, and the clear type far outshone anything the war-surrounded children remembered ever seeing. At that time the British could not buy even a two-guinea classic of such quality, let alone anything within the reach of a child's pocket. Deprived of their usual comics and adventure papers, the under-twelves and the over-elevens alike fell upon this food for their phantasies, as earlier children had fallen upon the first issues of *Comic Cuts* and *Illustrated Chips*.

The busy and war-weary parents saw that one little word *comics* and were delighted that their children should no longer be deprived of Tiger Tim, Teddy Tail, and the rest. As in America, so in Britain, children of all ages began to develop a taste for these easily interpreted exciting grown-up stories. When responsible adults, prompted by such writers as George Orwell, began to examine the so-called comics, they found that their children were deriving the greatest enjoyment from stories of extremely low moral standard, without of course having any idea that these lovely booklets were in any way irregular. They were also extremely surprised to find that the over-elevens were not at all averse to looking at picture stories – at least, not to picture stories of such a nature.

Almost before the few adults who had grasped the situation had recovered from their amazement enough to take steps, the war was over and the American soldiers had returned home. With a sigh of relief their hosts thought that this unfortunate gesture of friendliness would no longer constitute a public danger. But alas, in the post-war economy drive, it was mistakenly decided that children's comics were still not an essential commodity. Even Amalgamated Press and D. C. Thomson could not obtain sufficient quantity or quality of paper to produce what they at least recognized as an essential commodity for children, who are also citizens with rights. What they did manage to produce was pathetically below American standards of production. The children were contemptuous and angry. All ages complained bitterly at the loss of American comics, and the older ones especially despised the feeble British stuff; for by then they were too old for traditional British comics.

American publishers began sending American comics direct to Britain and these sold rapidly. To their horror many adults in Britain found that the children were actually prepared to forgo sweets in order to spend their pocket money on these sensational publications. The younger children had grown accustomed to sensational material and the older children had grown accustomed to pictures; moreover, both were now accustomed to transatlantic standards of production. Then the dollar bar prevented the importation of periodicals of any kind. Once more responsible adults sighed with relief over what they took to be a bar also to this public danger.

The shrewd and irresponsible American publishers of what were now called 'horror comics' were beginning to experience a serious drop in circulation, due to public inquiry and private initiative against them at home. They realized that what had made their comics of universal appeal to multilingual America could make them intelligible to other countries; in fact, they found their market already prepared wherever American soldiers had been stationed all over the world, because their comics were already well known. They hit on a most ingenious idea for developing this market, which arose from the British ban on importation of publications. They offered moulds of a substance not unlike papier mâché of whole comics, together with copyrights, to European publishers. These moulds or matrices, known to the printing trade as mats, were light for transport and relatively cheap. Whereas it costs hundreds of pounds to produce an original comic, these mats were offered for a mere sixty pounds or so. Naturally, the mats they were offering by now were of the very worst comics, which no longer sold well in America.

This business proposition did not appeal to the publishers of traditional British comics. Their own experts were now back from the war and expecting employment. Moreover, they had studied the material and were far more aware of its sources than were the general public. High standards are not maintained without integrity and they knew it was not right for the children. However, a number of firms with fewer scruples came into being and commenced production of British editions of American comics. A glance through the advertisements of these alone would demonstrate to any observant adult that they were not for children; there were advertisements for electric razors, for reducing busts, for elimination of menstruation pain, and so on.

By this time the horror-comics hurricane had blown a number of gusts. The Authors' World Peace Appeal had convened a panel which endeavoured to bring out an Evaluation List, along the lines of the Cincinnati one. I was a member of this panel, and night after night pored over dozens and dozens of horror comics. It was not a little annoying to be told by innocent adults who could not buy them from their respectable newsagents that they were not really obtainable. 'Go to a children's ward!' we used to say crossly. 'Go to any street market in London, Leicester, or Liverpool!' I do not think they ever did. Innocence is not a valuable moral attribute in adults. Perhaps they did try; perhaps they asked in their cultured tones for them. Nurses did not want their interference, because horror comics kept the children's ward quiet; street vendors did not want them spoiling a handy little side-line market. Indeed, I must confess that I put on an off-white accent and an old coat before I won the vendors' confidence. Then, realizing from my precision in asking for specific comics that I was something of an expert, they would produce one and offer to buy it back at half price 'termorrer'.

British attention was drawn to the international implications of the American reprinting of comics in Europe by a startling anomaly. Steps were being taken in almost all European countries to preserve the children from these very worst of American comics. In France a Watching Committee was set up in 1949 to look after children's literature. Like the American Joint Legislative Committee, the members sought *législation pour la protection de l'enfance.* In several countries, including Italy and France, churches posted lists of unsuitable comics at their doors for the guidance of parents. In Germany, at Bad Harzburg, a group of children who had had no opportunity to become accustomed to American comics, went to their newsagent and told him that they were being sold comics that gave them nightmares.

Newspapers in every country gave reports of public anxiety on the subject. In France it became illegal to sell the comics to French children. But England had freedom of the press! There was nothing illegal about the French producing American horror comics from the cheap mats and exporting them to us. So there we were, allowing our children to have American comics rejected by the Americans, which had been printed in France, but were rejected by the French as far as their own people were concerned. This seemed a very forceful argument but it arrived here just after a hurricane and nobody wanted to hear anything at all about comics just at that time. There were several more years of work to be done before the authorities could be made to take steps to stem the tide.

In 1950, when one of the hurricanes was at its height, Hulton Press entered the battle with a new and very constructive coup. Instead of saying, 'Naughty children over eleven to drink poisoned pictures!' they designed an illustrated comic for older children which would not poison them. The Editor was Marcus Morris, and he called the paper *Eagle*. It held its own against American reprints in quality of paper, brilliance of colour, clarity of type, and excitement of adventures. It upheld British traditions by combining the good quality both of our comics and of our juvenile literature. Above all, it was what the children wanted and so they began to turn away from the reprints. Its circulation rose rapidly to a million a week.

In the same year Amalgamated Press brought out *School Friend*, which enjoyed a similar circulation. In 1951 Hulton Press issued *Girl* as companion to *Eagle*. In 1952 D. C. Thomson and Company brought out *Lion* for older boys. In 1953 Amalgamated Press changed the format of the long-established older girls' adventure paper *Girls' Crystal*, so that it became a comic for older girls. From 1950 onwards there has been a new style of British comic available, designed for older children. Marcus Morris has already told some of the inside story of his venture; it will be interesting when we may have the whole of it.

These new comics for older children did not oust the comics for the under-twelves. Many of the old favourites for the younger children began to regain their previous standards and new ones appeared. Hulton Press produced *Robin* in 1953 and *Swift* in 1954. D. C. Thomson and Company produced *Topper* in 1953. And in that same year those who were following developments felt a nostalgic pang when *Comic Cuts* quietly expired. It richly deserved its obituary in *The Times*.

Shortly after the first appearance of *Eagle* two things became very clear. On the one hand, the rapid rise in circulation of this fourpenny comic, which was double the price of traditional comics, demonstrated that we had been starving the older children of quickly grasped dramatic tales. On the other hand the state of the reprint business showed that Hulton's had shown considerable enterprise in being the first to produce a picture paper for older children. The reprinting of American comics was now such a flourishing industry that 'mats' were dispensed with as soon as restrictions on paper slackened. (It was in any case much more convenient to print, as this meant that the more patently revolting sections could be eliminated.) These shilling British editions of American comics must have had a print run of not less than fifty thousand per issue in order to make a profit. There were regular advertisements for them in trade journals. In London the Atlas Publishing and Distributing Company were advertising their group, which consisted of *Batman*, *Superadventures*, *Superboy*, and *Superman*; T. V. Boardman were advertising *Buffalo Bill*, *Blackhawk*, *Roy Carson*, and *Crack Western*; Miller and Son were advertising twenty-three comics, including the Marvel group; Streamline were advertising *Crime Detective*, *Astounding Comic*, *Real Clue Crime*, *Airboy*, and others. In Leicester the Jenson Book Company were producing *Eerie*, *Saint*, *Boy Detective*, *Black Magic*, etc. Other comics were being produced in other industrial towns. All had *British Edition* printed on them and the price in British currency. Solways, in the East End of London, advertised extensively that they always had at least two hundred different comics in stock.

In Hansard, August 1952, the report can be read of exactly what the Member for Coventry quoted in Parliament from some of these British Editions. Here are three examples:

1. *Manhunt*: 'He was dipped into a chemical vat . . . his skin quickly tightened and split! Already starved he looked like a skeleton when he was pulled up.'

2. *Eerie*: 'The thing picked up the body of the unfortunate girl and threw it into an underground pit filled with sulphureous smoke and a strange flickering blue fire that did not burn like an ordinary flame! . . . From out of that pit rose corpse after corpse . . . shrunken, withered.'

3. *Crime Exposed* (advertisement): 'Relax! Keep Slim at home with relaxing, soothing massage! Also used in relief of pain.'

He assured the handful of members in the House that the pictures were even more horrifying than the text.[1]

The question of these British editions had to be raised half a dozen times in Parliament before steps were taken. The evaluation lists were not proving as helpful as had been hoped. It took an hour to go through a single copy with due care, and it took no time for the publishers to realize that they had only to change the titles for the list to be useless. That was what they were beginning to do. Intensive study confirmed Dr Wertham's claim that they contained every known form of sexual perversion, right down to the obscurer forms of vampirisim, etc. The plots were not even being invented anew; they were being plagiarized, lifted wholesale, from the most decadent and putrid failures of literary history;

---

[1] A later example (quoted in *The Times*, 7th July, 1960). The illustration: a girl tied by her feet and dragged face downwards behind a jeep. The caption: 'Gritty roads are bad for tyres, but they make fine face-erasers.'

but much work had already been done for them by degenerate scholars of the Romantic Movement, such as Schwob and de Sade.

In 1952 I decided to ask several hundred children just what comics they were seeing and what they thought of them. The answer to these questions will be seen in the next two chapters. In 1953 the 'Comics' Campaign Council asked me to convene a panel of experts to examine comics and give our views. This panel decided that it could not be much longer before legal steps would have to be taken about horror comics; we therefore concentrated upon comics designed for children being published at the time the panel was working. The report was published in 1955,[1] just before the opposition suddenly collapsed.

When the tycoons behind the major reprint industry realized that they faced growing public criticism, they sought psychological and psychiatric opinion in defence of comics on the ground that 'children need horror'. This approach met with scant response. Thereafter the publishers moved into the classics. Here they felt sure they would be safe from censure. Strangely enough, they *were* safe from censure for quite a time because critics were dumbfounded. It is quite extraordinarily difficult to *explain* why a classic ceases to be a classic when it becomes a comic. In order to discuss the matter at all one needs to have given quite a lot of study to the nature of artistic media. Since this has been done here, one can say quite briefly: remove the medium of art, and the basic plot that remains is no longer literature; it is little more than an infantile phantasy. Laughter was the lethal blow to classics as comics. Too many people laughed at, for instance, Lady Macbeth, hands dripping blood, crying 'Ouch!' and 'I got 'em!' Then the publishers tried the entire Bible, but this did not really go well, though the advertisements stated that it was in chronological order. In any case, what could be more impossible than the central figure of the New Testament playing the role of a comics hero? As a cinch for money-getters the Bible fell between two

---

[1] Pickard, P. M. (Ed.), *British Comics: An Appraisal*, 'Comics' Campaign Council, 23 Tillingbourne Gardens, London, N.3.

stools, being neither true religion nor true comics. This is just as well. Their production was fundamentally inaccurate.

Although the measures taken by Parliament were not very impressive, they must have caused considerable financial loss to some of the promoters in Britain. Several new series of the worst horror comics had just appeared in 1955 and had to be suppressed after their second and third issue. Their main themes were corpses, ghosts, vampires, skeletons, and the like. One example should be enough to give the tenor: an Egyptian seductress embalmed in her coffin and trembling lest after all there should be no resurrection; a tale nicely calculated to reach the deepest anxieties of any sensitive child, and all children are sensitive about dying.

It is unlikely that the new form of British comics for older children would have enjoyed its spectacular rise to fame unaided by the active fight against unsuitable comics. But there is no doubt whatsoever that the timely arrival of these comics made the fight against horror comics much easier. Children bought the new style of comics with their own money. In doing this they handed to responsible adults incontrovertible evidence that this was what they wanted.

Now, why were the comics so much wanted by the children? In the world of experimental science the one characteristic unique to experiments involving human beings is that the subjects of the experiments can give their views. Comics appear to be most extensively read about the age of ten or eleven, which in Britain is the end of the primary-school phase. If children can take an examination for secondary-school selection by this age, they are capable of giving their views on comics. It seemed a good idea to catch them in that post-examination period of relaxation, the spring of 1953.

CHAPTER 7

What children like

'You never see a nasty horror comic, do you, dear?' Thus Some People, as Keats would say, were obliging the children to be forced into duplicity and deceit. If such adults managed to avoid seeing the nasty comics, one could be sure children quickly learned that they were not among matters to be discussed with adults. With nearly twenty years' experience of children of primary-school age, mostly in progressive schools, I was familiar with the light, casual, brief conversations with children through which one gets the not-for-adults information. In 1951-2 I had ascertained in several industrial towns that children were seeing horror comics. Of all the many street vendors from whom I got copies, only one man spontaneously told me that he did not let little children have them; as a matter of fact, he fixed me with such a stern eye that I felt bound to ease his mind by explaining that I was no middle-man in that racket.

Well-informed people in the campaign against horror comics talked with such understanding about children's right to their own loved comics, that the idea of demonstrating the conformity of ideas between these people and children looked promising. All that was needed was to record the opinions of about fifty such adults and of several hundred children. Of course, as always in research, such a task would be difficult to organize and might prove the opposite of what one had anticipated. At this time the new form of comics was only just emerging and their immense popularity was not yet known to the general public. However, as nothing was being published about the children's views, the plan seemed worth carrying out for the sake of their views alone, whatever might emerge from collating the opinions of adults and children.

The first problem was to get together a group of well-informed adults, or at least of adults willing to become informed through my now quite spectacular collection of horror comics. The 'Comics' Campaign Council allowed me to use their file of people who had asked for their evaluation list, grading available comics from suitable to very unsuitable for children. These people had at least felt sufficient interest to bother to write for the list. I wrote to a hundred of them, asking if they would be prepared to give their views on comics sent to them. Finally sixty-six, agreed to do so. Fifty of them were teachers, seven head teachers, twenty-four parents, two children's librarians, two Justices of the Peace, one a parson, and one a psychologist; several belonged to more than one of these categories. They were scattered all over the British Isles, from Inverness to Donegal and Dover.

The plan was to get their views without giving any directive to opinions by asking specific questions. I sent round batches of four comics and four open questionnaires, one for each comic. All respondents had to do after studying a comic was to grade it on a five-point scale, from *E. Very objectionable* to *A. Suitable for children*, giving reasons for the decision and exact page and picture frame referred to, with rough estimate of age for which the comic appeared to be designed. In most cases this was done with exemplary precision. The four comics chosen ranged in my opinion from good to bad; but this I did not state.

One hundred and fourteen post-war comics were circulated in this way and three hundred and fifty evaluation forms came back. Thus most of the adults saw one or two batches of four comics, of wide range, and many comics were assessed by four or five informed adults. Only a very few comics got lost in the post or were never returned. The results are dealt with later.

The next step was to tackle the children. It would have been foolish to put the children on their guard by talking solely about comics; moreover, since considerable organization was required,

it would have been foolish while on the job to lose the opportunity to find out about their interests in general. If any quantity
of replies was to be obtained, the place would have to be school,
with groups of about twenty-five to thirty in number. Many
researches in America and Britain indicated that at least ninety-
eight per cent of children read comics, and the peak period is
about eleven years. Children of ten and eleven years could be
caught just after their secondary-school selection examination in
the spring of 1953. It seemed a little ironic to go into the schools
to inquire about out-of-school interests. But this would be a
moment when the authorities would not mind what looked like a
waste of time, and the children would regard chat about their
interests as good use of time at any season. Two kinds of district
were needed: one where street markets made horror comics
easily available, and one where lack of such markets might make
them more scarce. I decided upon the East End and the western
suburbs of London.

Altogether I got the views of over five hundred children of
nine, ten, and eleven years, as it would have been wounding to
omit nine-year-olds who belonged to a particular group. (Indeed,
tears came to the eyes of more than one child when I attempted
to do so.) There was a duplicated questionnaire which I went
through, stage by stage, first reading a question and then allowing them time to read it again for themselves before writing.
Many of the responses involved no more than underlining the
suitable word or crossing out an unsuitable word or completing a
sentence; occasionally the children were asked to write names of
games, comics, etc., or a whole sentence, and finally they could
draw a picture illustrating a story they would like to find in a
comic.

The questionnaire started with a group of questions designed to
obtain a relaxed atmosphere while incidentally obtaining insight
into spontaneous interests. Then there were groups of questions
about games, comics, radio, television, reading, etc. These groups
of questions asked first what the respondents liked about a
subject and then if there happened to be anything they disliked,

felt fear about, or had bad dreams about afterwards. It was only necessary to build a normal atmosphere about fears and dreams in connection with the first subject, which was out-of-school games. After that they were most reasonable about their fears; those who had none just waited or read ahead in the questionnaire; those who had some to record appeared to be writing with great attention. Several boys said regretfully that they had never had a dream, good or bad, as far as they knew.

The opinions dealt with here come from 382 children of ten and eleven in five London primary schools; there were 204 boys and 178 girls. Those in the East End were at Rotherhithe, Hackney, and Bethnal Green; those in the suburbs were at Putney and St Quentin Park, near the White City. What they liked is recorded in this chapter, what they disliked in the next chapter. The children were one-hundred-per-cent comics readers.

The schools kindly allowed me to see all the children's intelligence-test results, which ranged from the lowest level of intelligence considered educable in a primary school to intelligences high enough to win university scholarships. There were very few at these two extremes and the vast majority were round about average in intelligence. About seventy-eight per cent of the children were known quite well by two of the teachers. In these cases the two staff were asked to rate the children for various personality traits, to see whether their ratings corresponded. With one exception, this did not prove very profitable. The exception, concerning aggressiveness towards other children and towards the teacher, is dealt with in the next chapter.

Contact with the children was even easier than had been anticipated. What difficulty there was came from the so-called backward classes, whose reaction to pencil, paper, and reading appeared to be a frenzy of aggressive anxiety. But only one such class took as long as five minutes to relax. The children were warmed up to their task by a couple of sentences to complete in any way they liked: *I wish* . . . and *I am glad* . . . Then they had to say which of their possessions they would most hate to lose. There were over a thousand replies to these three questions, designed to find out what rose spontaneously to their minds, and only fourteen references were to comics. Comics did not appear to be uppermost in their minds. What did rise most frequently is worth examining. Of the 204 boys, 62 mentioned specific toys, 57 bicycles, 56 a football, and 55 their pets, and other things. Of the 178 girls, 73 mentioned their pets, 46 their school, 45 specific toys, and 31 bicycles, etc. Boys and girls shared interest in pets, toys, and bicycles. The pets were mainly dogs and cats, but also rabbits, goldfish, budgerigars and rarer animals.

Altogether there were 82 spontaneous references to school, 46 from girls and 36 from boys. Seven boys said in various ways that they were glad to be at school today in order to do this job. Only six of the 82 references were against school, one boy writing, 'I wish school was never thought of'. There were 66 references to their families, about equal numbers from boys and girls; eighteen of them were in the form of hating to lose some-one. Two girls wished to go out, 'But Mum won't let me'; two girls wished they had babies; and one girl wished she were the daughter of a rich man. One boy wished that 'Mum was rich'; another boy was glad that 'Mum is returning'. Other children, making virtue of necessity, were glad they were only children or had no brothers or no sisters or were eldest or youngest.

In these spontaneous references two subjects came up sufficiently often to warrant some attention. There were 25 references to health and 40 references about which sex they belonged to. On health the boys wrote such remarks as, *I wish* 'there was no disease', 'I was strong', 'Peter's leg would heal'; and *I am glad* 'I am healthy', 'I can see', 'I am strong', and (three boys) 'I am not ill'. On health the girls wrote such remarks as, *I wish* 'people in hospital would get well', 'grandma wouldn't go to hospital'; and *I am glad* 'I am strong', 'my Mummie is well', 'I am not in a home', grandma or mother 'got over her illness', 'I am not a cripple' or 'blind' or 'an invalid', 'the little boy is safe now', 'my dog's paw is better'. It is well for us to remember, as they sit in docility before us, that they have cares on their minds. Many of the remarks on health suggested quite realistic worries, though doubtless some of them were returns in the form of anxiety over earlier aggressive thoughts about other members of the family.

It seems extraordinary that as many references as forty should concern anything so unalterable as sex membership. One boy and one girl wished they were of the opposite sex. The other 38 completed *I am glad* . . . with stating their own sex. That ten per cent should, so to speak, throw away this opportunity for rejoicing on such an obvious matter should be noted, since it suggests that perhaps they were not glad at all. The adults had probably inculcated an attitude of doubt on the matter, as a hang-over from days when to be a boy meant adventure and to be a girl meant – well, boys will be boys, and so would girls! Here are two subjects that educators should bear in mind. Anxieties about health can be canalized into doing something for the sick, such as making or collecting gifts for children in hospital; and today it is easier than it was to build a realistic attitude about which sex one is, since girls can swim the Channel or win a show-jumping event.

The next question asked what they liked doing best when not at school. Over ninety boys and as many girls put something down. Many replies were unique, such as spring-cleaning, exams, and getting money. Where they could be tabulated, they indicated the most popular activities. For the boys, 75 put football first, and about 20 each put cricket, swimming, films, cycling, and reading. For the girls, 45 put reading first, and about 30 each put knitting or needlework, going to the park or common, and painting or drawing. The boys definitely preferred, or were allowed, more active occupations.

When they were asked to say what they would like to be, their replies were surprisingly realistic. The girls listed such occupations as nurse, teacher, hairdresser, singer, typist, etc.; one wanted 'a nice job'. The boys listed policeman, printer, mechanic, sailor, carpenter, chef, etc.; one put jockey, but he was slight in build and his father worked in stables. Only four per cent put jobs that might be unlikely; six girls put ballerina or film star, and eleven boys put footballer. This realism about the future in children of ten and eleven commands respect.

After this came the series of questions about specific activities. Out-of-school games came first. The most frequently mentioned games for the boys were football (143), cricket (86), hide-and-seek (19), racing (14), and touch or 'he' (14); and for the girls they were skipping (62), ball games (not team games) (58), netball (55), hide-and-seek (41), touch or 'he' (40), and rounders (39). Team games appear to have far more appeal to boys than girls, in this group; but hide-and-seek and touch (including French touch, chain touch, off-ground touch, and tig) are mentioned by both boys and girls.

Next came comics, which invariably met with incredulous amusement. In answer to which were their favourite comics this group of 382 children wrote down 1,670 titles. Every child mentioned at least one; they were all comics readers, or perhaps one should say comics viewers. The boys listed 87 and the girls 51 different comics; in all, 93 different comics were mentioned. This was in 1953, when traditional comics were barely back in full swing and the new form was only just becoming widely known. The favourites listed were the same for all children. There were no significant differences between the answers of boys and girls, the answers of tens and elevens or the answers of children in the East End and the western suburbs. On average, these children each saw two to three comics regularly every week, plus a couple more, probably swopped or borrowed.

Owing to the fact that comics were still scarce at the time of the inquiry the list of favourite comics is peculiar to 1953; but it is worth examination. *Beano* and *Dandy* topped the list for both boys and girls. *Beano* was seen regularly by 94 boys and 72 girls; *Dandy* was seen regularly by 92 boys and 75 girls. *School Friend*, still relatively new, was seen regularly by 83 girls. Other comics frequently mentioned as favourites were: *Girl*, 62 girls; *Eagle*, 56 boys; *Topper*, begun that year, 27 girls and 21 boys; and *Film Fun*, 24 boys and 21 girls. Boys and girls alike particularly relished *Beano* and *Dandy*, and to a lesser degree the long-established *Film Fun*. This last paper is designed for adults but probably reinforced the children's interests in films.

In the whole questionnaire the question for which I had to wait longest and give most encouragement was the one question that had really given rise to the inquiry, namely what it was that the children liked in their favourite comics. With every group the first reaction was to have absolutely no idea. There was no feeling of resentment; they just did not seem to know. However, they tried to think and eventually something was put down by 74 per cent of the boys and 88 per cent of the girls. Just 51 boys and 22 girls could write nothing down. Of course, what came was so diverse that it was extremely difficult to analyse, though this does not detract from its value.

There were two main groups of reasons. First came *exciting*, which was expressed in various ways by 37 boys and 68 girls, e.g. 'exciting stories', 'the way they put down and stop at exciting places', 'serials keep you guessing', '*Eagle* adventure stories', 'exciting adventures, makes you think it is happening to you', 'exciting, and serials can interest anybody'. To this group could probably also be added 22 boys and 31 girls who just wrote 'serials' or 'stories'.

Then came *funny*, mentioned by 33 boys and 46 girls, e.g. 'funny picture strips', 'to look and laugh at', 'amused', 'the comedians make you laugh', '*Beano* and *Dandy* funny'. Then came a smaller group, *interesting facts and puzzles*, mentioned by 20 boys and 25 girls. Two interesting points were mentioned by several children. One might be called *Reality and Unreality*, e.g. 'Brave deeds and things made up', 'Because they are a mixture of things that could and could not happen', 'because they tell the most impossible things'. The other might be called *Story Resolution*, e.g. 'When good men get the bad men in the end', 'Because the cowboy always gets the bad men'.

Excitement seems to be of prime importance, even more for the girls than for the boys. This is interesting, since the girls' favourite occupations had been quieter and their favourite games less competitive. It could be that convention was still expecting too much sedateness from them. It is almost with surprise that one sees they ranked humour highly, so solemn do children usually look as they study their comics. Twenty per cent had put funniness first. It would have been extremely interesting to make individual inquiry of the 19 per cent who had failed to answer this question, but this was not possible, as they were scattered through the five schools. It occurred to me that ability to analyse and state the characteristics enjoyed, particularly excitement and humour, might be a function of intelligence. I therefore correlated[1] level of intelligence and ability to give some explanation, but nothing significant emerged. Both answering and failing to answer came from all levels of intelligence.

Over three hundred comments, about the same in number for boys and girls, could not be classified. These included many thought-provoking replies, such as, 'It lets you get together with other people', 'exciting and sometimes interesting' (note the subtle distinction), 'nothing to scare you' (from a reader of *Eagle*, *Lion*, *Dandy*, and *Beano*), and 'murdering people is exciting' (from a reader of *Crime Never Pays*, *Tex Ritter*, and *Buffalo Bill* as well as *Dandy* and *Beano*). Incidentally, concerning the last reply, *Crime Never Pays* was a comic that indulged in great violence and ended stories *non seq.*, '. . . and so crime never pays'. This boy was not fooled; he recognized that murdering people was exciting and his insight compares favourably with that of most readers of detective stories who persuade themselves that their interest is in the evolution of the detection.

Other children gave as reasons for enjoying their comics thirty-two characters from fifteen different comics; but only two were mentioned twice. When asked directly who they would choose to be, if playing a character from a comic paper, 414 characters were named, only 6 of them humorous. Cowboys were given by 32 boys and cowboys or cowgirls by 18 girls. Dan Dare or Captain Marvel were given by 33 boys and a specific heroine from *Girl* or *School Friend* by 35 girls. Every character named had exciting adventures.

The next group of questions concerned television. It was not at all certain in 1953 that enough children would see television for

[1] Tetrachoric formula.

this series to be worth asking. However, it turned out that 38 per cent already had sets at home and so many visited friends' sets that only 12 per cent could not give any views on this subject. There was a difference between the two districts and it was the opposite of what economic circumstances would lead one to expect: 94 per cent in the East End and only 82 per cent in the suburbs were regular viewers. As many as 36 children in the East End and 10 children in the suburbs said the set was on all the time there was a programme. More children in the suburbs saw only *Children's Hour* and more in the East End stayed up late, many till the end. When half-way through the inquiry, at the suggestion of a headmaster, I asked children to put by their names what dinner money they brought. Thus I was able to deduce that quite a number who were having school meals free had television at home. This was an amazing revelation of the meaning of tales that do not have to be read, in what one might call sub-literate homes.

When asked what programmes they liked best there were nearly a thousand replies, half relating to *Children's Hour* and half to adult programmes. From *Children's Hour* 105 boys and 55 girls put cowboys first; Hopalong Cassidy and Tex Ritter were the only ones specifically mentioned, more girls preferring Hopalong and more boys Tex. Three other items were of interest to both boys and girls: *Muffin the Mule*, 26 boys and 38 girls; *S.S. Saturday Special*, 22 boys and 16 girls; and *Whirligig*, 21 boys and 27 girls. There was one divergence of opinion: 26 boys mentioned *Robin Hood* and 30 girls *The Appleyards*. Neither was mentioned by the other sex.

With regard to adult programmes, *What's My Line* was most frequently mentioned – by 40 boys and 19 girls. Next came plays (35 boys and 40 girls); then *Newsreel* (24 boys and 19 girls). The inquiry was made at the time of a murder serial called *The Little Red Monkey*. This will figure in the next chapter. But it was mentioned as a preference by 18 boys and 13 girls.

The next group of questions concerned films. More East End children went to the cinema, and in both areas more boys than girls went. The children who were not going at all were: East End 2 per cent of boys and girls; suburbs 1 per cent of boys and 8 per cent of girls. The children who were going four or more times a week were: East End 8 per cent of boys and 4 per cent of girls; suburbs 7 per cent of boys and 0 per cent of girls. In spite of their devotion to television, affectionately known as 'the telly', so many were going to the cinema two or three times a week that I mentioned this to a headmistress. She said she had asked one mother why on earth she let her boy go to the pictures every night of the week. 'What else can I do', she said, 'while his dad has tea? His dad needs a bit of quiet when he gets home.'

About a third of the children went regularly to a children's Saturday morning cinema club; and about the same number did not go at all. Those who regularly attended adult programmes said they decided whether to go by the trailer or the advertised stars. The boys and girls differed in their favourite kinds of film. Dancing and musicals were put first by 60 girls followed by cowboys or Westerns by 39 girls; but cowboys or Westerns were put first by 77 boys, pirates by 35 boys, murder and crime by 33 boys, and war or fighting by 20 boys. If the boys' favourites are lumped together as fighting films, then such films were preferred by 81 per cent of the boys but by only 22 per cent of the girls. Funny films were preferred by 25 boys and 18 girls; this is not very different for boys and girls but consistent with the girls valuing funniness less than boys in comics.

The next group of questions concerned the radio. All but 4 per cent had radio at home and three-quarters of them said they could have it on whenever they liked. Since the wireless was long established and on for so many hours, to save the children writing, a list of fourteen programmes was given and they were asked to put one, two, and three by their favourites. Each group made the gayest little whoops of joyful recognition as they read the list. Some went on numbering to the very end. One boy said, 'But they are all lovely'. *Educating Archie* topped the list, given as first preference by 78 boys and 80 girls. Then, a long way below, *The Mounties*, 34 boys and 21 girls; and *Flint of the Flying Squad*,

29 boys and 19 girls. Fortunately there was space for addition of any favourite left out; here *Life with the Lyons* was added by 37 boys and 44 girls, and *P.C. 49* added by 32 boys and 43 girls. The most popular radio personalities were: for the boys, P.C. 49 (29), Ted Ray (22), Max Bygraves (14); for the girls, Barbara Lyon (25) and Mrs Lyon (11). No one else was mentioned as much as ten times. Here again humour and excitement were the favourites, though the humour of *Educating Archie* was most popular. Its appeal can well be understood, since Archie and Monica are in constant league against authority, though all usually ends well.

The last group of questions concerned reading in general. The answers showed no statistically significant difference between boys and girls or between districts. Books were owned by 69 per cent of the children and borrowed from the library by 21 per cent. Only 6 per cent said they borrowed from friends. Eighty-six per cent said they looked at daily papers. The reason for their interest was easy to find; 90 boys and 101 girls said they looked at the comic strips. No other reason was given more than ten times, except sport, which was mentioned by fourteen boys.

More than half said they never read adventure papers. About one-third said they sometimes did. *Rover* was given by 4 girls and *Girl's Crystal* by 54; but the latter changed to comic format during the experiment and this was discovered too late to find out whether they were referring to the new comic or old adventure form. The references from the boys were: *Rover* (43), *Hotspur* (21), *Adventure* (14), and *Wizard* (8). What reading of adventure papers there was, was mainly done by the boys.

A question about favourite stories, in any form of reading, resulted in the following preferences: boys–adventure (33), Westerns (28), and mystery (26); girls–Dr Doolittle (52), true stories (49). Here, as with films, the boys sought more fighting excitement than the girls. (Dr Doolittle was, by the way, not being read in any of the schools at that time.) Then they were given five kinds of stories to put in order of preference. *Mystery* came first with 95 boys and 99 girls; then *Westerns* with 79 boys and 28 girls; then *love* with 14 boys and 15 girls; then *humour* with 11 boys and 22 girls; lastly *travel* with 10 boys and 9 girls. The great appeal of mystery, presumably without too much waiting for suspense to end, is of interest. Their excitement may be more enjoyed through suspense than is generally realized. More than half the children said they read something every day; and three-quarters owned what they read. If their favourite possessions were mystery tales, then they were learning to tolerate mystery by reading and re-reading the suspense.

When the evidence for the various out-of-school interests of these boys and girls of ten and eleven is arrayed, it appears that they have a very great deal in common. It suggest that more could be designed for them to see and hear and read that is not specifi-cally for one sex or the other. They love their toys and bicycles and animals, their schools and families; they enjoy similar wire-less and television programmes, which anyway cannot be separated for them. They enjoy mystery, adventure, excitement, and humour; and their family backgrounds are the same. Further-more, from their realistic replies about what they would do when grown up, they are beginning to enter into adult activities; adult programmes on radio and television, plays and newsreels, comedies and games, are immensely popular with them. Yet in so much that is designed for them, adults are either non-existent or solely curbing. It appears that they are, by this age, ready for more realistic presentation of adults and of children's relation-ships with them, at least for part of the tales. Moreover, this group showed concern over family troubles, sickness, accidents, etc. Neither the adults nor the children want to be together too much, but each party is greatly enriched by the other's com-panionship with common interest for short periods.

Results from several of the groups of questions certainly showed that the boys were pursuing more active and exciting games and wanting more fighting films. But there were signs of something rather suspicious about this. The girls, for instance, were wanting excitement from comics even more than the boys; and if the boys were getting their excitement from games and general activities, why should so very many more boys than girls not only go to the films but go to see specifically fighting films? These facts suggest that the boys and girls were not being given a balanced diet of the needed excitement. It may be that society is expecting the girls to be too docile and the boys to be so extremely belligerent that they have to seek compensation in the cinema. That there is a real difference between the majority of boys and girls is clear to anyone who is familiar with them; but the danger of expecting it to be greater than it is needs careful watching. As we have seen from some of the basic phantasies of the world's literature, the hand that rocks the cradle can wreck the world for the occupant; this is not feminine docility. Moreover, boys pressed to be too manly may go to the cinema to have their fighting done for them, or even to be fought. At any rate, it is as well to bear in mind the fact that society, with the best intentions, might be imposing a greater difference between the sexes than is actually there.

Before closing this chapter we must return to the subject of comics in order to compare the comics that the children approved with those that the adults approved. From the adults' comments and gradings it was clear that what they expected of comics for children were characteristics such as these: harmless slapstick or clean fun; good attitudes to morality (right triumphant without excessive encouragement of sympathy with criminals), to sex (no offensive bias), to racial problems (nationalities working together), and to animals (information and pleasant stories about them); stories well told, with exciting and healthy interest; and good drawings with clear print.

It will be remembered that questionnaires for adults and children were designed upon completely different lines. The adults received a wide range of comics and upon each one they answered an open questionnaire; the children were asked merely about comics they had seen, and the questionnaire consisted of many specific questions. Moreover, the adult opinions were completed before the children began to give theirs. Therefore there was quite an element of chance in their having seen the same comics at all. Unfortunately, *Girl*, which had only just come out when the batches of comics were first circulated and which later proved popular with the children, was one of the ones to be lost in the post, so no adult opinion was given of it. But in spite of these difficulties some interesting information emerged.

The children referred most frequently to *Beano* and *Dandy* as favourites. The adults classed *Beano* B, B, B, B, A, and *Dandy* B, B, B, B, C, A. Next on the boys' list came *Eagle*, which the adults classed A, A, A, B, B, B. Next on the girls' list came *School Friend*, which the adults classed A, A, B, B, B. Thus, when the informed adults came to class the children's four favourites in order of suitability for children, out of twenty-two assessments only one falls below the two highest grades. Each favourite comic was studied by at least five completely independent adults, who probably did not even know of the existence of each other. Yet children and adults were in very good agreement on what constituted an enjoyable comic. Moreover, children and adults had both cited fun and excitement as desirable characteristics, although the adults had on the whole laid more stress on humour than excitement.

CHAPTER 8

What children dislike

_____

Everyone who has good *rapport* with children knows that the one thing that must not be done, if we want to find out what is bothering them, is to make a fuss about it. *They* may make a fuss; they may scream and kick and refuse something, but this is simply infantile dependence upon adult ability to find out for themselves what is the matter. If the adult wants the child to explain, then an exquisite degree of indifference must be sustained on both sides if the matter is at all complex. Therefore the questions concerning dislikes, fears, and dreams were planned so that they could be easily answered. Each subject had a series of questions on these lines, which were read out with light indifference:

Do any of the games ever frighten you? YES/NO
If so, what sort of games?
Have you ever had a bad dream after any of the games? YES/NO
If so, what made you dream?

All the children had to do was to underline the appropriate word and if the answer was YES, then to add an explanation if they could.

Each time the group grasped at once the fact that the questioner was in the know about fears that go with pleasure, and was asking about fears that were too bad for fun. They also accepted the fact that some had them, some not; some had them for one thing and not another. The way in which they waited for each other had the quality of high courtesy.

What the children said about their dislikes, fears, and dreams should be seen as if a curtain had been lifted for a moment. Much of their phraseology has the ring of truth; doubtless much was not admitted; very likely some was put in for a lark. With comics, at least, we shall be able to see whether what they said they disliked had any connection with adult views.

Fear and bad dreams over games were admitted by 18 per cent of the children. There was no statistically significant difference between boys and girls. But when a correlation was made between those who admitted fear and those who admitted bad dreams, it was found that those boys who admitted fear over games tended also to admit bad dreams, and this was not so with the girls. It was easier for all the children to admit fear than to say what the fear was about, which was to be expected, since repression would be involved. However, some could explain a little; 33 boys and 39 girls gave explanations such as these: games played in the dark (usually murder-in-the-dark); ghosts were mentioned by 23 children, football by five boys and hide-and-seek by six girls.

Some of the girls made interesting comments showing that they realized the moment when there was loss of true play attitude: 'hide-and-seek when they make you jump', 'games in the dark when someone screams', 'when people are chasing you in the dark and someone makes noises', etc. Two children indicated serious withdrawal through fear: a boy wrote, 'when boys get knocked over in football' and a girl wrote, 'scared ball would hit him'. As with fear, so with bad dreams over games, murder and ghosts were the main subject of the dreams. Neither murder nor ghosts is given as favourite games, so that it is fairly safe to assume that murder and ghosts are games liable to cause too much fear for the aesthetic play attitude to be sustained.

Regarding comics, there were 133 references to comics that were not liked, and there was no significant difference between the number of dislikes given by boys and girls. Some children, quite naturally, could not recall the titles of the comics they disliked. Needless to say, the possibility of producing horror comics for identification had not been overlooked, but it had been turned down for a number of quite obvious reasons. Among the 133 titles mentioned there were: *Eerie* (11 children), *Black Magic* (8), Westerns (14), 'Americans' (8), *Tarzan* (4), *Airboy, Gabby Hayes,*

Gene Autry, Jungle, Super, Superman, Superboy, Army and Airforce, Blue Beetle, Captain Vidor, Comet, Crime Detective, Ghost Gallery, (leach). Many of these are the British editions referred to in Chapter 6, pp. 120–1.

This group of children had seen more horror comics between them than I had; consequently the group of well-informed adults had not been sufficiently well informed. However, 17 per cent of the comics disliked by the children had been seen by the adults, who had ranked them as objectionable or highly objectionable; moreover one of them, *Eerie*, had been quoted in Parliament.

There was no significant difference between boys and girls in admitting fears and dreams over comics. Fears were admitted by 26 per cent of the children and bad dreams by 18 per cent. The causes of fear, where given, were mainly murder and ghosts, which were given by 19 boys and 24 girls; the next most frequent causes given were crime, horrid faces, skeletons, guns, and monsters. The causes given for bad dreams were again chiefly murder and ghosts, given by 9 boys and 7 girls; then came skeletons, horrid faces, etc. A third of the children who said they had bad dreams about comics could not say what had caused them or what they were about. Those familiar with horror comics can well understand that the dreams might be too terrible to recall.

Here is a synopsis of all the things that this group of children said they disliked about some comics: murder and killing (75 children), ghosts, rising from the grave, etc. (43), crime, gangsters, and shooting (32), horrid faces and ugly men (14), monsters (12), skeletons (11), and (5 or 6 each) torture and space and love and horror and mysteries; also (1 each) stoning, strangling, hanging, dead people, too much adventure, all mixed up, too far fetched. One girl expressed it, 'Happening after happening, there is no pause'. What a galaxy of sadism to give the children through their favourite medium of comics!

It is salutary to compare the levels of self-expression between these groups of well-informed adults and well-informed children on a subject about which they are so much in agreement. Where adults could discuss lack of good resolution to stories, the children wrote such remarks as: 'they kill innocent people' or 'good men shot or captured' or 'if the person you stick up for is going to be killed'. Where adults wrote of violence, sadism, or morality, the children used concrete terms such as murder, ghosts, skeletons, etc. In all there were 118 references to ghosts and murder, 43 per cent of the boys' objections being these and 28 per cent of the girls'.

Three examples from the same comic seen by both children and adults will emphasize the great contrast between their powers of expression over their dislikes:

1. *Eerie*. Adult assessment: E, E, E, E, E, D.
   Referred to by 11 children.
   A boy: *There are too many bad men in it.*
   An adult: *Horrific pictures, descriptions of dead bodies walking and claiming victims, outrageous, obscene, blasphemous theological implications; pointless sadism, etc. Terrifying to sensitive child.*

2. *Black Magic*. Adult assessment: C, C, D, E, E.
   Referred to by 7 children.
   A boy: *When you read them you dream.*
   A boy: *Skeleton and ghost.*
   An adult: *Eight of the thirteen stories deal with death. Much is horrible. Moss scraped from skulls of executed men, faceless people, flagellation of women.*
   An adult: *Would give child night terrors, particularly as stated clearly 'True amazing account . . .'*

3. *Airboy*. Adult assessment: D, D, D, D, E, E.
   Referred to by one child.
   A boy: *More killing than the others.*
   An adult: *Horror, death, drowning, revenge.*
   An adult: *Pretends to be scientific but gives quite false terrifying ideas of science, e.g. magnetic starlight. Enervating substitute for real adventure.*

When the curtain was raised so very briefly upon what frightened the children, there was so very little to see; but there can rarely have been so much in so little. One boy wrote of *Eerie* and *Black Magic* together, 'because they are frightening'. Just that; no more. Those who were struggling to get an inquiry as to whether the children were receiving their citizens' right to protection had to suffer seeing very distinguished personalities on television, chatting and laughing about the childhood horror which had 'made them what they were'. What we said about what they were would scorch holes in any publication!

The agreement between the adults and children in this inquiry about unpleasant characteristics in comics was much more extensive than can be stated numerically. A number of the children objected to unpleasant things seen in Westerns and 'Americans', without being able to recall titles. The adults made a great effort to be tolerant and classed many Westerns and 'Americans' as C, neither suitable nor objectionable, while citing such examples from them as these:

1. *Crimson Comet*. Vilely drawn faces.
2. *Super Yank*. Constant play on emotion by fear and mystery.
3. *Sam Hill*. Constant recurrence of love interest of casual type, definitely intended for adults.
4. *Straight Arrow*. Frightening, unnecessarily bloodthirsty. Torture, stoning, elements of sadism.

Little wonder that some children classed 'love' among the horrors. Knowing, as we do, how much adults 'forget' their childhood, we can scarcely indulge ourselves in much righteous indignation about Victorian horrors for children, after allowing this to happen to our children in the name of freedom. It was murderous sentimentality to ignore the children's views: 'when you read them you dream', 'they are frightening', 'more killing than the others', 'there were too many bad men', and so on.

Since the parliamentary Act has banned but by no means obliterated the danger of the worst horrors reappearing in comics, let us inform ourselves in a little more detail about what the children object to in them. Here are a few of the children's criticisms:

BOYS

When horrible faces coming in at you and you take it in your
head.
I thought it happened to me.
I keep it in my mind.
Love, all about kissing. Because he keeps kissing.
They have inside killing in them (*The Worm*).
They scare me. The Faces. All the faces (*Crime*).
Yes, the man from Planet X and he is so ugly as anything never
seen (*Black Magic*).

GIRLS

Sometimes when its murder I dream a nightmare. The ugliness
about it. I read a comic and then I keep remembering it
(*Murder*).
When animals start jumping on men.
A girl went into a cave and when she came out she was a mole.
With a man being pushed overboard and roaming about the sea.
When the man rode the sea when he was dead (*Eerie*).

This sound criticism came from a little group of less than four
hundred children who had listed one thousand six hundred and
seventy dearly loved comics, which they enjoyed for their excitement and fun.

After the horrors of comics and dislikes, television dislikes
presented an amusing complication. There were no dislikes –
absolutely none whatsoever was admitted. Though the comics
horrors have been taken seriously here, with the children, as has
been explained, they were taken with light and airy disdain. Thus
we swam gaily on to the delights of television. This complication
of no dislikes about TV was realized right at the start, with a pilot
experiment upon five boys and five girls of ten and eleven, with
wide range of intelligence. They cried out indignantly that there
was nothing wrong with the telly, *ever*! So an extra question was
hastily fitted into the questionnaire; was there ever anything
which they would not specially mind missing? Even so, children
would look up while answering and say earnestly such things as,

'You understand, don't you, that I don't *dislike* this but I *might* want to do something else?' When asked what they might like to do instead, with the exception of fourteen boys who said football, all the other pursuits which they gave were activities which could be carried on in the room with half an eye on the set – drawing, painting, needlework, and stamp collecting; and 49 per cent of the children said they would never prefer to do anything else when they could watch television.

The programmes that they so grudgingly admitted that they might possibly not mind missing were: *Muffin the Mule* (17 boys and 23 girls); *Ballet* (16 boys and 7 girls); *Newsreel* (8 boys and 14 girls); *In the News* (13 boys and 8 girls); *Children's Hour* (8 boys and 7 girls). No other item was referred to more than once. Most of these appeared among their favourites and this consistency suggests that they knew their own minds.

However, the fact that these programmes, which did not require the laborious task of reading, were so popular, does not mean that the children experienced no fear or even no bad dreams over them. If this had been so, television would not have been assisting them to resolve their problems in the way that games and free activities were doing. There was no significant difference between boys and girls in admitting fears and dreams. Fears were admitted by 24 per cent of the children and bad dreams by 5 per cent. This is a very big drop from fears to dreams; it suggests that something which was really helping them happened during television watching. What it might be will be discussed in the next two chapters, where the great oral tradition is touched upon.

The only causes of fear given more than five times were the now familiar bogies, murder and ghosts, which were referred to 27 times by boys and 42 times by girls. The current thriller, with bloodcurdling signature tune, was *The Little Red Monkey*; it was mentioned as a cause of fear by 29 children, three boys and three girls specifically mentioning the music. The B.B.C. stated that they hoped the children were in bed. The B.B.C. perhaps were not thinking of the site of some of the sets in the East End. I have seen homes in which the beds were seats for the audience. One boy told me he could not go to bed till the set was turned off; and two boys said they could see the programme from their beds.

There was a difference between boys and girls over disliking murder; 18 per cent of the girls said they disliked it but only 10 per cent of the boys did so. With only 4 per cent having bad dreams, there was practically nothing to report. Murder was given as the cause by five boys and five girls; ghosts were given by three girls; the rest could not explain. From what is to be seen of murder and ghosts in other media for children, it might well be that these ten children who had bad dreams over television murder and ghosts, were having anxieties over murder and ghosts from other sources re-awakened by television; in other words, television was not the prime cause of the trouble.

Regarding films, the situation for the children was akin to that of comics. They saw their comics on their own, and very few adults bothered to examine them; also very many of them went to the cinema alone, so there was no adult to calm their fears or raise a voice against the unsuitability of some of the films. Fear over films was admitted by 25 per cent of the boys; and 12 per cent admitted bad dreams over them. But 44 per cent of the girls admitted fear over films and 24 per cent admitted bad dreams over them. The fact that nearly twice as many girls admitted to fears might arise from the fact that they were more timid; but it must be remembered that society allows girls to say they are afraid. The boys were seeing more films but expressing less fear. This might be due to a number of factors; they might be less timid than the girls, or they might be afraid to admit fear, or – a sinister thought – they might be becoming adapted to brutality; and we must not forget the suggestion that they might be in need of compensatory phantasies about the manliness that society might be over-imposing upon them. Whatever the explanation, the drop from fear to bad dreams for both boys and girls was only down to about half; and this was not nearly so promising as the drop from fears to bad dreams in relation to television.

There was a marked difference between what the boys and the girls disliked in films. Murder and crime were objected to by

32 per cent of the girls but by only 13 per cent of the boys. With one exception, nothing else was referred to as disliked by more than eight children. The exception was musicals and/or romance, which were objected to by 24 per cent of the boys. This would have been extremely interesting to follow up. Did they really dislike musicals and romance? Did they find them too erotic, as in horror-comics love? Or were they just bored by items that kept them from the fighting they seemed to need? It may have been an idiosyncrasy of this particular group of children. If it should prove not to be this, then it would be too superficial to pass it off as the boys regarding musicals at any rate as sissy, because as many boys as girls have gifts of music and movement; since we now know that excessive aggression is linked with sexual disturbance, an over-reaction to romance is also suspect.

Answering questions about radio, very few children admitted fears or bad dreams. Fears were admitted by 8 per cent and bad dreams by 2 per cent. Murder plays were disliked by fourteen children. One might say that if the children were glued to television they could not be expected to know much about radio programmes. Yet they had had a good deal to say about their preferences. It therefore seems clear that they enjoyed the radio and did not hear much that they disliked.

With regard to books, dislikes, fears, and dreams were almost non-existent. Only 2 per cent admitted to fears and only 2 per cent to bad dreams over reading. It is easier to stop making the intellectual effort to read and to put down the book without knowing more, than it is to walk out of the cinema or avoid happening to see some of the pictures in a comic that are disliked. Since more than half the respondents had said that they read something every day, it would seem that they were simply not reading what they disliked.

Before making a summary of what the children said they disliked in their out-of-school interests, there is one matter concerning school itself that might be examined. It was said in the last chapter that out of 82 spontaneous references to school only six were derogatory. This speaks very well for the modern primary school, for the five schools were chosen carefully as representative. The remarks about school had not been asked for; they came spontaneously in connection with 'wishes' and 'being glad'.

It has been explained that 78 per cent of the children were assessed by pairs of staff members who knew them; the kinds of trait they were asked to assess were: sociability, maturity, tendency to fear, cheerfulness and depression, and so on. This voluntary labour by the staff might have proved intensely valuable. But there had been tremendous school readjustments after the war and so many staff changes, with the men coming back to teaching, that not enough children were known well by two of the staff together for the assessments to be reliable. However, something very curious emerged, which may possibly have an indirect connection with the inquiry; or may throw some light on a possible connection between what the children did in school and what they chose to do out of school.

One of the traits that may be relevant to children's love of excitement and fighting and wrangling is aggression. Since a child may show one degree of aggression to teachers and another to children, aggression was broken into two parts:

(i) Shows aggression towards the teacher.
(ii) Shows aggression towards other children.

The pairs of teachers, working quite independently, were asked to indicate on a five-point scale how they would assess each child's aggression under (i) and (ii). Now, of all the eleven traits that the pairs of teachers assessed, (ii),[1] the children's aggression towards each other, was the one on which the greatest agreement between all pairs of teachers was to be seen; and (i),[2] the children's aggression towards the teacher, was the one on which there was greatest disagreement. From (ii), the reliable one, a few drops of information could be squeezed; for instance, that many children who were aggressive towards each other were very fond of Western comics and stories,[3] though there was no indication of

[1] Average of cor. 0·54 (ii) } Bravais-Pearson Formula.
[2] Average of cor. 0·15 (i) }
[3] Tetrachoric cor. 0·55.

whether the hen or the egg came first, whether Westerns made them aggressive together, or being aggressive together made them like Westerns.

It is not at all surprising to find that the pairs of teachers had pretty shrewd ideas about which of the children were aggressive little monkeys together, and which could do with a bit more standing up for themselves. Each teacher's assessment for this trait in the whole group showed a normal distribution, with very few at either of these extremes, and most somewhere about average. Each teacher's assessment for every trait except (i) shows aggression towards the teacher, had a fairly normal distribution of the same kind. But their assessment of (i), the children's aggression towards the teacher, went quite haywire; it was skewed in a very peculiar way. This could not have been because they did not understand the given definition of aggression, because they had understood it very well in connection with the children among themselves; it was only where the children's aggression concerned the teachers themselves that all sign of normal distribution was lost. We must go into what had happened, in order to see if there could be any possible explanation of the teachers' irregularity in this one judgement.

The number of children on whom two opinions for the eleven traits were given was 291. As there were two opinions for every trait, there were twice that number of opinions about (i), the children's aggression towards the teacher, that is 582 opinions. All the traits were assessed from E, *very little*, to A, *very much*, and all but the one under discussion went roughly like this:

	E	D	C	B	A
582 opinions	50	100	282	100	50

But when the teachers had to decide *which* children showed *how much* aggression towards them, the strangest things happened. First there were not nearly enough children classed as middling; then there were even more marked E, as showing absolutely no aggression towards the teacher, than were placed in the middle as average; and then scarcely a child was marked A as showing much aggression towards the teacher. This is how the teachers' opinions about (i) actually went:

	E	D	C	B	A
582 opinions	221	94	210	55	2

Nobody expects the actual numbers to fit at all closely to the made-up numbers of a normal distribution; but the differences here just cannot be overlooked. Let us fit them together:

	E	D	C	B	A
Roughly expected	50	100	282	100	50
Actual	221	94	210	55	2

The reason why all this is important is that far too many teachers were refusing to see any signs of aggression in the children's attitude towards them. And where are those scally-wags who are for ever having to be suppressed? There are at least a couple in every class, frequently many more. With nearly six hundred opinions, one could have expected a minimum of a couple of dozen classed as very aggressive towards the teacher. Only two! It does not make sense. Teachers often have to be very annoying to children, with *Stand up straight!* and *Have you washed your hands?* and *You have forgotten to carry the nine again.* What would children do with their healthy aggression if they were never allowed to show it? They would have to spend valuable play activity in working it out. Since, as they showed by their spontaneous references, these children loved school, they would try hard to get rid of this normal reaction, and much the easiest way would simply be to repress it, which is no resolution of the problem at all; this would waste an immense amount of their energy. Moreover, we need to encourage them to stand up for themselves at times; otherwise they are in danger of becoming little yes-men to authority for life.

A hundred of the children's questionnaires were handed over to an experienced graphologist, a refugee to Britain, without any indication that it was for this particular problem that I wanted her opinion. When she handed them back she said, 'What has happened to these children's aggression? I could find practically no sign of it in their writing. Is it possible that, in spite of your wonderful new Education Act, you are still suppressing the children too much in your lovely schools?'

Years of teacher-training have taught me that teachers' anxiety lest they cannot manage the large classes with which they are confronted, at least at the beginning of their careers, penetrates frequently to nightmare levels of anxiety. What they are afraid of is the class getting completely out of hand. What every progressive educationist should be afraid of is their dominating the class too competently. We are only just beginning to give the teachers in training something of the real insight that they need over the matter of class discipline. It might help them greatly if we were to explain more clearly that a certain amount of apparent insubordination from the children is a good sign; if the children find that they can speak frankly without upsetting the teacher, they are less likely to feel bottled up and thus to spend time planning retaliations, or repressing healthy reactions, or working out the trouble in play. That this school problem must affect the children's out-of-school activities to some extent is certainly true. From it springs some of their startling caricatures of teachers while playing schools.

When we come to summarize the children's fears and bad dreams in their out-of-school interests, as indicated in this inquiry, it is only over films that the boys and girls reacted differently. If we eliminate radio and reading, where their anxieties were negligible, then the pattern is as follows: *Fears Admitted:* Girls 44 per cent over Films, Children 26 per cent over Comics, Boys 25 per cent over Films, Children 23 per cent over Television and Children 19 per cent over Games. *Bad Dreams Admitted:* Girls 24 per cent over Films, Children 18 per cent over Games, Boys 12 per cent over Films, Children 4 per cent over Television.

We have seen, in Chapter 4, what extensive work children carry out in their games; it is therefore not surprising that the subject of their games should show little drop between fears and bad dreams. But the films and comics and television are given to them by adults and should be planned to maintain sufficient aesthetic distance to come to their assistance. There is no doubt that, with this group of children and particularly at the time the inquiry was made, television was helping them most. It is to be hoped that a similar inquiry today, with banning of horror comics and development of better comics, would show a more striking drop between fears and dreams over their dearly loved comics. On the matter of films, there are, in various parts of the country, groups of parents who are visiting performances seen by the children. When they are able to publicize their findings we may be in a better position to relate the frequency with which boys and girls are visiting films to the kind of films that they really enjoy. There has been a tendency for research on cinema-visiting by children to concentrate on the statistically manipulatable *amount* of going rather than on the more awkward *suitability* of the films for them.

There is just one last point that might be of interest about the fears and bad dreams admitted by these children. It may have occurred to some readers that it might not be the same children who admitted fears and admitted bad dreams. Correlations were made[1] and it was found that, with the exception of the girls and their games, on the whole it was the same children who were admitting both fears and bad dreams. The section of replies where it was most noticeable that fears and dreams were being admitted by the same children was the one concerning boys and their comics; next came both boys and girls over films. Thus it was where most fear was admitted that the greatest number of individual children were admitting both fear and bad dreams.

It is interesting that their bad dreams over the games they chose to play should be so great. If we fit the percentages of fears and dreams together in a table, this becomes evident:

[1] Tetrachoric correlations:

	204 Boys (S.D. 0·21)	178 Girls (S.D. 0·21)
Games	r 0·57	r 0·17
Comics	r 0·86	r 0·48
Television	r 0·59	r 0·58
Films	r 0·66	r 0·64

	Fears Admitted		Bad Dreams Admitted	
		%		%
Films	178 Girls	44	178 Girls	24
Comics	382 Children	26	382 Children	18
Films	204 Boys	25	204 Boys	12
TV	382 Children	23	382 Children	4
Games	382 Children	19	382 Children	18

It is not at all surprising to see that the games they choose for themselves come bottom of the list for causing fear. What is noticeable is that in games alone there is practically no drop in the number of bad dreams admitted. This is not actually so surprising, if the seriousness of play as explained in Chapter 4 is accepted. Since it is the underlying problems that motivates the spontaneous play, then they would seem likely to emerge again at night.

Relatively speaking, the whole inquiry was a very small one. However, its importance lies in the fact that the children were well able to make their contribution to the problem by giving psychological introspections on their views. Where the children's views could be directly compared with the views of adults who were well informed, the similarity of views was noteworthy. With the exception of the children's own games, the material investigated here could all be classed as mass media produced by adults. People inveighing against mass media frequently appear to forget that books are also a mass medium. Moreover, it is often overlooked that books written for children's enjoyment are a very recent phenomenon.

Now let us turn our attention to the times before the advent of films or comics or television or even of books for adults. How did children slake their thirst for stories before anyone enjoyed tales through any of these mass media? If we can find out this, we shall be more likely to get the whole problem of tales for children into perspective. It may be that insisting on their reading too soon has not only given far too many of them a distaste for the printed word, but has also thrown too great an onus upon their play.

CHAPTER 9

Stories through the ages
1. The great oral tradition

Until this century, the telling of stories by adults with children listening must be the nearest approach that adults have ever made to the play of children. The characters and objects in a tale that children love are so many larrikins upon which the children can work out some of their split-off tasks. The stories cannot supplant the children's own projections in play; their own personal problems must, for long periods, be presented to themselves by themselves through whatever strikes each child as a suitable symbol for a specific problem. Such play frequently borders on art but is too personal to be true art. Though the stories cannot supplant play, they can, and must, supplement play. Through the art form, tales perform a treble function: they bring to children experience as yet unknown to them, they demonstrate manipulation of that internalized action which we call thought, and above all they break down the isolation of phantasy life in all its lonely guilt-ridden anxiety.

These three points should be elaborated. Adults, in their tales, bring to children characters and objects and events of which the children may never yet have heard, thus bringing to the children's phantasy life a healthy outer reality. The tales, though arising from the inner life of the people, are a species of outer life for the children both because they come from without and because they are in art form. When next they return to their own play they will be equipped with a whole new battery of previously unknown arms for outmanœuvring the enemy. In the expert hands of adults, the most appalling conflicts are not only acknowledged to exist but are brought to satisfactory conclusions.

What, by the nature of childhood repression, was thought to be not permitted by adults is suddenly revealed by the adults as known to exist in the inner world of man; what is more, there is a cool, calm, and collected manner in which the fiercest monsters can be subjected. Practice and faith, a handful of pebbles, and a sling were all that David needed to outwit the most terrifying giant. Through practice and faith a child took on a task too formidable for the adults. Children feel deep gratitude to adults who possess sufficient detachment to tell this tale against themselves; it is one of the most encouraging stories children ever hear.

A reliable story-teller does not transgress the boundaries of art. There will be new experiences, and skilful manipulation of action brought to permissible conclusion, and sharing of 'forbidden' thought. Thus a well-told tale can become a criterion for successful play, an example in keeping sufficient distance from events for mastery to become a possibility. Stories, far from being a waste of the children's time, are as important as play for their healthy psychological development; and the children have left us in no doubt that they recognized their importance.

Before there were any books children widened their experience, learned facts of interest and importance, and absorbed the subtler aspects of the culture into which they were born by overhearing stories. From intonation they learned *finesses* of behaviour that elude the writings of all but the great masters of literature; what they could learn from hearing tales was therefore not something that they could have learned from books if there had been books. ' "Oh, you *poor* little mouse!" said the old man . . .' instructs tenderness far more surely than a dozen maxims. Moreover – and this is very important – the maxims of behaviour are usually given to children at moments when they have failed in some way, so that the maxims are distastefully confused with shame and guilt. It is much more valuable for the children to experience tenderness for a little mouse because they enjoy the old man's kindness, than to show signs of tenderness in order to win adult approval or to dodge feeling guilt.

Many things that children have to learn are too complex to

put over to them in a form less profound than a story. For instance, they have to learn to consider others but they also have to make decisions for themselves; at times, there may be so many people to consider, or one person demanding so much consideration, that the child is paralysed. A solution to such an impasse can be presented in a tale and can leave a child with much food for extremely interesting thought.

Yet for stories to be designed for children is a comparatively recent phenomenon. This new form of art dates only from the end of the seventeenth century, when wise people were beginning to grasp what Locke and Comenius had to say about the nature of immature minds. Between then and now, the quality of literature for children has developed to a very high level; but it is literature, and the stumbling-block has been learning to read. We shall probably never know how much this bogy of literacy was a publishers' racket, promoting sales of books. The first intimation of how much children learned through ears alone came to us through early radio listening; they chatted of radio personalities with acumen or backchatted comedians with astounding facility. Some time in the thirties a boy of seven came to me and said, 'Isn't it sad, we are losing Henry?' Thinking Henry must be one of his family of eight brothers and sisters, I started off cautiously by asking how he thought he would miss Henry most. It was not long before I discovered that this pinched expression of bereavement was caused by the prospective visit to America of Henry Hall.

If to what children learn by hearing people we add what they learn by seeing people, then we have some indication of the true meaning of television to them. The whole atmosphere of a tale can be rescued from disaster by a shrug, a raised eyebrow, and a few notes whistled from the haunting refrain in Schubert's Ninth Symphony; with their own eyes and ears they behold their hero collecting himself for the task of overcoming the disaster. Television gave back what printing took away, and none dares say the children have left us in any doubt about their views on the importance of television.

What they get from television was theirs centuries before the hideous word literacy was coined. But it would be quite untrue to say that, in listening to adult tales, they heard only unsuitable stories. They could always preserve themselves from boring parts by falling asleep or wandering off on their own affairs, as they do in a family party today. As we saw in Chapter 7, children are rarely bored by a well-told adult story. Moreover, the tales told in olden days were in the main really believed; this fact alone would act as a form of censorship upon the raconteur, for he would be unwilling to overstep the bounds of art and find himself in the limbo of great boasters. A virile and flourishing community is composed of individuals with sound ego-formation, and listeners would insist upon a reasonable measure of credibility.

When the stories become too terrible for the children, they would be with adults who could allay their fears – as happens with television today – speaking reassurance to the older ones, hugging reassurance to the tiny ones, and reminding them all that it was only a tale, that of course everything would come out well in the end. Even a decadent society could hardly have allowed its children to meet worse stories than our own children met during that brief period of horror comics.

Children's interest in adult problems has been seriously under-rated. Those earlier adult tales that the children may be said to have overheard concerned adult problems, but problems that we now know were rooted deep in childhood. Thus, unbe-known to the adults, much would have direct appeal to the children. Moreover, much in the telling, characteristics such as adventure, tolerable suspense, or humour would appeal to the children as much as to the adults. Many of the adults would recall their own childhood delight in certain tales and make sure that their children did not miss these, whatever else they might miss; through their children's delight they would, as happens today, re-live their own childhood delight in stories long since out-grown by themselves. Above all, every gifted story-teller would first have been enthralled in childhood, and those first tales to charm would never be forgotten; few raconteurs would be indifferent to the magnetic attention peculiar to a child audience, and for such an audience there would be the priceless repertoire of unforgettable childhood favourites.

Thus for a variety of reasons tales specially suitable for children would be perpetuated. It is incorrect to imagine that the adults were indifferent to the children's needs. They were probably unaware of the function of the stories for themselves and unaware of certain adaptations necessary before particularly disturbing stories could perform the same healing task for children as for adults. What aided the children was the adult mastery of the art of story-telling. Through this discipline the extremes of horror and beauty were preserved from wanton cruelty and sickly sweetness; confined within the framework of aesthetic distance, the horror and the beauty were within the adult audience's powers of integration. Art of this high quality would rarely be too strong for the children.

Stories overheard in these islands have probably been influenced for more than two thousand years by stories from all over the world. Aided by inflection and gesture, song and dance, stories are the most tradeable commodity of all, once the sketchiest knowledge of a few foreign words had been attained. If the Phoenicians really did reach as far as the British Isles, they would surely have learned something of the Celtic tongue from the inhabitants of the west coast of France. A people renowned for craftsmanship, cultivation, mining, navigation – as far as we know the first ever to leave sight of land – who traded gold and silver from Spain, perfume and spice from Arabia, fine linen from Egypt, and many other commodities, they would make a point of knowing the gods and myths of their clients. The little figurines that they bartered for iron and tin were doubtless named by the Phoenicians after Celtic gods as far north as Britain. These people, who gave their alphabet to the Greeks and who made many of their stone memorials bilingual, might well have brought tales from Tyre and Sidon, many of which had originated even farther east.

But in any case, it is found that stories springing from the human mind all over the world take two basic forms, myths

about supernatural beings and stories of the exploits of exception-
ally heroic men. These two basic forms are to be found in the
tales of the Celts, the Persians, the Indians, and far Cathay. From
all over the world there come stories of human problems in
these two forms. Thus it is comparatively easy for one version to
infiltrate another. The plots are known to us all: conflicting
adults, fatal children, strain between parents and offspring, tensions
between fathers and sons or mothers and daughters, the wicked
stepmother and neglected daughter, the cruel father and younger
son. Love, hate, and guilt bring in their train murder and panic,
with the dead returning to plague or devour the living. And
always there are the friendly talking animals and birds, who warn
men against love, against gold and silver, against certain plants.

It is curious to note the countless reference to plants in these
tales from all over the world. Some are nourishing, some are
curative, some are harmful and – most mysterious of all – some
harmful plants can be curative if not taken to excess. These harmful plants which can be curative in moderation might well be
taken as the symbol of all split-off work, be it the play of children
or the art of adults; the principle of *similia similibus curantur* is
rooted impressively far back in the history of mankind. It plays
such an important part in stories that its significance in mental
as well as physical matters must have been at least partially
realized. 'And with the juice of this I'll streak her eyes,' says
Oberon, 'and make her full of hateful fantasies.' He did not
mind whether these 'fantasies' were of lion, bear, wolf, bull,
meddling monkey, or busy ape; and as everyone knows, it
was one night with her hempen homespun half-human that
clarified the forgeries of jealousy. Innumerable plots hinge upon
the right plant given to the wrong person or the wrong plant
unintentionally or deliberately administered.

Over and above it all there are the super-beings who, for
reasons of their own, help or hinder man in his various enterprises;
but also, shot through the very fabric of every brand of tales,
there come those troops of super-larrikins, the fairies and the elves.
Always there is the necessity for hospitality to all, lest the meanest

beggar should turn out to be a super-being in disguise; always there is some land of the blessed where human effort may cease for a while – or to all eternity; and all over the world this land of blessed respite is in the west, across the ocean, where the sun goes down, in sleep . . .

A number of devices were used for preservation of accuracy in passing on the oral tradition. It seems that in the very beginning the tales were told to the accompaniment of symbolic movement; in addition to aiding memory, this movement would probably also help to subordinate alarming excess of novelty in the dawning tradition, thus restoring artistic balance. When the Greeks invented the lyre, tales were chanted to music. Rhyme was then added to rhythm and it seems that rhyme is more than just a mnemonic, a peg upon which memory can arrange sequence of ideas; rhyme enables the listener to make a forward movement, ahead of the teller, and prepare for developments; rhyme also connects words in sound associations outside the manifestations of reasons, and this illogical quality is ideal for bringing together illogical but psychologically logical concepts which are the essence of poetic unreason. Thus all that had to be passed on by word of mouth, both sacred and secular tradition, was accurately preserved. Moreover, the nature of movement, melody, rhythm, and rhyme was such that, in addition to preserving accuracy, they formed an ideal matrix for expression of original creative thought.

Tales with the perennial plots were told in these ways by Celtic bards before the Romans invaded Britain. The bards are mentioned in records as early as 200 B.C., and the Welsh bards reached the height of their influence in about the sixth century A.D. They led armies into battle, sang to princes and chieftains in their halls, and competed together in their renowned Eisteddfods. They were granted the protection of special laws and accorded degrees of privilege commensurate with their attainments. They so inspired the people that their power was at times regarded as highly dangerous; there were sporadic attempts by monarchs and the Church to suppress them, but without success.

Through these Welsh bards much, including the Arthurian

Cycle, was passed down to us. All over Europe tales were told in this way. Nothing seems to have been written down until about the eleventh century, when certain monasteries made copies of some of the secular tales and concealed them among their religious manuscripts; they believed these tales to date back many centuries. Among the earliest manuscripts of this kind known to us are the Irish *Book of the Dun Cow* and the *Book of Leinster*, containing mythological romances of the Ulster Cycle, many of them ascribed to the court of King Conor of Ulster in the first century A.D. Although there must have been a fresh infiltration of tales from places such as Tartary, Egypt, Turkey, and Persia, brought back by crusaders, the first records bear no reference to them.

It seems to have been several centuries before the crusaders' tales were written down; by then their tales had become infused with romance, as well as reporting the conflict of idology between orient and occident. There is, for instance, the tale of Orlando (Roland of the Charlemagne Cycle with metathesis of initial letters) who loves Angelica, daughter of the King of Cathay. The way in which travellers spread tales across the world is depicted in the fourteenth-century *Canterbury Tales*, in which Chaucer's pilgrims tell tales originating in Tartary, Greece, and Rome, as well as in British lays.

By the twelfth and thirteenth centuries medieval legends had clustered round historic figures such as Alexander and Charlemagne, and myths had clustered round such beings as Siegfried, Arthur, and Rustem. Before these clusters of tales could reach epic quality they usually required a single great poet to mould them into unity. Firdusi brought the many Persian tales of Rustum together in the epic *Shahnameh*. In this great cycle the hero lives through several centuries, sometimes fighting men for days on end without pause, a constant conqueror who overcomes dragons and demons. He is eventually slain only by treachery, but not before he has unwittingly murdered his own son. This tale is now known to many through Matthew Arnold's *Sohrab and Rustum*.

In the great Hindu epic *Mahābhārata*, which is believed to date from 200 B.C., there is a tale destined later to infiltrate Christian tradition: Vishnu the Preserver saves the progenitor of the human race from the deluge by means of an ark. How old the tale was when it was raised to epic standards none can now say. In 1957 Frank Edmead published an article on Asia describing how he had attended a rendering of that twin Hindu epic the *Rāmāyana*. Here the passing on of the millenia-long oral tradition is not disrupted by modern communications:

'I went to the weekly reading of the *Rāmāyana* and apart from one or two hurricane lanterns there was little that I might not have seen and heard a hundred years ago. This was entertainment as well as religious ceremony – the ancient text was sung with all the verve and abandon devoted in the West to rock 'n' roll – but on other nights of the week the young men taking part might have been listening to the development officer's wireless set, or watching the films he was showing about hygiene or improvements in husbandry.'[1]

The tales told by raconteurs everywhere with the verve and abandon of rock 'n' roll were accepted by all classes, high and low alike, in the days of the great oral tradition. The minstrels, those gifted itinerant musicians and poets, accompanied their masters on their travels; by the thirteenth century most of the chief houses had a permanent staff of minstrels. The German minnesingers sang of military adventure, country life, and politics, as well as of love; they were themselves often of noble, even princely, rank.

So prolific in song were the minnesingers that by the fourteenth century one single nobleman had collected fifteen hundred of their songs. The French troubadours invented their own complex rhythm and rhyme to sing of chivalric love, tenderness, elegance, flattery, wars, and religion; in their themes and style and locality of southern Europe, they seem to have been the natural heirs to the Latin of the Decline. The French trouvères were a much more virile band; they were known as the men with a pen in one hand and a sword in the other; they raised much of their poetry to epic quality.

[1] *Manchester Guardian*, 21st May, 1957.

Ballads were sung all over Europe and Asia. In these islands the ballads reached a perfection of their own, for instance in *Kynge Horn*, *Sir Tristram*, *Havelock*, and *Sir Gawayne*. In these, too, the venerable plots are to be found. They tell of the girl who followed her 'fause luve', of 'fause Sir John', of the talking 'wee birdie', of the danger of 'the red goud' and the 'siller'; they tell of the ghastly crimes to the 'childe' who is drowned or smothered or stabbed and who always seems to be blessed or threatened with 'gouden locks'. Beware the red goud danger. The ballads had refrains not unlike those to be heard in the traditional games of children. Such refrains as 'down-derry-down' are linked to ritualistic movement by the names of country dances. This theme is developed by the Opies in *The Lore and Language of Schoolchildren*, Ch. 8.

An example from children's games may give some indication of the much greater antiquity of the refrains than of the ballads. In parts of Scotland children play 'Tappie, tappie tousie, will ye be my man?' and the singer seizes a child by the forelock. Experts have traced the origin of this game and find it to be a remnant of rhymed legal procedure, much older than the ballads, whereby an overlord accepted the surrender of a freeman; the freeman knelt at the appropriate moment and the overlord seized his forelock. Thus that superficially incomprehensible cliché 'seizing time by the forelock' falls into place; we would make time our serf. The refrains that we find in our indigenous ballads may well have been elliptical references to relevant procedures far too familiar to require more detailed exposition; the refrains might almost be described as a kind of telegraphese of oral tradition.

This magnificent oral tradition, in all its complexity, would be available to all children in hall and cottage and in the great public contests, where the camaraderie of the talents strove for recognition. From it they would take what they required, and few adults, if any, would note the virtual insatiability of the children's requirements. There would be the basic plots which the adults did not dream were so relevant to the children's affairs: the wicked young groom who seizes his master's horse and rides off with his mistress; Rustum unwittingly annihilating his own

Sohrab; Bevis of Southampton winning fame abroad though treacherously sold by his own mother to be a heathen slave; and many others.

There would be the countless tales in which children have a part to play. In the Ulster Cycle, there was Cuchulain, royal prince of miraculous birth, who entered the court when only four, slew a fierce hound when still a lad, and in manhood performed many mighty feats, the most renowned being the defence of Ulster against wicked Queen Maeve;[1] this same Cuchulain, while only a boy, fought his best friend Ferdia to the death. From the same cycle there is a tale of the boy corps which rushed to the defence of their hero and died protecting him. In the tales of the crusades there was the tragedy of thirty thousand boys, under the French lad Étienne, who perished on the way to the Holy Land; and the only slightly less tragic exploit of children under the German lad Nicholas, which never reached the Holy Land.

This tragedy of the children in their reality-attempt to reach the Holy Land raises a most interesting problem. It is understandable that the spectacular level of story-telling might carry the boys so completely away that they banded together to set forth themselves. What is not understandable is how the parents could have let them go. After all, obstacles such as the sea and mountain ranges must have given the parents ample opportunity to stop them – had they wished to do so. Why might they not wish to do so? It may be that the answer to this apparently unparental behaviour can be sought in some of the tales themselves, particularly in the Arthurian Cycle.

The Boy with the Mantle is a ballad in which only the child was pure enough to test the chastity at court. Sir Galahad, son by enchantment of Launcelot and Elaine, by his immaculate purity was alone able to find the Holy Grail. There would be the general talk about the Feast of the Boys, a ritual in some cathedrals and religious houses and schools, in which boy bishops performed

---

[1] Of whom Synge wrote, 'That poets played with hand in hand, To learn their ecstasy' See above, p. 24).

high office – presumably in an attempt to win back some lost state of innocence. An effigy to one of the boy bishops is to be seen still, in Salisbury cathedral.

In all these tales, told about children by the adults, there is a quality of insight and observation about childhood problems which would be a credit to any modern child-specialist. Consider for a moment the tale of *Parzival*. Medieval people were so profoundly preoccupied by the irreconcilability of vice and virtue that they were fascinated by any black-and-white symbol, from magpies and wagtails to check cloth and masonry. A much-travelled minnesinger, Wolfram von Eschenbach, who was a most noble knight, brought back to Germany a Spanish tale of a boy born of a black knight and a white lady, who grew up in such purity that he was able to find the Holy Grail. This attempt to fuse within one person the black and the white, vice and virtue, or horror and beauty, is of particular interest, as it is not again attempted in literature for half a dozen centuries. Then Goethe was to spend a lifetime on his *Faust*. The Parzival tale was transmuted by von Eschenbach into an unsurpassable lyric of considerable length. Much could be written about the exquisite delicacy with which mother and son are portrayed.

To spare him the corruption of court, she brings him up deep in a forest, knowing nothing of knighthood. As with all truly living relationships, both she and her son alternate between overwhelming insight and equally overwhelming blindness about each other. He is allowed a toy bow and arrow, for knights do not use them. One day he inadvertently shoots a bird stone dead. He cannot explain to his mother why his breast heaves with unshed tears; after deep thought she draws the wrong conclusion and has the birds driven away. Eventually he meets knights passing through the forest and mystifies them by asking in clearly cultured tones what knights are. Once he knows, nothing will stop him from becoming one of them, and his mother has to let him go; but for armour she gives him a kind of sackcloth suit, so that he will be driven back to her by ridicule. He is not driven back. He perseveres and eventually achieves supreme success.

The more one observes the enrapturing charm of these tales of
spotless youth, the more one must speculate upon what can have
given this aura of spotless purity to youth. We now have, as one
might say, inside information that the children, far from being
immaculate, are lacerated by guilt over their swings between love
and hate in their shatteringly aggressive phantasies. But those
parents of long ago must have seen that real children were stormy,
undisciplined, violent, and in need of guidance over behaviour.
Therefore, in one sense, the adults were mistaken in harking back
nostalgically to the innocence of youth. But we have to remember
that, knowing all this, we are still today profoundly moved by
tales of Sir Galahad, Parzival, and the boy bishops.

What is it that childhood has which is so profoundly moving to
us, even though we know it is a time of horror and strife? The
immaculate youths were not just unacquainted with sin or horror
or blackness; they made some moral effort, an integration of
personality, whereby they spanned the black and the white, the
horror and the beauty. The sixty thousand parents who let their
boys follow Étienne knew their sons were not perfect. What
qualities, then, did they think the children had, that they would
let them attempt what noble knights had failed to achieve? We
are forced to the conclusion that the parents must have realized
that the children had some secret access to techniques of moral
striving, techniques for making the effort to integrate personality.

There are, of course, other explanations as well. Adults forget
or repress the discomforts of childhood; they envy the hours for
idle day-dreaming, the freedom from adult toil, and the brilliance
of childhood experience. But it looks as if the ethically and
aesthetically superb tales of immaculate youth partly symbolize
the profound moral striving and progress that children can make
in their play.

We should therefore add to the list of reasons why children
were able to derive their own mental nourishment from adult
tales the fact that the adults themselves, for their own reasons,
poured into tales of childhood an awareness of something of
supreme moral importance lost by adults. Thus the children heard

tales in which children alone could play the leading roles. Far from being a golden age of innocence to which the adults wished to escape back, what they wished to retrieve was a golden age of moral achievement. During the period of the great oral tradition the approach which adults made to the play of children may have been very much closer than hitherto suspected. This puts in a different light some of the tiresome admonition that became current after the decay of minstrelsy, for the admonishers may themselves in youth have suffered serious privation of spoken tales.

But in addition to the serious contribution that could have been made by tales heard by children about children, there were exciting marvels. There would be the many tales of magic; the magic lamp and the magic carpet, tales of being carried 'amid the wind' like any modern superman. There would be those nursery-sized super-beings, which might be called the super-larrikins, the pucks and goblins, the elves and fairies, both trooping and solitary, as unaccountably for or against children as were the super-beings of adult tales. There would be the many famous magic fountains, such as the Fountain of Youth in which Alexander's army was restored to vigour after battle. Many of the children, like Hans Andersen later, would have been bathed in the local magic fountain for this or that childish ailment; and we can be sure that, steeped well in such tales beforehand, any ailment that could be cured by suggestion would miraculously disappear. There would be monsters galore, such as the invulnerable boygs, and Fenris-Wolf, the son of Loki, who burst his dwarf-made chains to fight the gods, and Fafnir the dragon, and perhaps even Ephialtes the giver of nightmares. There would be the talking animals and birds, to whom the children would feel even closer than the adults; and because of this closeness, the children would welcome the joyous love of nature in the tales of the far-travelled St Francis, whose followers reached Britain in the thirteenth century.

All this the children would hear told with as much conviction of truth as was to be heard in tales of the exploits of exceptional men, such as Charlemagne, Canute, Marco Polo, Vasco da

Gama, or Francis Drake. Indeed, the phantasy-laden tales of other lands must have been too deeply rooted to be easily extirpated by the true reports brought back by real travellers; strange truth would seem far less credible than familiar fiction. On every side there would be ample confirmation of all they heard, to support the magnificently high quality of the telling. There would be the drama, played before their very eyes; the plays and pageants and recurring festivals, such as Corpus Christi and Christmas; and always available for examination in minutest detail, the coloured pictures in the church windows, the statues and the *bas-relief* on walls and pillars. It is hard for us to realize today how the great oral tradition was supported and explained and corroborated by these tangible witnesses to events, not merely in mighty cathedrals but in every tiny village church.

It might be worth while to pause a moment and consider a curious error in the renovation of one such village church window a couple of centuries after the invention of printing; it was an error that could never have happened while the passing on of tradition was by recitation with illustrations in public buildings and churches. In the Berkshire village of North Didcot there is a beautiful old east window in the parish church. There, a dozen illustrations are set out in four lights, dedicated respectively to St Nicholas, St Peter, St Paul, and the Blessed Virgin; each light illustrates in stained glass worthy of the minute scrutiny for which it was created three well-known incidents; the colours are exquisite, the incidents dramatic and poignant.

During the Restoration the window was renovated and two illustrations were put back in the wrong place: the conversion of St Paul was put in the St Nicholas light and the enthronement of St Nicholas in the St Paul light. This was presumably not noticed, for by the time of the Restoration half a dozen generations had become increasingly accustomed to gleaning information from books – or perhaps it would be more accurate to say that half a dozen generations had become decreasingly accustomed to hearing tradition orally conveyed. So it has never been worth while rectifying the error, and the subjects can be seen in the wrong place today, accompanied by a notice explaining what each picture is about and which ones are out of order.

There are still churches where one can see parties being taken round by monks and other officials, who tell the tales and point out the details to enthralled pilgrims. Vézelay, in France, is such a cathedral, and here one can see a wide range of illustrations, including dragons, monsters, devils, magic mills, and fountains; David is attacked by the fiercest of lions; Daniel sits in the den surrounded by lions with expressions of puzzled docility; the miraculous plants and animals are minutely depicted. All is to be seen, together with a small percentage of the horrific, and all with the freshness of complete sincerity.

What children prize above all is this elusive attribute of sincerity, with its attendant freshness and accuracy. They are gifted with unerring insight about sincerity, perhaps because sincere people are consistent and therefore of more help to children in the difficult task of formulating the laws of behaviour through which they attain integration. At any rate, the tales that children accept without reservation show a superb mixture of vigorous simplicity, precise detail, and wide scope for the imagination. The hero cries: 'Bake me a bannock and roast me a callop for I'm going away to seek my fortune,' and the children are also away, laden with food, to seek their fortunes with him. Young Merlin Legasaich sees the little Cornish men go off in their tiny boat, 'curved like a new moon on her back . . . a burning wonder on the quiet water', and the children are spellbound at the beauty before their eyes. Kilhwch rides off to seek Arthur's help in winning his bride; he is mounted upon 'a steed with head dapple grey, of four winters old, with shell-formed hoofs and a bridle and saddle of gold'. Kilhwch has two silver spears, 'with an edge to wound the wind'. Imagery has been given a definition; the children have seen the gold saddle and bridle, heard the wind being wounded; if the teller forgets and says later that the saddle was leather or the spear blunt, then imagination falters uncertainly.

To satisfy children, not a statement may be nullified by careless contradiction, not a word be misplaced, not a phrase deadened by over-use. If Manwyddan's dragon is turquoise and sapphire and gold, then every time it appears it is to be expected that it will be exactly turquoise and sapphire and gold. The clear directives as to imagery free the imagination to leap confidently forth. In exactly the same way there must be trustworthy directives as to the characters. Kilhwch has ridden off to seek Arthur's help; the children already know and love Arthur, and they are excited about this splendid owner of a gold saddle and silver spears who, like them, trusts Arthur. Let Kilhwch or Arthur be mean and unworthy; then the children will lose confidence about whom to trust. Villains must be quite differently introduced, with a hint of suspicion right from the start. A well-introduced villain is treated by the children to comments such as, 'I don't quite trust that traveller. Who is he? And what's he got in that sack, anyway?'

The fine exactitude that enchants children must unfold the developing plot in such a way that their imaginations are expanding and dancing along with the utmost confidence that the teller means what they think he means. That the audience is with the raconteur is the acme of story-telling. In the days of the great oral tradition there were limitless feasts which the children could share with the adults.

It is unlikely that the monks of the eleventh century had any idea that, in making manuscript copies of the tales of their own day, they were sounding the pre-echo of the death knell to the great oral tradition. The first recognized blow to the masterly telling of tales was the establishment of stationary theatres, which became increasingly common after the fourteenth century. These co-operative efforts by bands of raconteurs at fairly regular times in stated places – usually at or near an inn – must have seemed bewilderingly unfair to many minstrels. They were in the position of vaudeville artists with the invention of talking films, of film artists with the invention of television. It is possible that they might have survived these setbacks, though many of the brilliant young ones would have seen the potentialities of the theatres and joined the bands of actors. But there was a still greater setback to come.

CHAPTER 10

Stories through the ages

2. The invention of printing

The final blow to the masters of the oral tradition was without doubt the invention of printing. Had they kept their heads they might have saved the situation; but what probably happened is that the young and brilliant minstrels went off to read and act, while those who could not grasp the importance of the new discovery plied their withering profession in disgruntlement. Since it was the old or the less able minstrels who were carrying on, they could neither abstract the telling quality peculiar to oral tradition nor advocate it if it were pointed out. The age-old tension between young and old, between gifted and less gifted, doubtless arose; those who could see the future for writing and printing grew impatient with the old stick-in-the-muds and left them to themselves.

Anyone learning to read at that time, in the fifteenth century, must have been gifted indeed, because there were no simple books from which to learn. The only primers were such classics as were printed. A high proportion of the eighty odd books printed by Caxton in this country were tales of many lands which had been told through the centuries, such as the *History of Troy*, the *Golden Legend*, the *Morte d'Arthur*, the *Canterbury Tales*, and a large part of the French cycles. The only aid afforded those who were learning to read would have been the illustrations, accompanying the text. There were as many as seventy woodcuts to the *Golden Legend* alone. Since the minstrels as a whole were classed as an outstandingly accomplished section of the population, a cartoonist might have depicted the situation in some such way as this:

> *The Great Hall.* A minstrel in his accustomed seat but relaxed and bowed over a huge volume of golden legends. A handful of princes, dotted about the hall, also relaxed and each lost in great volumes of his own. A disconsolate crowd wandering off in pursuit of entertainment, with the local inn as focal point upon the horizon.

There is no doubt that the quality of tale-telling in hall and cottage deteriorated rapidly, for the public contests swiftly fell into abeyance. Those of the bereaved majority who had some verbal facility did what they could in cottage and kitchen, but the dramatic incidents were no longer conveyed with high art and forgotten parts were eked out with untransmuted personal phantasies. The children played what they could remember of the rhythmic bits in their games, but, without real comprehension, the chants soon became nonsensical. The disturbing tales would be essential to the children, for they were below subsistence level in stories and their play would of course suffer. The tragic deterioration continued through several centuries.

Just before the mutilated remnants of this age-old oral heritage passed away, scholars saw the significance of this folk material, and began to piece it together as best they could. It is not quite correct to imply that it would all have gone. There was, for instance, the modern rendering of the *Rāmāyana* in regions of Asia only just being affected by books. The sudden publicity given to South Uist, in connection with rocket bases, drew attention to a form of oral tradition still chanted as it was many centuries before the invention of printing. Certain sociological investigations carried out in parts of Italy where people still live in caves have drawn attention to isolated areas where, here and there, one may find women gifted with a technique for keyless singing believed to derive directly from the trance-utterings of oracles. The point is that the heritage passed away wherever a small section of gifted or fortunate people were able to read books; and this was an inestimable loss to the non-reading majority, among whom were to be numbered nearly all children. It now becomes clear why the children devoured the mutilated remnants retrieved by the scholarly efforts of the Brothers Grimm, even though they brought in their train nightmares of a peculiarly horrific kind.

The disaster of printing from the children's point of view was not just the labour of learning to read, difficult though this has been, and slow though teachers have been in understanding how best to teach it. After four centuries we are just beginning to have an idea of how and when it should be taught, if children are to look upon books as their friends. The disaster was not even that the children were overlooked. We have seen with what loving care the adults regarded children, introducing them into stories and illustrations of the highest artistry. Caxton did not forget them. He printed special books for them but, far from being the glorious tales of old in simple form, they were manuals of edification and admonition, such as *The Book of Courtesaye: How Boys should Behave in Noble Houses*. He missed the point that the *Morte d'Arthur* might be a more reliable guide to courteous behaviour for children, in humble as well as noble houses. The pilgrim fathers did not forget them. The early settlers in New England published a book for their children in 1646 called *Spiritual Milk for Boston Babes in Either England, drawn from the Breasts of Both Testaments for their Souls' Nourishment*. To this stern diet was very soon added Foxe's *Book of Martyrs*, that they might be prepared to meet their Maker, possibly at a very early age amid the hazards of pioneer settlement.

The disaster of printing for the children was that, in one brief generation or so, they lost the glorious panoply of oral tales told by masters, from which they had been quietly imbibing a complex and concentrated nourishment of incalculable value to their balanced development. In due course most children have been taught to read, but even today not one in a thousand is sufficiently gifted to gain from reading before the age of ten a fraction of what was being derived from the magnificent tales magnificently told. It is quite ridiculous to pretend that children must struggle to read if they want to know their noble heritage. We might as well say that an eagle should walk up a mountain in order to know it, for stories bring the children an eagle's view of their world. Of course they must learn to read when they are sufficiently mature, but this has so little to do with their need for stories that it is really misleading to couple the two points.

Rescue from famine came, for the illiterate, the semi-literate, and the not-yet-literate, from a most unexpected quarter. This was broadcasting. It came first as sound, through which many spontaneously conjured up such vivid visual imagery that they could describe and even paint what they had seen. When vision was added, it was found that mime, at least for short periods, could hold its own without any spoken word. Vision and sound together, actually by the family hearth, meant that the great oral tradition was potentially back.

Parallel with the scientific work through which broadcasting had become possible, there had been carried out scientific work in psychological laboratories showing that a medium as complex as television enables people to receive the communication according to their own physical and mental make-up. Those with most vivid auditory imagery could follow predominantly through their ears, those with vivid visual imagery predominantly through their eyes, and those with most vivid kinaesthetic sense – one of the senses that Aristotle missed – through movement and rhythm.

There is probably nothing of the great oral tradition that cannot come across by way of television, and there is every reason to suppose that the new medium may surpass the old. Yet a new medium has new disciplines, and, curiously enough, it so happens that one of the weaker techniques for communicating a dramatic tale on television is the single raconteur. On sound radio it is ideal – for listeners with good auditory imagery; but television technique has access to other types of mind, and does not seem to excel when not fully exploited. The rapid evolution of television techniques is in itself a fascinating drama, and one which intrigues many adults who are accustomed to regarding themselves as able and enthusiastic readers.

Now let us trace the history of children's stories during the four centuries between the decay of the minstrels' art and the advent of television. The majority of children were hearing fragments of great stories round their own hearths. Some were also learning to read. But of course nothing was known about, for instance, suitable reading age, preliminary work, individual differences, or the age at which children can be expected to abstract the principles underlying the alphabet; and the resultant loss in terms of child hours from genuine education became astronomical. Adults had no idea that the alphabet, which seemed such a logical approach to books, had been discovered three thousand years before the great enlightenment; reading had not spread during those three millenia because people could not understand what the alphabet was supposed to be doing. Even now four-fifths of the people in the world are illiterate. In spite of these problems, the more gifted children, when given the opportunity, learned to read. If they belonged to a social class with free access to private libraries, then, in the absence of masterly tale-telling, they would be able to experience something of the thrill of stories from their own reading. Let us not be misled by accounts of little geniuses lost in *Canterbury Tales* at the age of four. The chance of our meeting one of these is not much higher than our chance of winning a football pool; and in any case such a child, preferring solitary reading to a well-told tale, may well become socially retarded.

But writing for print developed a *malaise* of its own, which was to increase the burden of learning to read widely, for the less gifted members of the community. It is one thing to be speaking directly to people before you; quite another to sit writing in studious isolation. A live audience becomes restless when the speaker loses vigour and simplicity; without this real contact, the pen can become more and more involved and abstruse. It was against this excessive elaboration that writers such as Perrault and Andersen struck, with their beautifully written tales for children; Perrault supremely aware of what he was doing and Andersen quite unaware. Both wrote in this way specifically for children; and how much the children needed this greater simplicity will be evident if we recall for instance the title of the seventeenth-century book for Boston Babes.

In spite of these problems, during the four centuries under review an ever-increasing number of children learned to read. They made their own many an author who never dreamed that there would be a multitude of children to pay homage to his swift narrative, vivid wording, clear-cut delineation of characters, and humour. The children's favourites ranged from Caxton's editions of *Æsop's Fables* and *Reynard the Fox*, through Defoe and Swift, to Fenimore Cooper and Scott, none of whom was thinking of children as readers. Countless examples of books never intended for children spring to mind. Such children as loved these authors for adults, and were able to master the reading with reasonable ease, really could get from books something of the thrill of the great oral heritage. But let us not lose sight of the facts that these were the more able children, that appreciation of real literature would inevitably come later than appreciation of masterly telling, and that none could get from reading just what can be got from listening and seeing. Whereas the minstrels could see before them the number of deeply absorbed children, the authors did not know of their child readers.

It was two centuries after the invention of printing that Locke first drew attention to the fact that parents were in need of instruction concerning their duty towards children; that they required instruction in how to cherish and spare the children's young minds. Those two words, *cherish* and *spare*, are today fundamental to all educational ideas of value. 'When by these gentle ways', he wrote, 'he begins to be able to read, some easy pleasant book should be put in his hand, wherein the entertainment that he finds might draw him in.' He said children loved animal stories but could suggest nothing other than Caxton's *Æsop* and *Reynard*, published some two hundred years before.

About the same time similar understanding was coming from abroad. Comenius conceived the idea that, since nothing was known that did not first reach the mind through the senses, children should learn through pictures as much as through print, if learning was to be a delight. 'Schools', he cried, 'are slaughter-houses of the mind where ten or more years are spent in learning what might be acquired in one.' Comenius published *Orbis Sensualium Pictus*, the first picture-book for children, to the end that they should 'absorb knowledge of the fundamental things of the world by pastime and pleasure'. The pictures are, to our modern eyes, truly execrable; yet in Hoole's translation this was said to be the most popular book for children in England for over a century.

It was really two hundred years before the concepts of Locke and Comenius concerning the nature of education for the maturing mind began to be at all widely grasped. They must have struck hard-headed citizens as so much philosophical fiddlefaddle, utterly unrelated to real children, who obviously got on with their alphabets quicker with a little touch of the birch. Let us not delude ourselves that there are no teachers of the same opinion today. But at least we now know that they are using the children as their split-offs for unintegrated aggression. Many of them will frankly say, 'I had corporal punishment as a child *and look how wonderful I am.*' They do not actually say the part in italics, but wait in hopeful naïvety for the listener at least to indicate that this has been grasped.

The delay in evolution of stories for children cannot really be seen in perspective unless we pause a moment to get the feel of what was holding it up. Let us use these two examples of the alphabet and corporal punishment. Mankind did not learn to read for a very long while after the invention of the alphabet, because fluent reading is not done by the alphabet at all, as anyone knows who suddenly comes across a foreign phrase, such as *Ein Gefühl der erreichter Leistung*. If we were accustomed to alphabetical reading, we should have no difficulty in seeing what we think this ought to sound like, but in fact we have to pause and read it carefully. Regarding corporal punishment, those who maintain it does work are at least reporting what can be seen in a classroom when the stick comes out; the children's heads can be seen to go down to their books. The two arguments put forward by the progressive educationists, who have made a study of developing minds, are these: first, learning to read should not commence with the alphabet, as children are ready to take an interest in printed words and phrases before they are ready to abstract the alphabet: second, many of the people who can read, but will not, were taught by punishment and threat of punishment; moreover it is found that the one child who is beaten may be less affected than many of the forty or so watching, whose reactions may range the whole way between sadism and masochism.

These are two interesting points, not difficult to grasp; moreover, in these days of specialization, we have all grown accustomed to relying upon the opinions of experts. If we can understand what kind of mind refuses to take in a new, habit-breaking concept, then we shall better realize why the ideas of Locke and Comenius and their followers were so slowly grasped by parents and educationists, and therefore so slow to affect children's literature.

Let us make a physical analogy. Consider the source of modern locomotion. Imagine Hero of Alexandria demonstrating his little steam engine. The hard-headed Alexandrians must have laughed at his ridiculous idea that he had discovered an important new form of power. 'Why,' they must have sneered together, 'obviously the weediest little worthless starving slave is stronger for heaving baggage!' Only the imaginative and the well informed could possibly see what Hero might be talking about and trying to demonstrate.

This analogy suggests that we are asking much of people in expecting them to adopt practices the educational principles of which they do not grasp and the educational application of which presents fresh problems. Lack of imagination and lack of study were what held up the acceptance of the ideas of Locke, Comenius, and their followers. It is highly probably that imagination deteriorated through lack of suitable stories overheard when the hearers were children, but this would be hard to prove. Anyhow, the remaining two centuries, which bring our history of children's literature up to date, show three clear strands: first, adult stories which some children were able to read for themselves; next, stories written for children to enjoy; and last, books of edification and admonition, which sank from Caxton's well-meaning manual of courtesy to a baleful infliction of advice certain to wither and stunt any sensitive child. To the eternal glory of the imaginative and well-informed, the third sort, the books of mental cruelty, died.

During the last two centuries the stream of children's books has grown to a mighty river; at times it was driven underground only to emerge strengthened from many sources. In the first fifty years the chapman booklets showed comprehending attention to children's interests. There is testimony to their meaning for children in Boswell's diary for 10th July, 1763, when he chanced to find himself in Bow Churchyard printing office, from which the chapbooks originated. There his eye fell upon some of his own childhood favourites and he underwent that strange emotional churning known to many of us on seeing in after years a childhood favourite. 'I saw the whole scheme', he wrote, 'with a kind of romantic feeling, to find myself where my old darlings were printed.' He said that *Jack the Giant*, *The Seven Wise Men of Gotham*, and other stories had amused him in his dawning years as much as *Rasselas* did in adult life. He obtained a few to add to his collection of *Curious Publications*, and noted on the flyleaf of one that he would one day try to write such a tale for children, if he could find 'the nature and simplicity and humour'. He concluded by saying, 'I shall be happy to succeed, for he who pleases children will be remembered with pleasure by men'.

With the Romantic Revival, other writers were beginning to recall the importance of these early favourites, now being so laboriously assembled by the scholars. Steele reported on the utter absorption with which children could be seen reading chapbooks and other old tales, wherever they could find them.

By the mid-eighteenth century books designed for the entertainment of children were beginning to appear. There was *The Child's New Plaything*, the very first 'A. Applepie' book, published 'to make learning to read a diversion instead of a task'. Then, with a foretaste of publicity to come in children's books, *A Little Pretty Pocket-Book*, attractively bound and gilt-embossed, with an advertisement stating, 'The Books are given away, only the binding is paid for.' In these, Newberry, the publisher, had set forth advice to parents and correspondence with Jack the Giant-Killer. From then onwards the quality of publication for children rose higher and higher, till it reached the level of such publications as *Aunt Judy's Magazine*, a periodical that reviewed straight from the press such books as Hans Andersen's *What the Moon Saw*, Lewis Carroll's *Alice in Wonderland*, and Charles Kingsley's *Water-Babies*. The remarkable scientist editor of this magazine was Mrs Gatty, and she did not hesitate to criticize Kingsley's slip in describing exactly how a dragon-fly sheds its skin. Copies of her journal are to be seen in the British Museum, treasured not with the journalistic material at Colindale but at Bloomsbury itself.

Thus progress was being made in appreciating what the old favourites designed for adults meant to children, and in preparing material designed for the children themselves. Now what about the third, the well-meaning but baleful, strand? If writers of these books had ever read of cherishing and sparing the developing young minds, they must have interpreted this as swaddling them in admonition. It is hard for us, trained to think in terms of winning the confidence of children, to understand what they thought they were doing for the children; and there is no doubt that these adults were at times seduced into orgies of contemplation of sin, ostensibly for the preservation of future generations. Their lack of awareness of what was going on was so humourless that it is not surprising to learn that they actively condemned imagination and phantasy as error and untruth. They were the sort of people of whom Keats said that they compelled children to deception.

They banned *la bonne grâce de Perrault*. Translations of his *Histoires du Temps Passé* were harshly condemned by such as Mrs Trimmer, who regarded Cinderella as 'a monster of deceit'. Yet in Europe alone there were between three and four hundred forms of this tale in circulation as told through the ages, including the Italian Cenerentola, the Spanish Cenicienta, the Catalan Venta-fochs, the German Aschenbroedel, the Russian Chernushka, the Hungarian Popelusha, and the French Cendrillon, which the gawky young Andersen had danced. The chapbooks had been crude and not designed specifically for children; but banning Perrault meant banning the very first fairy tales written for children ever to reach this country. In her preface to *Holiday House* Catherine Sinclair reports that Walter Scott had said to her: 'In the rising generation there will be no poets, no wits or orators, because all the play of imagination is now carefully discouraged.'

The pressing need which these adults felt to administer admonition and their rejection of imagination were not the only troubles. There were some quite serious misapprehensions of educational principles, resulting in faulty practice. It was stated that children needed simpler stories, so Lady Eleanor Fenn brought out *Fables in Monosyllables*; but they were not monosyllables at all; the book consisted of a hyphenated polysyllabic adult vocabulary. When the idea of genuine monosyllables was grasped, whole books of three-letter words poured on to the market, so cramped by this limiting selection factor that they were destitute of interest e.g. *Dan is a man with a pan and the dog has a log*. Nobody seemed to have noticed that words of striking variety and interest were easier for children to disentangle, e.g. *Orlando the Marmalade Cat*.

Perhaps the most serious misapprehension concerned Locke's idea that we should gently lead the child. Rousseau, that brilliant and inspiring comet across the educational skies, had gone farther and said that we should accompany the child and educate him upon the way. Rousseau's imagination enabled him to appreciate the need for care over the early impressions because, he said, they were written upon the child's mind *en caractères ineffaçables*. He awoke people to their responsibility for children.

But some mistook the idea of guiding by going with them as an opportunity for further lectures, so the poor children suffered a plague of pertinent facts, whether they were interested or not. Others would have nothing to do with Rousseau because he was the same nationality as Perrault of the deceitful *Puss-in-Boots* and Galland of the newly translated and shocking *Arabian Nights*. A fresh upsurge of admonition discredited Rousseau.

People like Hannah More produced tracts and pamphlets in which, little though they realized it, they were guilty of most aggressive phantasies, as they dwelt upon the horrors of sinful reality. Not only were they obtaining vicarious pleasure from the horrors they described; they were also eluding responsibility for those social evils and thus indirectly perpetuating them. Mrs Trimmer had no thought of raising the status of the common people when she started her *Family Magazine* for 'instruction and amusement of cottagers and servants, calculated to improve the mind and lead to religion and virtue . . . and to counteract the pernicious influence of immoral books'. This mother of six sons and six daughters condemned Mother Goose for confusing children; yet she herself indulged in interminable phantasies of admonition in her *History of the Robins*, in which father robin covers pages of admonition of his little Dicky, Flapsy, and Pecksy.

Now let us turn to the imaginative and well informed, who studied and understood the views of the educationists. From them there was coming a healthful stream of creative writing for children. If, instead of studying the books, we have a look at some of the authors, we may gain some insight into the sources of this entirely new branch of art, high-quality literature designed for children. Let us take some of the more outstanding authors in chronological order and see whether we can find some of the most notable characteristics in them.

Perrault, whose eight exquisite folk tales were soon translated from the French, was a scholar, a member of the French Academy, assistant superintendent of public works, and had several distinguished brothers. His devotion to children can be seen in one of his last acts, which was to ensure that the Tuileries Gardens remained open to all, particularly the children; for, he wrote: 'I am persuaded that the gardens of Kings are made so great and so spacious that all his children may walk in them.' His son was nineteen when the *Histoires du Temps Passé* was published and – possibly because it might have been thought a peculiar thing for an academician to do – he pretended that the boy had written the fairy tales. Perrault cut out a great deal of the horror, though not as much as would be cut out today. The latest, unabridged, translation by Brereton is dedicated *For Richard, Later*. Here one may read how Sleeping Beauty's mother-in-law eats first her two charming grandchildren and then her daughter-in-law, or so she thinks; when she finds she has been duped, she commits suicide in a vat of reptiles.

Maria Edgeworth was brought up by her father along lines suggested by Rousseau, though reality-practice necessitated her father's adapting several details. She and her father brought up the rest of the family, educating them, telling them stories, playing games, and making endless direct observations of their reactions. Her stories for children were never seen by the public until they had been written on a slate, tried out on the children, modified according to their reactions, and then set out for publication. It was her successful novel for adults, *Castle Rackrent*, which inspired Scott to apply to his Scottish countryside the same keen observation and sympathetic interpretation that she had given to her Irish countryside. The developing reality of her characters for adults is to be seen in the characters she created for children.

Mrs Gatty was a scientist, artist, linguist, writer, editor, and mother of ten, eight of whom survived. Her gifts must have been evident at a very early age. When she was eight she had made up her own secret language, a game enjoyed by many outstandingly intelligent children. Her etchings are to be seen hung in the British Museum and her treatise on *British Seaweeds* is still a standard work. The beasts and birds and insects in her writing for children are accurate in every biological detail. This busy woman fought prejudice everywhere and even persuaded her local doctor to overcome his prejudice against chloroform. Of all her children, the one she depended upon most was the second, known in the family as Judy; it was after this one that she named the famous magazine. Dame Ethel Smyth, who was to become a pupil of Judy's husband, says in her memoirs that Aunt Judy had a positive genius for people.

Edward Lear, landscape artist and illustrator, said of *More Nonsense* that it was written when most of his time was spent in a country house where children and mirth abounded, and so no assistance was given him save their uproarious delight at every fresh absurdity. These were the grandchildren of his patron, the Earl of Derby. He published accounts of his travels in Greece and southern Italy, with his own illustrations. He had been for a time art master to Queen Victoria. Of his first *Book of Nonsense*, Ruskin said that it was 'first in the list of a hundred delectable volumes of contemporary literature'. When Lear died Tennyson wrote a poem to 'E.L.', '*Illyrian woodlands, echoing falls . . .*'

Charles Kingsley was a clergyman and novelist, in his younger days associated with the Christian Socialist movement. In *Yeast* and *Alton Locke* he used a virile pen to attack various social abuses. He had a great command of language and was a master of scene-painting. He wrote the first chapter of *Water-Babies*, about the underprivileged Tom, during the half-hour after his wife had said to him, 'Rose, Maurice, and May have their books, and baby must have his'. In *The Heroes* he rewrote for children the stories of Perseus, Theseus, and the Argonauts. He published several volumes of sermons, many of them remarkable for their style, interesting subject-matter, and broad spirit of humanity.

Charlotte Yonge was a Victorian writer of best-sellers who had been educated by her father. She published various historical works, including a monograph on Hannah More, and wrote over a hundred novels for adults and children, as well as running a magazine. All told, she published over one hundred and sixty books. Something of her pleasure in children can be seen in the account of her visit to the Moberleys in Iremonger's *Ghosts of Versailles*. She first began writing when urged by the vicar of a neighbouring parish to put his religious views into fiction.

Lewis Carroll was a mathematics lecturer at Oxford, who had taken a First in mathematics before being ordained. His mathematical speculations were intricate and ingenious. He took great delight in children, particularly little girls, and wrote half a dozen books for children, the most famous being for the daughter of the Dean of Christ Church, Oxford. He was a frequent visitor at the house of George Macdonald, whose children he greatly enjoyed.

Mrs Ewing, the second child of Mrs Gatty, known as Judy, pursued a brilliant career, contributing to her mother's magazine and also to Miss Yonge's *The Monthly Packet*. Her stories were illustrated by such distinguished artists as Cruikshank and Caldecott. She and Randolph Caldecott were in such perfect harmony that the reports of their discussions make delightful reading; both used as the source of their inspiration real humans and animals, and both were particularly fascinated by diversity of character. Mrs Ewing, whether at home or travelling with her soldier husband, delighted everyone, for she was raconteur, mimic, and actress. People of widely differing backgrounds said of her that she was such good fun that there was always stimulation when she was about. Prolific though she was, writing did not come easily to her and she spent many hours arranging and rearranging her sentences. She was a devoted admirer of Hans Andersen, the value of whose work she correctly appraised. Of her *Old-Fashioned Tales* she wrote that it was one of her theories that all fairy tales should be written down as if they were oral tradition.

Such were the authors of the first masterpieces written specially for children – and many other names could be added to the list. They were outstandingly gifted people, accustomed to happy households of children and familiar with concepts of educational and social responsibility. They were cultured, imaginative, observant, and informed. If they had no children of their own, then they borrowed them. Their tales grew with real children and so they were filled with simple exactitude, adventure, and humour.

But there is something else that these great authors brought back once more to the children. Accomplished in the art and the craft of writing, learned in their works for adults, they brought back a masterly level of tale construction. Previous writers, grossly underestimating the complexity of immature minds, had rushed to the end of the story anyhow, thinking this was all the children needed. These new writers, true to the highest canons of art, introduced nothing irrelevant; they picked up each threat at the appropriate time, and the conclusion became a matrix of the whole story. A really magnificent denouement brings back into consciousness the many threads of the story, so that, in the last few moments the total story is seen as a whole instead of a sequence. All the misunderstandings, all the mistakes and mis-judgements, the hero and even the half-loved villain, are brought into a pattern that is truly satisfactory.

Children had not experienced this quality of story-telling since the days of the great oral tradition and even then story-telling was not designed specifically for children. Nor would it have been so now, had these writers not been familiar with educational works. They were people who would have known about Locke, Comenius, Rousseau, Pestalozzi, and Froebel. They would have seen the implications of Pestalozzi's discovery that even waifs and strays responded to sound educational treatment, and of Froebel's discovery that the earliest years were already too late unless the educators themselves were well educated. They put into practice Froebel's request that we should learn from our children, and they acted upon his belief that children were not told nearly enough stories.

CHAPTER 11

The merry judgement-day

At last the discussion of the nature of stories for children begins to clarify itself. Enough has been examined in detail for the position to be stated briefly, without long pauses to explain what each step of the argument implies. It is now quite clear that valid conclusions cannot be drawn unless the principles underlying storytelling to children are coupled with its practice. Principles without practice would quickly become unrealistic; practice without comprehensoin of principles produces so many paradoxes, such as the children wanting and not wanting some characteristic of stories at the same time, that all appears to be confusion.

Investigation of principles and practice conjointly has produced such surprising facts that what Ernest Jones has said of one particular kind of plot, namely vampirism, might well be said of stories for children as a whole: The paucity of psychological explanations of children's stories in itself indicates that essential factors have been overlooked.

At one moment in the inquiry it looked as if the search for principles was going to land us in a plethora of high-sounding psychological terms. But there are two equally important reasons why this was not the solution. The first is that psychological jargon only gets into a general discussion when not very experienced people have gone rushing after principles without due awareness of practice and are not yet sufficiently at ease with the meaning of the terms to put them into simpler words. It makes such people sound as if they are more engrossed in appearing informed than in communicating information: but few of us would have the temerity to claim that we have never done this at any time.

The only out-and-out bit of jargon which became necessary was *ego-formation*. This seemed to be unavoidable for an interesting reason. The central factor in the importance of stories for children was this very aspect of, so to speak, jokingly widening and closing the boundaries of the ego *with adult connivance*. This sharing between adults and children of the disintegrative phase, together with adult demonstration of how to bring back a more advanced stage of integration in the conclusion, seems to be one of the essential factors to have been overlooked. There are no terms in common parlance for factors that society has been overlooking; it therefore became necessary to use the scientific term ego-formation.

One might argue that *split-off* or *projection* was jargon; but this is not really tenable, for we all realize that we project ourselves upon the people we admire in stories and plays. The tender little diminutive *split-off* was preferred for a very special reason. The extent to which we do project ourselves can at times be so embarrassing that we prefer to turn a blind eye and deny that we have done so. However, altruism can reach sublime heights in our care for the young. Let us take one example, reform of the penal code, which looked as if it would never come. The changing attitude towards young criminals, towards juvenile delinquents, is now recognizing changes that must be made in the penal code – for the young; but already changes for young criminals have begun to effect changes for those not yet old; eventually attitudes towards hardened criminals, we hope, will become less rigid. All this has crept in through our insight over *young* offenders. In order to be sure that we kept our distance on this question of projection, it seemed advisable to call up altruism by use of a nursery term as aid to our insight over this tricky problem. What can be tricky about projection, of course, are the projections we make during the disintegrative phase – just for short periods – upon not very savoury characters.

The other important reason why it was not necessary to load

the discussion with psychological terms was that much under discussion is already familiar from the world of art. The play of children and the art of adults are quite clearly differentiated, but they cannot be completely separated. Both are concerned with profound moral striving towards integration of personality. Moreover, artists and child psychologists agree that there is an overlap of play and aesthetic attitudes. It is authoritatively stated by great artists that there is an element of play in creative work; for instance, Keats speaks of being and not being concerned at the same time, and Synge speaks of poets playing with wicked Queen Maeve to learn their ecstasy. Conversely, scientific research on the nature of child development shows an element of aesthetic awareness in the play of children at an extremely early age.

Thus it might be argued that the two reasons why it has not been necessary to use much psychological jargon could be given as the explanation of why the one term ego-formation was adopted. First, the process of forming a sound and healthy ego occurs when the individual tries out situations in playful practice, whether in actual play as a child or in creative art as an adult. Then, the moral striving in both play and art is towards better integration of the various aspects of problems, some of which have to be laboriously drawn up from repressed regions of the mind.

Had Synge succumbed to the wickedness of his Queen Maeve all would have been horror; had he succumbed only to her beauty all would have been prettiness. There are works of art that go to both these extremes, thus failing to make the great synthesis that harmonizes the strain. On the one hand there are the domineering men and women of literature discussed in Chapter 2, and on the other hand there is the original day-dream in *The Little White Bird* from which the Peter Pan of the stage evolved. This original Peter Pan in Kensington Gardens met his enchanting Queen Mab, queen of the fairies, and consequently never grew up. It is not at all surprising to learn that Barrie went through a prolonged period of uncreativeness. When, to the surprise of those who knew him well, he plunged into his final play, *The Boy David*, he had been stimulated by meeting Elisabeth Bergner, whose physical resemblance to his own mother was most striking. Thus we see the difference between the individual escapist day-dream about the Garden of Kensington and the basic human plot of the Garden of Eden; the one maintains immaturity and the other goes forward to the stress and strain of maturing.

The stories that children need, as examples of how to undergo ecstatic decomposition with final composition, to use the phraseology of Keats, cannot go far wrong if they conform to adult aesthetic laws; but they will be more enjoyable if they conform to the aesthetic balance suitable to the maturity of the children, an aesthetic balance just as rigorous as the adult one but slightly different. Eventually a high proportion of the children will be able to read the tales in literature. But long before this stage, which in any case will not be reached by all of them, all children urgently need to be told such tales. This is a need which was, perhaps unwittingly, supplied before the invention of printing. We now know that children vary in what they need, not only according to their level of maturity but also according to the speeds at which individuals reach the various levels. But we also know that conformation to aesthetic laws is more important than content of plot. Nothing is really too bad for them to hear about, since the terrible basic plots are already within them; what matters is how they hear about these things. The epitome of wrong telling is to hand back infantile phantasies in infantile forms of aggression, as with the ghastly night-owl tales of the *strigidae* discussed under the nightmare in Chapter 2. We can now see why: the child projects his horrific phantasy and, instead of being helped by the adult to become more realistic, is told that what he projects exists in outer reality. What the adult has done is to take the phase of decomposition and plunge it into worse decomposition.

On the one hand, we can condemn ourselves severely for having been too preoccupied to notice that some unscrupulous publishers were giving our children inartistic infantile phantasies of aggression in horror comics. But, on the other hand, we can congratulate ourselves for an educational system that brought up children healthy enough to make such sound criticism of horror comics as is to be seen in Chapter 8. As we read their objections, on pages 140–4, it becomes patently clear that what they disliked was having back their own horrid nightmares of evil faces, skeletons, bad men, ugliness, and murder, without any assistance towards surmounting them. What these children had come to expect from adults was example in retaining detachment, excitement which would be well resolved, interesting and useful information, all of which they would spontaneously exercise later in their own play.

From the definition of art put forward in Chapter 1 as a starting-point to the discussion, the sliding scale whereby aesthetic balance is maintained at each stage requires adjustment of novelty and tradition, and of 'high' and 'low' elements of the mind. The adjustments are required according to the age, the gifts of temperament and intelligence, and the previous experience of the children. Art develops from the completely personal communication of an artist with a child, their relationship being already established, to the impersonal communication of artists and appreciators, who not only may not know of each other's existence but may not even live in the same millenium.

The first problems that we have to solve appear to each one of us as absolutely unique. But our vision is gradually widened through the integration that comes from constantly widening and closing the boundaries of our ego. Each maturing individual learns to become aware of common elements in his problems and the problems of other people. The artist goes so far that he can set forth in some medium his problem and his solution; these are in sufficiently general terms for people unknown to him to appreciate his communication. Mature art calls for mature appreciation.

Man, be he artist, appreciator, or scientist, cannot afford to forget how to play. Once out in the lonely region of pioneer thought, there is a remarkable similarity between the mental activity of artists and scientists. One example may bring this home. We are already accustomed to accepting the idea of

Mulberry Harbour, even of the Sputnik; but the early thinkers concerned with these projects must have tried and tossed aside countless fantastic schemes before they saw the solutions. If we take an example of an hypothesis which never made headlines and is therefore not familiar to us, we can feel the absurdity of a scheme that could have worked though it was never used. During the war the Admiralty accepted many schemes from Geoffrey Pyke for unexpected forms of destruction on the Continent. A plan that was not used was this: 1. Dress some monkeys in copper chain-mail. 2. Train them to climb up and get bananas from the top of power pylons. 3. Train them to fall by parachute and bite off the cord. They could then be dropped all over the Continent. They would bite off their parachutes, climb the nearest power pylon and cause a tremendous explosion, ruining the circuit, through their copper chain-mail. Ridiculous? Not more ridiculous than Mulberry Harbour seemed to some of its designers as they paced the courtyards of Westminster the evening before D-Day.

There can be no high creative thought, in art or science, once loss of play flexibility brings to a standstill the capacity to leap to unexpected relationships. All pioneer thinking shows remarkable powers of alternation between disintegrative impossibility and integrative possibility. The playful aesthetic detachment is essential. Thus we find outstanding scientists writing or reading science fiction and outstanding artists producing or enjoying works the frivolity of which shatters the inflexible. Each has his own way of communicating the seriousness of play. Educationists who wish to foster the sporting and jesting with serious undercurrent have to treat children's play with understanding.

Much of children's work consists of undoing misconceptions, such as those about adult domineering and victimization, as experience and maturation give them further opportunities for forming sounder conceptions of the world in which they find themselves. Much adult development is on similar lines. Stories, by bringing apparently impossible situations to good resolution, give the children criteria for 'undefeatism' about their problems.

Constant review and revision in the light of fresh knowledge can be preserved from falling into disuse; moreover, this important work is done with the connivance of adults. Those who have made the most mature resolution of infantile problems seem least resentful of the humble source of much that troubles us. This need no longer surprise us, for maturity can be attained only by flexible facing of what the infant mistakenly and uncomprehendingly thought was completely forbidden.

It would seem that the uncritically forbidden becomes a weight and terror just because it appears incommunicable. Does this mean that all adults should seek psycho-analysts upon whom to unburden their private anxieties? There are two reasons why the answers is a categorical *no*. The first reason is a practical, economic one. Training for taking on the responsibility of receiving these private confidences is long, arduous, and expensive. Not only does the analyst have to sort out his own problems, but he has to be carefully trained in not treating a patient as his own split-off, two matters necessitating the utmost integrity. The community could not at present spare either enough able people or enough money for this training; nor could many individuals spare the money for the inevitably high fees. Those already qualified are working to capacity on the treatment of people in mental distress and on training future analysts. It looks as if the next extension of training in depth psychology will have to be to those occupying key positions in education; for normal children have been undergoing mental distress that could have been greatly alleviated if educationists had grasped what was happening. The idea of an educationist having to inflict mental pain for its own sake as a discipline is not only as outmoded as the Chinese idea of binding women's feet to make their gait more trippingly feminine; it is as suspect in sadistic origin as the long-discarded Chinese custom.

The second reason for not demanding enough analysts for everyone to become a patient is, of course, that all cultured people are already making most encouraging efforts to help themselves towards integration through greater awareness of art and through greater objective awareness of outer reality. Culture is by definition and by derivation a form of development and growth. This even applies to intellectual growth, for intellectual clarity depends upon resolution of obstructing emotional confusion. There cannot be development of the 'high' (intellectual) levels of the mind unless there is development of the 'low' (not conscious) levels of the mind; the two levels become increasingly integrated with maturity. The difference between the *Faust* of Marlowe and of Goethe is that Marlowe's Faust succumbs to hell in the disintegrative phase and Goethe's Faust, by colossal moral effort, drags himself out again towards integration.

The uncommunicated terrors of the earth, which Thomas Nashe described before the decay of the great oral tradition, as *the sinnes of the night* which surmount *the sinnes of the day*, must be communicated if they are to be resolved. In this sense the appreciator does actually commune with the work of art, much as the artist communes with his creation; and both can, during the process, go through the whole gamut of emotion from darkest despair to brightest ecstasy. It is childish to haggle over who suffers most, artist or appreciator. If it is a Shelley looking at a painting of the Medusa, none could say; and the irony in this example is that nobody is quite sure which of the two pictures of the Medusa in the Uffizi Gallery so moved Shelley that he expressed his appreciation in verse, from which the quotation on page 31 comes.

Shakespeare, whom Keats classed as possessed of superlative negative capability, communicates these terrors at all levels, from that of Macbeth who stops at no terror only to find that all is sound and fury signifying nothing, to Malcolm who is stopped by all terror, not even daring to claim his rightful throne. Shakespeare's sporting and jesting with serious undercurrent goes on almost without pause, with tokens such as rings, chains, and names showing that things are not what they seem. Take one example: characters from four different plays, Julia, Viola, Imogen, and Rosalind practise deception by pretending to be men; but the names they assume counterbalances the idea of deception. Julia and Viola call themselves Sebastian, which means honourable; Imogen calls herself Fidele, which means faith; and Rosalind offers herself in place of a lovely youth by calling herself Ganymede, cupbearer to Zeus himself.

Why, Shakespeare cannot even resist tossing the audience up on to the stage, perhaps with intent to point out an active part for those who have come to see the play. There is *A Midsummer Night's Dream*, where a house-party calls upon some hempen homespuns to entertain them, but all is brought to confusion by a shocking tiff among the super-larrikins. There is Hamlet's play, which he put on as a communication to his mother and step-father. At this stage our sweet and gentle Will had reached a maturity where he was sufficiently far out on a lonely limb of pioneer thought to create the first hesitant hero of all recorded time. Hamlet had the strength to hesitate. So had Macbeth, but not enough to withstand the expectations of the so-called weaker sex. The Lilith quality of Lady Macbeth becomes clear when we hear that she would kill her children (were they not already killed) if they should prove as weak as their father.

At the time of writing *Hamlet* it must have been touch and go whether Shakespeare could successfully project upon Hamlet the desire to use the play as a lethal weapon, with intent to communicate by destroying aesthetic distance. Something of what he was going through at this time can be surmised from the despairs of *Troilus* enmeshed with a Cressida whom Hazlitt describes as 'a giddy girl, an unpractised jilt'; and from the nothingness of the fury of *Macbeth* and the barren dream in which *Lear* ends. But his resilience, his ability to retrieve negative capability, is to be seen in the lighter veins still to come, such as *All's Well that Ends Well*.

It is not just the old masters who reveal these things. Great modern poetry has the same preoccupation. Once again we can perhaps take just one example: Theodore Roethke's *Words for the Wind*. In *For Sale* he includes such things as 'an attic of horrors, a closet of fears'. In what he calls 'sprattling's prattle' apparently inconsequential remarks such as 'It's a piece of a prince I ate' take on meaning. In one poem, concerned with people who busy themselves with trivia, he writes:

> *And the lives of their children?*
> *The young, brow-beaten early into baleful silence,*
> *Frozen by a father's lip, a mother's failure to answer.*

This covers parental sins both of commission and of omission. When he pleads 'O to be delivered from the rational into the realm of pure song', we should plead to go with him, if we are to continue our balanced development.

At first sight it appears much harder to summarize the principles underlying the telling of stories to children than to summarize the practice. But in fact the position is the other way round. With a little patience one can list the basic plots, the reasons why children need to hear them and the sliding scale whereby aesthetic distance can be maintained at each stage of children's development. But to summarize the practice when every circumstance presents different contingencies is well-nigh impossible. A whole volume of practical application might be written about telling stories to one child, and yet miss some unique circumstances presented by this single child; when several children maturing in different ways at different speeds are dealt with, the position is correspondingly complicated.

Yet children are being herded in groups of thirty to fifty from the age of five onwards for their education; and they are regularly hearing stories while at school. However, we need not be too despairing about the hopelessness of this aspect of our task. Experienced and sensitive teachers are accomplished in noting loss of distance in just one child in the class, and moderating the telling. The signs that they observe are remarkably similar to the summary of nightmare symptoms given by Ernest Jones: the nightmare agonizing dread with sense of oppression and weight, alarming interference with respiration, and a conviction of helpless paralysis. Experienced story-tellers always watch the eyes of their listeners and observe the dilation of the pupil caused by discharge of adrenalin attendant upon the nightmare sensations. This is a reflex action of which the children are unaware and which they have therefore not learned to conceal. A story vivid enough in content and presentation to disturb one child in a class so much, will almost certainly be of importance to all the children; it will thus stand several repetitions and can easily be moderated for this first telling. On later occasions something of familiar tradition will enter the tale, thus reducing the excess of novelty; then the 'low' (not conscious) elements will not grip any child to excess, and balance of 'high' and 'low' elements can be restored. Thus the signs of anxiety are an indication that the theme, far from being unnecessary, is very necessary but requires different handling.

Once the principles underlying story-telling have been grasped and the children's loss of distance can be diagnosed, then what to do in practice is comparatively easy. In this way it becomes possible to foresee that we can cope with the unforeseen. As we cannot cover a wide range of practical examples, let us thoroughly examine a single case. We will take one child in a happy and well-regulated home and follow through the kind of crisis that could happen in any family, until the parents call upon oral tradition for assistance. It had better be a girl, because convention assumes that girls know less of the horrific than boys; and she had better be under seven, because the early and most sensitive years are least understood. It will take a moment to build the atmosphere, so we may as well put it in the form of a story about a little girl of five years.

Mark and Mary Harrison had been invited to New Year's Day lunch by their friends, the Rileys, at the Essex farmhouse that had been their home since John Riley had joined the research department of an industrial concern on the north-east of London. Mark, who was enjoying the brief Christmas holiday respite from teaching in a nearby grammar school, had been sternly instructed by John's wife, Jane, to bring his five-year-old daughter,

Melanie, along with them, since the child always seemed to enjoy walking round the few acres still attached to the farmhouse and seeing the poultry, the pigs, and the two cows that Jane kept as her contribution to the family exchequer.

The forty-mile drive over to the farm in the Harrisons' somewhat ageing car was uneventful. Mary, as she shepherded Melanie into the hall on their arrival, sniffed the air as she greeted her friends.

'I smell goose,' she said.

Melanie accounted for a Coca-Cola while her parents and their hosts drank a couple of sherries; then the party moved into the dining-room. The melon came and went, and John Riley then applied himself to the task of carving the goose. As he poised the knife for the first cut, Melanie turned to her mother and asked with an undertone of anxiety:

'Mummy, is that Mother Goose?'

The question was inaudible to her father and to Jane Riley who were talking together, but John heard it and sensed the threat to the child's phantasy world.

'Oh, no!' he said with rather emphatic reassurance, 'this is an old gander that we killed off on account of his age.'

'Then it isn't one of her twelve goslings either,' said Melanie, still full of apprehension.

'No, no,' her mother replied, 'people don't eat goslings, only old, old, grown up birds.'

By this time Mark had picked up the drift of the conversation and turned to assure his daughter, 'Most people have to eat *some* meat or they would not keep strong and well,' and Mary chimed in with, 'I tell you what, darling, we'll talk about this together, later.'

'Promise?' said Melanie.

'I promise,' she answered, and Melanie joined rather tentatively in the general laughter that followed. Thereafter, nobody was so thoughtless as to remark that Melanie had eaten only a little of the vegetable and none of the meat on her plate.

On the drive home Melanie, now weary but still excited, did

not at once drop off to sleep. Presently Mark began to hum a tune and his wife joined in.

'What's that song?' Melanie asked.

'Oh,' said her mother, 'just a song about a bad old fox who had to go out hunting to find food for all his hungry little cubs, eight, nine, ten of them.'

'Sing it, please,' said the child, and Mark started off supported and prompted by Mary. The story unfolded verse by verse each one followed by a jovial refrain, and so to the last verse, which ran:

> *Well, the fox and his wife, without any strife,*
> *Cut up the goose with the carving knife.*
> *They never had such a supper in their life*
> *And the little ones chewed on the bones, O, bones, O, bones, O*
> *And the little ones chewed on the bones, O.*

The singing died away and the only sounds that remained were the hum of the engine and the whirr of the tyres on the road below. Suddenly, a chuckle from Melanie.

'I chewed on the bones, O, with my mummy and daddy,' she murmured. 'Why aren't *we* eight, nine, ten?' and was asleep.

Mother and father looked across at one another and held up their thumbs to signify the conclusion of a successful operation.

Anyone who is familiar with a happy household where there are children knows that this is exactly the kind of storm which may threaten on the sunniest day. It so happens that the storm may burst when everything seems to be going well, just because the children's defences are down. The children themselves are quite as devastated as the adults by the unexpectedness of it all. If only the adults would instantly ally themselves with the perplexed child, instead of distracting their own attention by worrying about what Some People might think, they would greatly raise the probability of having a sound inspiration about what to do in the emergency.

These parents sensed at once that Melanie, just for the moment, was so completely identified with Mother Goose that to eat her would be as cannibalistic as to eat her own mother, carved up by Mr Riley. They also knew that to force her to do so might have resulted in something approaching a temper tantrum or alternatively in a harmful submissiveness. Either would have been bad for Melanie; on the one hand, it is as wounding to a child as to an adult to suffer the shame of behaving badly in public, and on the other hand it is unspeakable to be made into a real cannibal – real in the inner sense of such poets as Swinburne, who wept his cannibalism into exquisite verse.

Having made the correct diagnosis, this young couple acted upon an assumption known to us all: that Melanie could be eased into identification with someone else, if not rushed. Let us grant that her father, being a teacher, was pretty shrewd in spotting that the salient point for Melanie was that it was *Mother* Goose. So he took it upon himself, being emotionally out of the picture for the moment, to sing the song when she did not fall asleep.

It might be argued that normal families cannot be expected to know so much. It might also be argued that thoughtful parents, if they go back over crises that they have averted by the skin of their teeth – and these are many – will find it is just some such sound inspiration that has come to them. Obviously sublime heights of inspiration are more reliable if the adults concerned have made themselves well-informed upon child psychology. There was a girl of six whose parents had no outstanding knowledge of psychology. She came dancing home from school and was so appalled to find the grandmother she adored in place of her mother that she stormed and sulked and kicked the furniture and could not eat her tea. No inspiration helped the poor grandmother and she finally decided something terrible had happened at school. When the mother came back she was hastily informed. She looked at her strangely ill-mannered daughter for a moment and then said, 'Jane, did you do something well at school?' The child burst into tears and sobbed that she had come top. How one could come top at six it is hard to guess, but the disappointment of there being no mother to tell about it had been too much for her. Normally happy families should take more note of their successes. Reasonably mature parents are parents who have not forgotten what it is like to be a profoundly upset child.

Adults who grasp the principles of child development adjust and readjust their practice until they have found a way to come to the rescue of a child in distress. Physicians and psychiatrists would agree that the skill is required for the diagnosis; once the diagnosis is made, then the cure is comparatively easy. In telling stories to children, skill comes in knowing what stories they are ready for and adapting the telling to their circumstances. Once this awareness has been reached through study of childhood problems, then the telling is comparatively easy. It is only by trying out stories upon real children, as masters such as Maria Edgeworth, Mrs Gatty, and Aunt Judy did, that one learns how much excitement can be endured and how to draw all the disharmony safely back home to secure harmony. When this is achieved, then the children are led forwards in their development towards the adult world of literature.

The complete novice in telling stories to children is often in need of down-to-earth practical tips, such as the following. First it must be remembered that children are so far below subsistence level in hearing stories that they will overlook a multitude of errors while the teller is learning. Then with both younger and older children it is better to start off with a story they do not know; thus there is no risk of younger ones thinking you need correction when your version differs from theirs; and it helps to gain attention with older ones, if curiosity is kept alive as to what the solution could possibly be. It is fortunate if the story they do not know is one you have at some time enjoyed yourself; then, no matter how scared or embarrassed you may feel, your own enjoyment will surely shine through somewhere.

As a matter of fact, that first story you tell to a group of children with whom you are not familiar is almost certain to be a success for a very surprising reason. The children are fully occupied because they are doing two things: they are enjoying the story and they are sizing up the new teller of tales. The shrewdness with which children assess newcomers is proverbial and too complex to be put into simple words. It is very largely by intonation that we give away our attitudes to things and events and people – in fact that we give away our attitude to life. They will know whether the teller had real pity for the frog with a bandage on his left toe, if there was an ironic undercurrent to our laughter at the child who fell over, or if we really think knighthood magnificent. During that first story they have plenty of time to make up their minds whether they can accept you.

When students are training to become teachers it is always helpful to explain to them that huge yawns at the end of a story are caused by the children having listened so intently that they have failed to breathe sufficiently. ('Is *that* what it is?' cries the student, dilated pupils revealing the horrific fear of becoming nothing but a boring teacher.) It is a great step forward when a student can pause after a story instead of rushing full tilt into some activity 'before the children get out of hand'. At first the pause may be only a few seconds but with experience it can become a minute or so, to allow the children to come back to themselves, or even to chat quietly to each other as people do coming out of a theatre. Adults after a fine performance may not want to talk about the play. The children may not want to talk about the story – yet.

With all this to attend to, it would seem a simple solution to read a story to begin with, till experience comes. This will not do at all, for the simple reason that the kind of experience we have in mind does not come with one's head bent down over a book. Nobody reads a story well to children who has not first told stories to children. Reading to them comes after telling has been discovered, for discovery it is.

In some twenty years' teaching children of primary-school age, I only got caught out once over reading to children, and it was not over horror but over tenderness. The book was Grey Owl's *Sajo and the Beaver People* and we had reached the point where one beaver finds the other dying in a zoo. I looked up and round the class, as every reader should do constantly, and was so startled to see tears in the eyes of both boys and girls that tears came into my own. That is *not* the way for a story-teller to maintain aesthetic distance. Over tenderness it did not matter so much, but over horror it could have been very serious. The difficulty with reading is that the time for glancing round at all the children is so very brief. One needs to become sensitively well informed about the signs of loss of distance. They can be learned only with one's eyes upon the children.

As people become more aware of the significance to children of the loss of the great oral tradition, they will tell more stories to children and they will find out how to tell them well. In their search for what is of great interest to children they will study comics, television, the Bruin Boys of pre-Caxton *Reynard the Fox* and, of course, what has been preserved of the great oral tradition. They will understand how the sequence of pictures in the comics brought back a touch of what was theirs when minstrels related dramatic events and no one was in any doubt about the villain losing and the hero winning.

Incidentally, one mystery is now cleared up about the excitement adults showed over comics, which so obscured the horror-comics issue. Those harmless comics which the adults had enjoyed long ago must have touched on so much that had been uncritically repressed that repression was causing serious gaps in their logic. Even many who were sure comics had done them good did not dare risk an inquiry for fear of what might emerge as sources of enjoyment. This is a good example of how intellectual clarity can be obstructed by uncritical repression. Had the earlier comics of which they spoke contained the untransmuted infantile phantasies of aggression to be seen in horror comics, then the situation might by now have been as serious in Britain as in America, where youngsters have come to idolize daring criminals.

Another mystery can also now be cleared up. This is why Some People, as Keats would say, cannot bear to see children really enjoying themselves over comics or television. They assume that a child deeply absorbed is up to no good, because they have uncritically repressed their own childhood absorptions. The more profoundly absorbed a child is, the more certain are Some People that whatever he is doing should be forbidden.

If the main body of stories for children, whether told, read, televised, or communicated in any other way, is to be substantially raised to the highest standards of the last hundred years, then writers for children must take their work seriously. They must study both children and writing. But they must also work through their own creative powers. Each writer for children has to search for his own solutions, in exactly the same way as any other artist.

The position with regard to publication of children's stories is promising. According to the *Bookseller*, 20,719 works were issued in 1957 and nearly 2,000 of them were for children. This figure represents a marked rise in the proportion of works for children. Some of these are by writers of the highest competence, for instance Geoffrey Trease and Noel Streatfeild, to name only two. They stand up to the most rigorous aesthetic analysis, and exhibit an exquisite balance between excitement and vigorous simplicity supported by sound construction.

There are two books that may be recommended for study. The first is *Books Before Five* by Dorothy White. This is a diary kept by a children's librarian about her own daughter and reads more as a case-study than as a work of art. But in this diary, covering about three years, every phase of aesthetic appreciation can be traced. The detailed account of this lively child runs from the two-year-old, who loves her first book to ruins, to the five-year-old, who is far too rational a being – provided one understands what she is talking about – to be regarded as an infant. There is precise evidence of the links between reading and experience, of how exciting experience ousts stories for a while, of how the child cannot appreciate stories unless her own experience is wide and varied, and of many other aspects. There is most revealing information on the development towards humour and imagination, neither of which can become prominent until the child can distinguish between the 'true' and the 'not true', and how this affects her appreciation of illustrations.

Perhaps one of the most interesting points is the division of laughter into three classes: extravagant, *touché*, and happy laughter. Those who, for instance, would wish to have a clearer understanding of the outrageous laughter of the young Keats, could well study the clear accounts in this book of exactly what caused this child to go off into gales of extravagant laughter. This librarian author, trained to recognize the tastes of others, can see what amuses the child intensely even when she is not herself amused by the incidents. 'I could not see what Carol saw,' she writes of *Two Bad Mice*, 'an *intense* funniness. At such moments I feel separated from my daughter by some unbridgeable gulf.' Moreover, she noticed that books which later caused this response were not laughed at at all on first reading. Of books like *Orlando the Marmalade Cat Keeps a Dog* she noted that child and adult both find jokes, but contrapuntally, which probably accounts for their great popularity.

We should be deeply grateful to this mother for troubling to keep this careful record of a child's introduction to stories. It was not an easy task; and the birth of a second child made it extremely difficult. From the point of view of any adult who knows the fury of not being able to force practice to keep step with accepted principles, quite one of the funniest sections is a moment where irony pours into the diary. The distracted mother feeds the infant, knowing it should be in peace and quiet, but actually while fixing the older child with an Ancient Mariner glare and allaying her jealousy by discussing everything under the sun, from circus lions to the feeding habits of butterflies. We are in great need of such careful records of the earliest years. The reason why there is such a dearth of them does not lie solely in the effort involved in keeping a diary; the real difficulty is that creating children is so satisfying that mothers lack further creative urge in the first years. However, it might be better for the children later if the mothers would widen their horizons a little from the start.

The other book worthy of study by anyone interested in writing or telling stories to children is *Four to Fourteen* by Kathleen Lines. This is a manual grading some two thousand stories for children. To the latest edition have been added a number of examples of illustrations. Illustrations are of great importance, because really good ones assist the children to move away from the intensely personal aspects of the problems being resolved through stories. This immensely patient review of children's books enables us to widen our knowledge of titles available today. Having myself enjoyed with children many of the books listed by Miss Lines, I find that on the whole I am in close agreement with her views.

Now, at last, we begin to understand what it is that the children require of us. We see what it is that we have to do, so that they will follow us as for ever they follow that 'strangest figure whose queer long coat from heel to head is half of yellow and half of red'. They want good stories and they want them well told. There must be no doubt, right from the start, about who is the hero and who is the villain. If the villain is to be of real assistance to them, then they must enjoy being shocked at him, which means that they will care for him too. While marvelling at the hero's undefeatable courage and preparing themselves to achieve the apparently impossible with him, they must care for the villain's downfall. The conclusion must be a merry judgement-day.

Glossary of Mythology

ALEXANDER: Born 355 B.C., surnamed the Great, son of Philip and Olympias. The night he was born the temple of Diana at Ephesus was burned and magicians foretold his coming greatness. When he tamed Bucephalus, a horse which none of his father's courtiers could control, the King said with tears in his eyes that his son would have to seek another kingdom, as that of Macedonia would not be big enough to contain such greatness. During her pregnancy Queen Olympias claimed that she was with child by a dragon. For five years Alexander was pupil to Aristotle, whom he greatly respected throughout his life.

ALTHAEA: Mother of Meleager. According to the oracle, he was to live only as long as a brand cast in the fire continued to burn. Althaea kept the brand until Meleager slew her brothers, whereupon she threw it in the flames and he expired with it. She killed herself in remorse.

AMAZONS: A famous nation of women in Cappadocia. They had no commerce with the opposite sex, except for purposes of propagation, when they visited the men of a neighbouring country. All male children were either returned to their fathers or maimed.

ANACTORIA: A woman of Lesbos wantonly loved by Sappho.

ARGONAUTS: Heroes who went with Jason to Colchis on Argo about seventy-nine years before the fall of Troy. The cause of the expedition was strife in the family of the King of Thebes. The king divorced his second wife for her fits of madness and returned to his first wife. There was conflict among the stepchildren over the inheritance. The adventures of the Argonauts included a two-year stay in Lemnos, where a new race was started from women who had murdered their husbands. Jason raised an armed multitude by sowing dragons' teeth and caused them to destroy themselves by throwing a stone among them.

ARTHURIAN CYCLE: The romantic figure of Arthur may have some historical basis in fifth or sixth century. Some of the other figures originate from the Celtic pantheon. In epic form it is English. (Geoffrey of Monmouth, twelfth century, *Historia Regnum Britanniae*.) Further details accrued from war in this century. Many French writers added to it, till it became the core of a mass of legends in many lands. Only the early forms make the central figure, Arthur, a model of purity and valour. In the fifteenth century Malory used the mass of legends in the *Morte d'Arthur*.

BEVIS OF HAMPTON: A popular verse romance of the fourteenth century amounting to four thousand lines. The mother of Bevis had his father murdered, married the murderer, and sold the Christian Bevis to a heathen king. Bevis refused to marry the king's daughter till she became a Christian. He was banished and she married twice, murdering the second husband on her wedding night. For this she was to be burned, but Bevis rescued her from the stake and they married.

CARYATID: Sculptured female figure used as pillar. From Greek *Karuatis*, priestess at Caryae in Arcadia.

CELTS: See Ulster.

CHARLEMAGNE, A.D. 742–814: King of the Franks and emperor of the west, son of King Pepin. He and his paladins are the subject of numerous *chansons de geste*, of which the most famous is *Chanson de Roland*. According to legend he is not dead but sleeps in a mountain, awaiting the time to avenge the blood of the saints.

CHEMNOS: A Moabite god (1 Kings xi, 7).

CLYTEMNESTRA: Wife of Agamemnon. He left his cousin to guard her while he went to Troy. Hearing of their infidelity he returned to murder him but was himself murdered by the adulterous cousin. The lawful children were Elektra and Orestes. The adulterers married Elektra to a lowly man and planned to murder Orestes. Seven years later Orestes was falsely reported dead and, aided by Elektra, Orestes avenged his father's death by murdering the adulterers while they were celebrating his supposed death.

COMNENA, LA: Daughter of the Emperor Alexius, eleventh century. She wrote the *Alexiad*, a history in fifteen books, mainly concerned with her father's life. Figures in Scott's *Count Robert of Paris*, in which her husband plots to dethrone her father.

CRESSIDA: No basis in classical antiquity. Originates from Benoît de Sainte-Maure, a twelfth-century *trouvere*. Cressida deserts Troilus for Diomede; they fight but neither is killed. Chaucer's *Troylus and Cryseyde* develops the character of Cressida. Shakespeare makes her a 'giddy girl' who deserts Troilus out of thoughtlessness and temper. Henryson's *The Testament of Cresseid*, a sequel to Chaucer, invents tortures from the gods for her blasphemy.

CUCHULAIN: A principal hero of the Ulster Cycle of Irish mythology. He has a miraculous birth, prowess at an early age, defends Ulster against Queen Maeve single-handed, and is murdered by the children of men he has slain.

ELECTRA: Daughter of Clytemnestra and Agamemnon. She incites her brother Orestes to murder their mother and he, ignoring the lowly marriage imposed upon her by her mother and stepfather, gives her in marriage to his devoted friend Pylades.

ENDYMION: A shepherd to whom Jupiter gave lasting youth and prolonged sleep. He was loved by Diana but married a mortal, by whom he had three sons and a daughter, Eurydice. He so lacked ambition that he gave his crown as a prize to the son who won a race.

ERECHTHEUM: A temple dedicated to the worship of Erechtheus, on the Acropolis at Athens. He was an Athenian hero, secretly reared by Athene; she concealed him in a chest which was not to be opened; those who disobeyed her were so frightened by a serpent twining round him that they committed suicide. When he became king of Athens he instigated the worship of Athene.

FAFNIR: The dragon guarding the Niebelung's hoard of gold. See Siegfried.

FAUST: A wandering conjurer who lived in Germany about 1488 to 1541 and is mentioned in various documents of the period. He was the subject of great dramatic works by Marlowe and Goethe. Goethe began his drama in 1770, but did not complete it until 1832, just before his death.

FIRDUSI: Persian poet (*c.* 950–1020), author of *Shahnameh*, the great epic of Persian heroes and kings from earliest times.

GANYMEDES: A beautiful shepherd of Phrygia taken to heaven by Jupiter as his personal cupbearer. It is said that he was carried up by an eagle to satisfy the shameful and unnatural desires of Jupiter.

GALAHAD: By enchantment the son of Launcelot and Elaine, daughter of King Pelles, in Malory's *Morte d'Arthur*.

GAWAINE: A hero in the earliest Arthurian legends. The perfect knight, courageous, pure, and courteous. In later developments his character deteriorates.

GORGONS: Three hideous daughters of Phorcys and Ceto. With hair entwined with serpents, hands of brass, golden wings, bodies covered with impenetrable scales, and teeth as long as the tusks of wild boars. They turned to stone anyone on whom they fixed their gaze. When Perseus, with the aid of the gods, cut off the head of Medusa, the drops of blood turned to serpents.

HARPIES: Harpylae. Winged monsters with the faces of women and bodies of vultures; their hands and feet armed with sharp claws. Daughters of Neptune (sea) and Terra (land). They emitted an infectious smell and spoiled whatever they touched by their filth and excrement. They plundered and carried off people and property.

HECTOR: Son of King Priam. A most valiant Trojan chief. When Achilles drove back the Trojans, Hector was too proud to flee till he beheld Achilles himself. Hector was killed and his body dragged ignominiously round the battlefield in cruel triumph.

HERCULES: Celebrated hero, ranked among the gods after death. He was the son of Jupiter and Alcmene. There were miraculous events at his birth and Jupiter said he would be the greatest hero the world had known. His great deeds began in infancy and he performed twelve famous labours, the last of which was to bring up to earth the three-headed dog Cerberos. He was one of the Argonauts, q.v.

HELEN(A): The most beautiful woman upon earth, sprung from the eggs which Leda, wife of King Tyndarus, brought forth after her amour with Jupiter disguised as a swan. Helen was stolen when ten years old and, some say, ravished; she was rescued by her brothers Castor and Pollux. Her suitors included Ulysses, Antilocus, Diomedes, Amphilocus, and many others. They were so numerous that her father was afraid to choose one for fear of offending the rest. Ulysses, renowned for sagacity, suggested that she should herself make the choice. She chose Menelaus. After three years she was seduced by Paris, son of Priam, and taken to Troy. When Paris was killed she married another of Priam's sons. Eventually she returned to Menelaus. Throughout she retained her matchless beauty. Some chronologists maintain that, if she was born of the same eggs as Castor and Pollux, she must have been about sixty when the Trojan War began.

HUBRIS: Insolent pride or security, resented and punished by the gods.

ICARUS: Son of Daedalus. He and his father flew with wings from Crete to escape the resentment of Minos. Icarus flew too high; the sun melted the wax which cemented his wings and he fell into the Aegean Sea. Daedalus, descendant of Erechtheus, was the most ingenious artist of his day. He constructed the Labyrinth in which King Minos confined the bull for which his wife had an unnatural passion. When he helped the Queen to satisfy her desires, Minos confined him with Icarus in his own Labyrinth.

JUPITER: The most powerful god, saved from being devoured by his father as an infant, through his mother substituting a stone.

LAOCOON: Son of Priam. Priest of Apollo. While offering a bullock to Neptune to render him propitious to the Trojan War, two huge serpents came out of the sea and attacked his two sons, standing by him at the altar. The serpents attacked him as he defended his sons and squeezed him to death. This was punishment for dissuading the Trojans from bringing in the wooden horse, since it had been dedicated to Minerva, and also for hurling a javelin at it when it was brought in. Some say it was for marrying and knowing his wife when he was a priest of Apollo.

LÉLIA: Said to be a form of Lilith, q.v.

LESBOS: An island in the Aegean Sea, 168 miles in circumference. The inhabitants were renowned for their music and their beautiful women. The Lesbians became debauched and extravagant. Many natives became illustrious, such as Alcaeus, inventor of Alcaic verse, and Sappho, inventor of Sapphic verse.

LILITH: Assyrian demon vampire, associated with the night. In Isaiah (xxxiv, 14) translated as 'screech owl' – revised version 'night-monster'. In Rabbinical literature, the first wife of Adam, dispossessed by Eve. Thus Eve had a nightmare predecessor, unknown to her. In Goethe's *Faust* she appears in the *Walpurgisnacht*. Probably Babylonian, since Lilu and Lilitu are Babylonian spirits which plague men by night. Amulets were worn by children as protection against her hostility.

LOKI: Spirit of evil and mischief in Norse mythology.

MAEVE: See Queen Mab.

MAHĀBHĀRATA: One of the two sacred Hindu epics. Believed to have originated before 600 B.C. but the present form dates from about 200 B.C. It is eight times as long as the *Iliad* and *Odyssey* together and appears to be a compilation. The leading story relates a contest between spirits of good and evil; evil triumphs only temporarily and good ultimately prevails.

MEDUSA: See Gorgons.

MELMOTH THE WANDERER: A powerful tale by Maturin full of mystery and terror. The theme is the sale of a soul to the devil in return for prolonged life, the bargain transferable if anyone can be persuaded to take it over. None can be persuaded, not even a lunatic, a victim of the Inquisition, a father of starving children or Melmoth's own wife. When Oscar Wilde, a connection of Maturin's, came out of prison, he called himself Sebastian Melmoth, Sebastian suggested by the broad arrows on his prison uniform.

MOLOCH: Canaanite idol to whom children were sacrificed as burnt offerings (Lev. xviii, 21, and 2 Kings, xxiii). Since Milton made Moloch a chief fallen angel, the name is now applied to an object of horrible sacrifices.

OEDIPUS: Son of the King of Thebes and Jocasta. Descended from Venus on his father's side, he was destined to be persecuted by Juno. His father was informed by the oracle as soon as he married Jocasta that he must perish by the hand of his son. He resolved never to approach Jocasta, but did so when intoxicated. When she became pregnant, he ordered her to destroy the child at birth. Lacking courage, she ordered a servant to expose him on the mountain; but in pity he only bored the infant's heels and suspended him from a tree. He was found and reared in a neighbouring court. When grown to manhood he was envied by his companions, who, to mortify him, told him that he was not the king's son. He consulted the oracle and heard that he must never return home, that he would die on foreign soil, and that he would greatly enrich the land where his bones lay. Thinking home was where he had been reared, he set forth. Rudely obstructed by a stranger he killed him, not knowing he was the King of Thebes, and travelled on to Thebes. Finding the Thebans troubled by the enigma of the Sphinx (q.v.) he resolved the symbolic riddle, was crowned King, and given Jocasta as wife. When, with the aid of seers and by his own persistent effort, he discovered that he had killed his father and married his mother, he put out his own eyes to punish himself and left the homeland. Led by his daughter Antigone, he reached a grove sacred to the Furies; here the ground opened and he disappeared.

OLINDO: See Sofronia.

ORLANDO: Italian form of Roland (q.v.), one of the twelve paladins of the Charlemagne Cycle.

ORESTES: Son of Clytemnestra and Agamemnon, saved from his mother's dagger by his sister Elektra (q.v.). He was brought up by his uncle Strophius, to whose son Pylades he formed an inviolable attachment. Later, ignoring a misalliance imposed on Elektra by their mother, he gave Elektra to Pylades in marriage. Orestes died peacefully at the age of ninety.

PARIS: Son of Priam and Hecuba. In the first month of pregnancy the queen dreamed that her son would set fire to the palace and destroy Troy, so the king ordered him to be exposed at birth. But Paris was saved and educated by shepherds. He grew to be a princely youth and was identified by his sister Cassandra, who had received from Apollo the gift of foreseeing the future. He was acknowledged by Priam. (See Helen.)

PARZIVAL: An epic by Wolfram von Eschenbach, a Bavarian knight of the twelfth–thirteenth century, who claimed to be illiterate. It is based on the legend of Perceval, a folk tale of great antiquity, which may be identified with Peredur of Welsh mythology.

PENTHESILEA: Queen of the Amazons, daughter of Mars. She assisted Priam in the last stages of the Trojan War. She fought against Achilles, by whom she was slain. He wept at her dead beauty and treated her infamously. Achilles had been enamoured of her before they fought, and they had a son Cayster.

PERSEUS: Son of Jupiter and Danae. Danae's father, learning from the oracle that she would have a son who would kill him, had confined her in a tower. When Perseus was born, he threw mother and son into the sea in a slender boat. They survived and the young prince, after many adventures, inadvertently killed his grandfather with a quoit. Perseus, greatly depressed, refused the throne gained by parricide. He exchanged kingdoms with a neighbouring king and founded Mycenae, naming it after the pommel of his sword (*myces*), which rested there. After death he was honoured by a place among the stars.

PHOENICIA: An Asian country east of the Mediterranean. The chief towns were Sidon and Tyre, the chief activities industry and navigation. Among their colonies were Carthage and Marseilles. Their goods were so highly valued that anything elegant or outstanding was called Sidonian.

PRIAM(US): The last king of Troy.

PROMETHEUS: Brother of Atlas. He surpassed all mankind in cunning and fraud. He ridiculed the gods and deceived Jupiter. To punish him Jupiter took fire away from the earth but Prometheus, aided by Minerva (who had been produced from Jupiter's brain without a mother), stole fire from the chariot of the sun and brought it back to earth. Jupiter ordered Vulcan to make a clay woman; this he animated, named Pandora and sent, with a box of rich gifts, as wife for Prometheus. But Prometheus, suspicious of Jupiter's generosity, gave her as wife to his brother Epimetheus. Jupiter then had Prometheus tied to a rock in the Caucasus, where a vulture was to feed on his liver for thirty thousand years. Thirty years later Hercules rescued him as one of the twelve labours. Prometheus made the first man and woman of clay, which he animated with his stolen fire. He taught men many skills, such as the use of plants, cultivation, and taming of animals. He was such an infallible oracle that he was consulted even by Jupiter himself.

QUEEN MAB: Queen of the fairies. According to Drayton, Herrick, and others the wife of Oberon. Shakespeare called her Titania.

RĀMĀYANA: One of the two great Hindu epics, originally composed not later than 500 B.C. The present form probably dates from about 300 B.C. The main theme is war waged by Rama, son of the king, and an impersonation of Vishnu (the god of preservation), against the fierce giant Rāvan who had carried off Rama's wife, Sita. Rama slays this dread enemy of gods and men

ROLAND CYCLE: Romantic tales of the most famous of Charlemagne's paladins. They appear to be based on the historic fact of A.D. 778 when Charlemagne's army was returning through the Pyrenees and was attacked by Basque inhabitants and their leader, Hrodland, was vanquished. Basques are changed to Saracens, Roland is given a companion Oliver, and the pagan army is wiped out by Charlemagne. According to tradition a *jongleur* in William the Conqueror's army sang an early version of *Chanson de Roland* at the battle of Hastings. Roland and Oliver were so well matched in combat that the phrase 'a Roland for an Oliver' has become proverbial.

RUSTAN (RUSTEM, RUSTUM): The principal figure in Firdusi's *Shahnameh*, a great Persian national hero, who lived through several centuries, a constant conqueror until killed by treachery. His fights sometimes lasted for days, he overcame dragons and demons, and unwittingly fought and killed his own son, Sohrab. The subject of Matthew Arnold's 'Sohrab and Rustan'.

ST GEORGE AND THE DRAGON: Patron saint of England, Portugal and, formerly, of Genoa and Aragon. Arrested, tortured, and died A.D. 303 for Christian beliefs. His connection with the dragon was introduced much later and its origin is obscure; but as St George's remains were at Lydda, near where Perseus slew the monster which threatened Andromeda, this may account for the dragon.

SALOME: Daughter of Herodias. Her stepfather, Herod Antipas, was so enchanted by her dancing that he offered her a reward 'unto the half of my kingdom'. Instructed by Herodias she asked for the head of John the Baptist on a charger (Matthew xiv). Oscar Wilde's *Salome* (1893), written in French, was produced in Paris in 1896; it formed the libretto of Richard Strauss's opera; but licence was not granted for its performance in England until 1931.

SAPPHO: A woman born in the island of Lesbos about 600 B.C., famed for her beauty, poetic talents, and amorous disposition. Her passion for three women friends was so violent that it is, according to legend, regarded as criminal. She conceived a passion for Phaon, a youth of Mitylene, and when he refused to gratify her desire she threw herself into the sea from Mount Leucas. Of her nine books of lyric verse, elegies, and epigrams, only two fragments remain. These are so outstanding that the ancients appear to have been justified in calling her the tenth muse.

SCYLLA: Daughter of Nisus, King of Megara. She became enamoured of Minos as he besieged her father's capital and offered to deliver Megara into his hands if he would marry her. Minos agreed. As the prosperity of Megara depended upon a golden hair on the head of King Nisus, Scylla cut this off and Megara fell. But Minos ridiculed her and she destroyed herself. According to some authorities the dead father and daughter were changed to hawk and lark.

SHAHNAMEH: Firdusi's Persian epic of heroes and kings. (See Rustem.)

SIBYL(LAE): Certain women inspired from heaven; the exact number is not known and varies from one (Plato) to ten (Varro). The most famous was at Cumae in Italy, and had many names. Apollo loved her and offered her what she asked. She asked for life as many in years as the grains of sand in her hand but omitted to ask for perpetual health and vigour. During her thousand years she became decrepit and haggard while continuing her prophecies.

SIEGFRIED: Hero of the first part of the *Niebelungenlied*, a German poem of the thirteenth century, embodying a story from the Edda, of Norse mythological origin. Siegfried forges a sword from the fragments of his father's sword, with which he slays Fafnir, the giant snake which guards the stolen Rhine-gold.

SIRIUS: The dog-star. Its appearance was supposed to cause great heat upon the earth.

SOFRONIA: Sister of Olindo, in Tasso's *Jerusalem Delivered*. They faced martyrdom to save Christians in a beleaguered city.

SOHRAB: Son of Rustum, who killed him without recognizing him, since he believed his child to be a girl.

SPHINX: A monster with head and breasts of a woman, body of a dog, tail of a serpent, wings of a bird, paws of a lion, and a human voice. Sent to the neighbourhood of Thebes by Juno to persecute the descendants of Cadmus because he had married Hermione, daughter of Venus. The Sphinx had to propound unanswerable enigmas and devour Theban inhabitants when they could give no answer. From the oracle the Thebans learned that she would destroy herself if an enigma were explained, so the king promised his crown and queen to anyone who could do this. Oedipus penetrated the symbolism, and saw that it is man who walks on four legs in the morning, two at noon, and three in the evening. This correct interpretation caused the Sphinx to expire.

STRIGAS: Owl or vampire in Roman mythology.

TASSO, TORQUATO: A sixteenth-century Italian author, for many years at the court of Ferrara. He lived in such terror of imaginary plots against him that he had to be locked up for some years and was released only on condition that he left Ferrara. He wandered from court to court. Byron's *The Lament of Tasso* and Goethe's *Torquarto Tasso* are based on a now discredited legend of his love for Leonora d'Este.

THAMMUZ: A Syrian god. Milton in *Paradise Lost* (i, 446–52) relates him to Adonis, a beautiful youth beloved by Venus, who was killed hunting. He was also linked with Pan, god of huntsmen, because, according to Plutarch, the death of the great god Pan was announced by a loud voice calling from a ship to Thamuz. Panic fear was believed to originate from Pan.

THESEUS: King of Athens. One of the most celebrated heroes of antiquity. He was not acknowledged son of the king until his mother, Aethra, sent him with one of his father's swords for identification. Medea attempted to arrange for his father to poison him unwittingly but failed, owing to the sword. Theseus rid the lands of many monsters, including Phaea, Scion, Procrustes, and Cercyon. While attempting to kill the Minotaur he was himself confined in the Cretan labyrinth. He was rescued by the king's daughter, Ariadne, whom he married but deserted. According to some authorities Ariadne, who had the mental ability to comprehend the scheme of Daedalus's labyrinth, turned to Bacchus for comfort when Theseus failed her.

TROILUS: Son of Priam and Hecuba, killed by Achilles in the Trojan War.

ULSTER (CELTIC) CYCLE: Tales of Irish mythology, in which Cuchulain of the first century is one of the principal heroes. A number of these legends was translated by Lady Gregory at the turn of this century when she was cooperating with W. B. Yeats in the formation of an Irish National Theatre. The originals are to be found in the *Book of the Dun Cow*, written down by monks of the eleventh century from oral tradition, only fragments of which now remain, and in the twelfth-century manuscript, the *Book of Leinster*. Cuchulain figures in Macpherson's Ossianic poems as Cuthuilin, transposed in time so as to be contemporary with Fingal, who is Fion of the later Irish Cycle.

ULYSSES (ODYSSEUS): King of Ithaca, suitor of Helen, who thought out the way to find a husband for her. When she chose Menelaus, Ulysses married Penelope in despair. He joined other Greek princes in pursuit of Helen in the Trojan War. In war he was distinguished for prudence and sagacity. Returning home he met many adventures, including being shipwrecked on the island of Circe, by whom he had a son Telegonus, who later killed his father and married Penelope.

ZEUS: See Jupiter.

Bibliography

BUXTON FORMAN, M. (ed.) (1947). *The Letters of John Keats*. London: Oxford University Press.

FRANK, JOSETTE (1949). 'Comics, Radio, Movies—and Children.' Public Affairs Pamphlet No. 148. Washington: Public Affairs Press.

FROEBEL, F. (1889). *The Education of Man*. New York: Appleton.

GRUENBERG, S. M. (1944). 'The Comics as a Social Force.' *J. educ. Sociol.* Vol. 18, No. 4, p. 204.

HELWEG, H. (1927). *H. C. Andersen: En Psykiatrist Studie*. Copenhagen.

HEWLETT, DOROTHY (1937). *Adonais: a Life of John Keats*. London: Hurst.

JACKSON, LYDIA (1950). 'Emotional Attitudes toward the Family of Normal, Neurotic, and Delinquent Children.' *Brit. J. Psychol.* Vol. XLI, Pts. 3 and 4.

JONES, ERNEST (1931). *On the Nightmare*. London: Hogarth Press.

JONES, ERNEST (1957). *Sigmund Freud, Life and Work*. Vol. III, *The Last Phase, 1919–39*. London: Hogarth Press.

KARDOS, E., and PETO, A. (1956). 'Contributions to the Theory of Play.' *Brit. J. med. Psychol.* Vol. XXIX, Pt. 2.

KRAFFT-EBING, R. (1951). *Aberrations of Sexual Life. After the Psychopathia Sexualis*. New York: Associated Booksellers; London: Staples Press.

LINES, KATHLEEN (1950). *Four to Fourteen*. London: Cambridge University Press.

LOCKE, J. (1693). *Some Thoughts concerning Education*. London: Cambridge University Press, 1880.

MAUROIS, A. (1953). *Lélia: the Life of George Sand*. Trans. Gerard Hopkins. London: Cape; New York: Harper.

OPIE, IONA, and OPIE, PETER (1959). *The Lore and Language of Schoolchildren*. London: Oxford University Press.

ORWELL, G. (1940). 'Boys' Weeklies.' *Horizon*, Vol. I, No. 3.

PESTALOZZI, J. H. (1781). *Leon and Gertrude: A Book for the People*. (2 vols.) London: J. Mawman, 1825.

PESTALOZZI, J. H. (1801). *How Gertrude Teaches her Children*. London: Swan Sonnenschein; New York: C. W. Bardeen. (2nd ed.) 1900.

PIAGET, J. (1926). *The Language and Thought of the Child*. London: Routledge & Kegan Paul.

PICKARD, P. M. (ed.) (1955). *British Comics: an Appraisal*. 'Comics' Campaign Council, 23 Tillingbourne Gardens, London, N.3.

PRAZ, MARIO (1933). *The Romantic Agony*. London, New York: Oxford University Press.

REUMERT, E. (1927). *H. C. Andersen: the Man*. Trans. J. Bröchner. London: Methuen.

ROUSSEAU, J. J. (1762). *Émile*. Trans. B. Foxley. London: Dent; New York: Dutton.

RUDWIN, M. (1931). *The Devil in Legend and Literature*. Chicago, London: The Open Court Publishing Co.

TERMAN, L., and COX, C. M. (1926). *Genetic Studies of Genius*. Vol. II. *Early Mental Traits of 200 Geniuses*. Berkeley, Calif.: Stanford University Press; London: Harrap.

TOKSVIG, S. (1933). *Life of H. C. Andersen*. London: Macmillan.

TREASE, G. (1949). *Tales out of School: a Survey of Children's Fiction*. London: Heinemann.

TURNER, E. S. (1948). *Boys will be Boys*. London: Michael Joseph.

TURQUET, P. (1949). 'Aggression in Nature and Society.' *Brit. J. med. Psychol.* Vol. XXII, Pts. 3 and 4.

VERNON, M. D. (1948). 'The Development of Imaginative Constructions in Children.' *Brit. J. Psychol.* Vol. XXXIX, Pt. 2.

WERTHAM, F. (1954). *The Seduction of the Innocent*. New York: Rinehart; London: Museum Press, 1955.

WHITE, DOROTHY (1954). *Books before Five*. London: Oxford University Press.

COMICS

FLEETWAY PUBLICATIONS LTD
Begun by Pandora Publishing Co.
   Comic Cuts, 1890–1951
Begun by Amalgamated Press Ltd
   Wonder, 1892–1953
   Rainbow, 1914–1956
   Tiger Tim's Weekly, 1919–1939
   Film Fun, 1920–
   Chicks' Own, 1920–1956
   Playbox, 1925–1955

Illustrated Chips, 1890–1954

Larks, 1927–1939
Tiny Tots, 1927–1959
Girls' Crystal Weekly, 1935–
School Friend, 1950–
Lion, 1952–

There are a number of others now running, e.g. *Harold Hare's Own Paper*, *Jack and Jill*, *Knockout*, etc.

BIBLIOGRAPHY

D. C. THOMSON & CO. LTD
    Dandy, 1937–
    Beano, 1938–

                                      Magic, 1939 only
                                        Topper, 1953–

HULTON PRESS LTD
    Eagle, 1950–
    Girl, 1951–

                                        Robin, 1953–
                                        Swift, 1954–

ODHAMS PRESS LTD
    Mickey Mouse Weekly, 1936–1955

Index

Printed in Great Britain
in 12 pt Bembo
by Taylor Garnett Evans and Company Limited
London and Watford